Pugin's Builder

The Life and Work of George Myers

THE
UNIVERSITY
OF HULL
PRESS

Cover Illustration
The Tower of London and Moat from Tower Hill
by Thomas Shotter Boys (1803-74).
Reproduced by kind permission of The Bridgeman Art Library.

Pugin's Builder

The Life and Work of George Myers

Patricia Spencer-Silver

THE UNIVERSITY OF HULL PRESS
1993

© P. Spencer-Silver

British Library Cataloguing in Publication Data

Spencer-Silver, Patricia
    Pugin's Builder: Life and Work of George Myers
    I. Title
    690.092
ISBN 0-85958-611-1

Phototypeset in 11 on 12pt Plantin and printed by the Central Print Unit, the University of Hull.

Contents

Contents

Notes and References
Select Bibliography

Oil painting of George Myers c. 1860, artist unknown.
By kind permission of H. Myers.

Foreword

George Myers has gone down to posterity as 'Pugin's Builder', and this for most people is a not inconsiderable accolade. Even before the general recognition of the value of Victorian art and architecture, the name of Pugin was respected, both as an artist and a theorist. Yet this soubriquet and his rôle as a builder of churches has perhaps obscured Myers' claim to eminence as a well-known London tradesman and indeed one of the most important of Victorian general contractors. From his works on the site of County Hall, he managed a wide variety of contracts, everything from individual carved items, not only for Catholic, but for Anglo-Catholic and even Nonconformist, places of worship to the construction of whole hospitals and major Government contracts like that of the Staff College at Sandhurst. Thus in 1851, his men both completed the building of the Colney Hatch Asylum and prepared the famous Medieval Court for A.W.N. Pugin in the Crystal Palace. His work for the British Army was very considerable, at a period when some of the many deficiencies in its education, housing and medical care were being addressed. He constructed the original camp at Aldershot, the first barracks, garrison churches and Prince Albert's Officers' Library. In 1854 he built the Chateau de Ferrière in France for the Rothschilds.

Patricia Spencer-Silver has rendered a great service not only to the historians of Catholic Emancipation but also to students of architectural and building history. Drawing on family papers, as well as national and local archives, she has presented a picture of a great Victorian builder which illumines not only his methods and achievements but conditions in the building trade at the time.

Hermione Hobhouse
November 1992

Preface and Acknowledgements

George Myers was one of the great master builders of the Victorian Age. Born in Hull in 1803, he started work as an apprentice stonemason at Beverley Minster. He later worked for Pugin the eccentric Gothic Revivalist and other well-known architects. He moved to London in 1842 and by the 1850s was one of the country's leading contractors. In the press he was often referred to as 'the great builder'. He lived at a time of rapid social change. To study the list of his buildings is to realise a history of the 19th century. There cannot be anyone living in England today who does not know at least two or three of those which he constructed or restored. Yet little is known of his life and until now no attempt has been made to record it.

Myers' papers, which are mentioned in his will, no longer exist. Archive libraries, however, both public and private, contain copious information about him and his buildings, although this is often difficult to locate as builders' names are seldom indexed. A wonderful source of information has been the Hardman letters in the Birmingham City Library. These not only discuss business matters but also give insight into Myers' character and that of his colleagues and patrons. It is from these and other letters, the occasional contracts which have survived, as well as contemporary newspapers and journals, and visiting many of his buildings that I have pieced together the story of George Myers.

It was a privilege to be allowed to examine documents from the archives of their Graces the Dukes of Norfolk, Devonshire and Northumberland and to talk to the Countess of Rosebury about Mentmore. The Right Honourable Viscount Midleton gave generous permission to quote from the Midleton Papers in the Guildford Muniment Room and Lady Rupert Nevill allowed me to wander round her lovely house. The Right Honourable Lord Weatherill, former speaker of the House of Commons, and Lady Weatherill let me admire the beautiful George Myers furniture in their private apartments in the Palace of Westminster. I am most grateful to them all.

I wish to thank the President and Fellows of Magdalen College, Oxford, for allowing me to quote from their Pugin mss, also B.G. Hoare, Building Bursar, and the Provost and Fellows of Eton College for their help and hospitality, the late Lord Rothschild, Rothschilds' Bank, and Simone Mace for the fascinating days I spent in the Rothschild Archive, London. I had much welcome assistance from the late Brigadier Reed, Director of the Aldershot Military Museum, from Colonels Bailey and Newton of the Staff College, Camberley and from Colonel Long and Major Eller of the Headquarters Stamford Training Area, Norfolk.

My thanks are due also to Patricia Allderidge, archivist at the Royal Bethlam Hospital, to Jill Allibone, to Victor Belcher, Head of Survey and General Branch, English Heritage who read the manuscript and made many helpful suggestions, to R.T. Bratby of the Country Houses Association, to Paul and Arabella Burton who showed me round Lismore Castle and provided a delicious lunch as well, to Canon Cantwell of Derby, Fr Michael Clifton of Southwark, Robin Guard of Newcastle upon Tyne, P.W.J. Duffield of Travers Smith Braithewaite, Andrew Hamilton of Culverin, Peter Howell Chairman of the Victorian Society, John Kenworthy-Browne who provided much information which I would not have discovered without his help, to Professor V.A. McClelland who suggested that I should offer my manuscript to The University of Hull Press, to Dom Bede Millard OSB of Ramsgate, M.G. Moss, David Pollard of the Bath Stone Quarry Museum, Dr David Neave, Rosemary Rendel, Dr Ruth Richardson, Dom Martin Salmon of Downside Abbey, the Nuns at Rise Hall, Dr Jon Spence, and to David Stipetic of Hull who bicycled seven miles to unlock the Holy Trinity vaults, to Sir Francis and Lady Vallat, to Clive Wainwright, Lady Wedgwood who helped identify the working drawings, and to Mr and Mrs Whitehead of Shepshed.

Carol Boddington of the Humberside Archive Library and Jackie Johnson and Julie Oosthuizen of the Lavender Hill Reference Library gave unstinting help over the ten years of my researches. During that time so many people helped me that it would be impossible to mention them all. But there is a small group of people to whom I am especially grateful, who helped me from the beginning to the very end: my husband and other members of my family for work on the text and for producing some of the photographs, Ann King-Hall, for her expert advice and help, Timothy McCann for being the source of much information and for answering endless questions, Hugh Myers for many discussions and for his generosity and trust, and finally, Hermione Hobhouse. Had it not been for her encouragement, continuing help and interest in George Myers, which almost equalled my own, I do not think this book could ever have been written.

List of Maps and Illustrations

Note:
Figs. 11-18 are Pugin/Myers working drawings.
Figs. 11, 17 & 18 are drawn by Pugin.
Figs. 12-16 inclusive are Pugin designs, drawn by someone else, probably Myers.
Courtesy of the Myers Family Trust

I

The Early Years in Hull and Beverley: 1803-42

George Myers, known as 'Pugin's builder', was to become one of the great contractors of the Victorian Age. He was born in Kingston-upon-Hull in 1803, the son of a whitesmith also called George Myers, and of his wife Mary Benson.[1] Whitesmiths carried out the non-ferrous metalwork for the building trade, sometimes making church bells or working as shipsmiths. The family lived at 8 Ordovas Place, Chariot Street, in the parish of Sculcoates, a part of Hull which is near the docks.

At the beginning of the 19th century, Hull was a prosperous port, her shipping tonnage only exceeded by that of London and Liverpool. Sculcoates, outside the old town walls, had been much extended and improved. The wealthy wharfingers and many of the merchants lived in the old town High Street, in grand houses with gardens sloping down to the river Hull where they could watch the ships being loaded for trading ventures in the Baltic and in the Low Countries. It was in one of these houses that William Wilberforce, the leader of the campaign to abolish the slave trade, was born.

Patterson's Roads[2] described Hull, in 1826, as having 'a market place that is spacious and magnificent and presents a range of houses and shops that for beauty of appearance and richness of merchandise is surpassed by few in England ...'. It also described the shipyards, the mills and manufactories and drew attention to Holy Trinity Church where Myers was later to work and in which he was to marry his first wife. The well-regulated schools, the spacious theatre and the subscription library and museum were mentioned. Hull was a thriving, busy port with plenty to interest an intelligent lad.

But it was to Beverley, eight miles north of Hull, that Myers chose to go when it was time for him to learn a craft.[3] Beverley had seen its heyday in the 13th century when it was a centre for the woollen textile industry, but economic decline had set in when the industry migrated to the West Riding. In the 18th century Beverley had become a fashionable place to live but, having been bypassed by the Industrial Revolution, it became once more a sleepy market town. It was a staging post on the road from Hull to York. At the age of thirteen or thereabouts Myers left Hull to be apprenticed to William Comins, the Master Mason at Beverley Minster.

It would be interesting to know the reason for his choice; in his twenties he was to inherit his father's house, but he had not been apprenticed to a whitesmith which would have enabled him to take over his father's business as well. His resolution to become a stonemason determined his future.

He was to work at the Minster until the spring of 1829.[4] During the greater part of the preceding century churches had been allowed to decay, but with the turn of the century and the increasing momentum of the Religious Revival, they were once again being restored and rebuilt. In 1812 William Shout, Master Mason at York Minster, had carried out a survey at Beverley Minster and this resulted in the appointment of William Comins, who had worked under Shout at York, as Master Mason at Beverley. During the 18th century the Minster had been 'Georgianised' but, about 1815, the process of 're-Gothicising' commenced. This included the removal of Hawkesmoor's cupola and other Georgian additions. The Fowlers of Winterton were the architects and they did much of the restoration carving themselves. Comins' Day Book for the years 1827-33 still exists in the Beverley Public Library. Myers' name appears on the first and every subsequent page until the week beginning 27 April 1829. The word 'left' has been scrawled against his name on the previous page.[5]

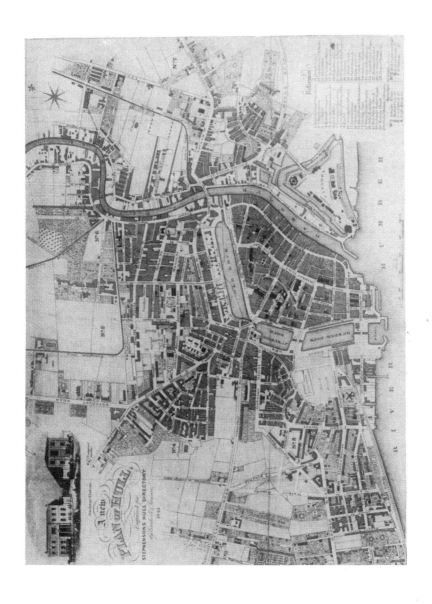

Figure 1   Map of Hull 1842.
Courtesy of Hull City Record Office.

The Day Book shows that Comins had under him a group of five masons, one apprentice and two labourers. When it snowed an extra labourer was paid 6*d*. a day to keep the paths to the Minster clear and, if much unskilled maintenance work was required, labourers from the town were taken on. The masons were paid 4*s*. 0*d*. a day for a six-day week and the apprentice 3*s*. 0*d*. Sometimes they worked on Sunday for the same wages. Comins was paid a flat rate of two guineas a week regardless of how much time he spent working at the Minster. He had a business of his own in the town. A stonemason is a craftsman of considerable skill; in the Middle Ages it was the Master Masons who designed and built the great Gothic Cathedrals. They were architect, engineer, contractor and supplier of building materials. In those days a Master Mason would have had a labourer or 'servant' to prepare his tools. It is said that some servants even had their master's boots warmed for them when they arrived for work in the morning.

When Myers was apprenticed to William Comins at the beginning of the 19th century, little had changed since the Middle Ages - except that holidays were fewer. Many saints' days had been abolished at the time of the Reformation and the Trade Unions had not yet come into being to demand more holidays for their members.

The Day Book records the work done by Myers and his fellow masons during those years which included the repair of the north side of the choir, the floor and the altar rails. The altar rails were removed some time between 1870 and 1880 and now ornament a Beverley garden.[6] Perhaps Myers also worked on the reredos which was restored in 1826. In his Will he refers to 'the drawing I made of the reredos as restored at Beverley Minster' and, as he left it to the eldest of his five sons, it may have had some special significance for him.

Comins travelled to the Tadcaster quarries to choose the stone required for the restoration work. Tadcaster stone had been used for the building of the Minster in the 13th century and later in the 14th century for St Mary's, which was built as a chapel of ease for the Minster. At that time the stone went by boat down the rivers Wharfe, Ouse and Humber as far as Hull, then up the river Hull and the little Beverley Beck. The stone

was finally unloaded at Beckside within half a mile of the
Minster and completed its journey on drays pulled, sometimes,
by as many as ten cart horses. The same mode of transport
was in use in the mid-19th century. In times of drought the
shallowness of the canals and rivers made it impossible to
transport heavy loads and the supply of stone and brick dried
up, as a letter written by Thos. H. Archbell, a quarryman, to
Mr Thomas Whiting, Churchwarden of St Mary's Beverley,[7]
makes clear.

Mr Whiting   Tadcaster, June 25th,1839.

Sir

I write to inform you I have shipped on Board of
the Wm of Tadr, Capt Beamand, 22 stones
containing 20 tons which I hope will arrive safe
and please.
You may expect them I should think about
Thursday, we have only had a flush of water one
day which was Sunday, the water began to fail
again on Monday morning. Knowing that both
you and the Minster was so much in want of the
stones, I thought I had better send you a part of
your respective orders. I have therefore sent you
20 tons and the Minster 25 tons. Your stone is
all marked with a black paint mark thus X. The
remainder of your order, 10 tons, I will send you
on their return if the water will permit, I will send
you also a proper invoice with the remainder of
the stone, waiting your further favours

I am, Sir, Yours Respectfully

Thos. H. Archbell

During these years there were many visitors who came to
admire the beautiful Gothic carving in the Minster. One of
these was E.J. Willson of Lincoln, the antiquarian and

Figure 2 Beverley Minster from the South.
Courtesy of Humberside Archives Services ref. DPX 62/1.

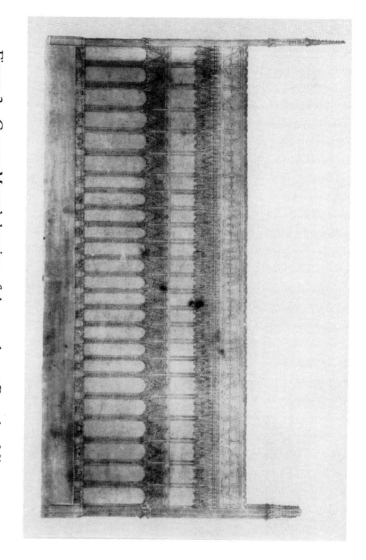

Figure 3   George Myers' drawing of the reredos at Beverley Minster
before its restoration in 1826.
Courtesy of the Myers Family Trust.

architectural historian, who went there to draw, and it is probable that he came to know Myers and possible that it was through Willson that Myers met the architect A.W.N. Pugin. So, it is worth recounting how Willson came to be acquainted with the Pugin family. According to legend, Augustus Charles Pugin, the architect's father, escaped from France, the Revolution and the guillotine and landed in Wales. Here he met John Nash, who was to become the Prince Regent's favourite architect but who at that time, *c.*1793, was bankrupt and living in Wales to escape his creditors. Nash engaged Augustus Charles as his draughtsman and when he moved back to London and fame, A.C. Pugin moved with him. There they heard talk of the Gothic Revival on all sides and Nash sent his draughtsman on a tour of the country to gather information. When he reached Lincoln it was inevitable that he should meet Willson, the renowned authority on Gothic buildings in the area. Their friendship dated from this time and in 1821 Willson helped A.C. Pugin publish *Specimens of Gothic Architecture*. The Willsons were not the Pugin family's only acquaintances in the county. A.W.N. Pugin's mother had relations in Lincolnshire, and visits to these relations and to the Willsons are noted in Pugin's diary. Perhaps Willson and A.W.N. Pugin went together on a sketching expedition to Beverley and it was to please Willson that Myers 'procured ladders and scaffolding' for the young Pugin, as described in Benjamin Ferrey's biography many years later. Ferrey does not record the date of this meeting but George Godwin, the editor of *The Builder* from 1844-83, did so in his obituary of Pugin published on 25 September 1852. He states that the meeting took place '25 years ago', which would have been in the year 1827 when Pugin was fifteen and Myers, still working as a mason in Beverley Minster, was twenty-four.

On leaving his work in Beverley in April 1829, Myers returned to Hull. On 10 May he married Isabella Patterson, the elder daughter of William Patterson, breeches maker, who lived in one of the Georgian cottages which stand in Highgate, the street which leads up to the Minster's 15th century north porch. The wedding took place in Hull's Holy Trinity Church. The witnesses were Richard Wilson, soon to be Myers' partner, and

George Craven, the sexton. They were married by Mr Davies the curate. Myers described himself as 'stonemason' and Isabella as 'spinster'. Isabella signed the register with a cross which was quite usual in those days when literacy could not be taken for granted in any stratum of society. Holy Trinity is one of the largest parish churches in the country and a very rare example of 14th century English brick work, but at the time of Myers' marriage it had, 'through the ignorance and indolence of the churchwardens' more remote predecessors, been permitted to lapse into mutilation and progressive decay'.[8]

Myers took his wife to live in the house, in Chariot Street, Hull, which had belonged to his father since the early days of the century. His father's name had not appeared in the directories at this or any other address after 1823, so we presume that he had died. Myers lived in Hull until 1842. Richard Wilson, Myers' partner, also lived in Hull. The first documentary evidence of their partnership was a contract drawn up in 1831 whereby George Myers and Richard Wilson

> ... carrying on business as stone masons in co-partnership in Carr Lane in the Lordship of Myton in the Town of K/H do hereby severally and jointly promise to agree with and to Pearson Fox the Surveyor to the Commissioners for the better paving of the Parish of Sculcoates to find and provide all necessary and requisite materials for flagging New George Street and Caroline Street ...

This document is in the Hull City Record Office. The day and month were not entered.[9] Myers & Wilson's builders' yards and workshops in Carr Lane were in a central position in the new part of Hull. It is not known how their business was financed initially. Perhaps Myers had inherited money from the whitesmith's business; possibly he had influential connections and those who had known his father had been willing to lend him money to get established. If so, their confidence was justified. From 1832 onwards, there are documents to show that Myers & Wilson continued to work for the council and that they were building terraced houses in Vincent Street and in Medley Street which they were developing on their own account. They built more houses in Popple Street and Edward Street and towards the end of the decade they were building better-class houses with quite large gardens in Queen Street and English Street. Loans to the business were secured by mortgages and the lenders were names well-known in Hull: Grimston, Thurnbull, Cross and Mr Foale, Surveyor to The Trinity House who acted as surety when Myers & Wilson borrowed money from The Hull Banking Company.[10]

This was a time of great industrial expansion in Hull and Messrs Myers & Wilson built many mills and factories. This is evident from a letter written by Myers on 7 May 1841, in answer to one from 'the Gentlemen of the Groves Church Committee' who sought his advice concerning the foundations of a new church which they were proposing to build.[11] Myers replied that they were right to be concerned, as the use of concrete, which was the usual material used for foundations, was unwise. Concrete had been used at Hull College and in several other instances, but 'though done in the best fashion, had failed in all cases ...' . He explained that the reason why concrete did not answer in Hull was 'that we have about 4 ft of strong clay on the top, below which is a very soft silt which will not carry great weights'. Myers reminded the committee that Myers & Wilson had built the Wilberforce Memorial using piles 20 ft long and, though the Monument was within 30 ft of the lockpit which was 28 ft deep, it had not given way in the slightest degree. They had also built 'heavy engineering chimneys and several heavy buildings close to the Humber side' using the same method, all of which had stood very well. This was the way to ensure stable foundations in this part of Hull. Myers & Wilson prospered, their building yards were extensive and their wharf in Queen Street was situated where the River Hull flows into the Humber.

Myers & Wilson did restoration work at Holy Trinity Church, Hull.[12] The surviving vestry account books show that they were working there in March 1833 repairing the stone. They supplied new coping for the north wall, restored the Great West Window and supplied two figures at a cost of £1. 10s. 0d.

John Hardman Powell in his manuscript *Pugin in his Home,* says that Myers was Foreman of masons here when Myers and Pugin first met. Powell described how 'when one of the masons could not understand some sectional drawing, taking up a mallet and chisel, with a few strokes, he, Myers, chipped it out. This was enough. Pugin invited him to Town to be his builder'.[13] There are several stories relating how these two men met which were published in Myers' lifetime, but he never confirmed or denied them.

Myers & Wilson were still working at Holy Trinity when, in 1842, the churchwardens decided to call in the Yorkshire architect H.F. Lockwood to restore the church to 'good order and decent splendour'.[14] The cost of restoring Holy Trinity was expected to be £3,000 and the churchwardens were confident that they could raise £1,200 from pew rents and the sale of burial vaults in the crypt of the church. The sum remaining was guaranteed by 'a few gentlemen who had taken an interest in the subject'.[15] One hundred spacious vaults were built under the nave at a cost of £1,000 but few had been sold when, in the spring of 1855, a letter arrived from the Under Secretary of State for the Home Office instructing the churchwardens that 'burials were to be discontinued forthwith in the parish churchyard, vaults and church of Holy Trinity'. The churchwardens were appalled. They wrote back hastily to the Under Secretary and explained: 'with reference to such intimation we ... state that in the year 1846 upwards of one hundred spacious vaults were built under the nave of the church at a cost of a thousand pounds or thereabouts, very few of which were sold'. There had been only thirty-one interments so far, producing a profit of a mere £87. The whole of the surplus funds of the church had been spent on the vaults.[16] The churchwardens went on to point out that theirs was a very healthy parish, (despite all the graves in the centre of the town), and that the Vicar, Mr J.H. Bromley, who was eighty-four, had lived there all his life. Mr Bromley was Vicar for nearly seventy years. He died on 25 March 1868, aged ninety-seven.[17] But Queen Victoria signed the Order of Consent on 1 May 1855 and burial in Holy Trinity became illegal. The Burial Act of 1852 had empowered local vestries to acquire new burial

Figure 4   Holy Trinity Church, Hull, where George Myers married Isabella Patterson in 1829.
Courtesy of Hull City Record Office.

Figure 5   Wilberforce Monument and St John's Church, Hull.
Courtesy of Hull Museums and Art Gallery.

grounds outside the towns and in 1853 the closure of urban cemeteries was ordered. A campaign against such burials had been waged for many years before this law had at last been passed, and there had been gruesome stories in the press. The churchwardens of Holy Trinity had obviously missed the descriptions of putrefying corpses in lead coffins exploding in vaults. Only the rich could afford coffins; the poor were deposited coffinless in common graves in the churchyards which were covered over with earth when they were full.

Holy Trinity's new vaults were a disaster for another reason. They disturbed the medieval foundations, and floods over the years further endangered the building. It was not until the 1980's, that, bucket by bucket, the mud and water were ladled out of these subterranean passages. The vaults are now dry and lit by electricity.

Twenty-one years before the drama of the vaults, in 1833, William Wilberforce had died, aged seventy-three. A public meeting of the inhabitants of Hull and its neighbourhood was held on 12 August in the Guildhall to decide a proper means of honouring the town's most famous son. It was decided to erect a pillar, to be surmounted by a statue, in a prominent place in the centre of the town. A committee was set up under the chairmanship of Richard Bethel Esq., M.P. J. Clerk of Leeds was appointed the architect and as already mentioned Myers & Wilson were the builders.[18] The site eventually chosen was the end of Junction Street at the head of Junction Dock, the site requiring the use of 20 ft piles to ensure the stability of the Monument. The foundation stone was laid on 1 August 1834, the day the Bill abolishing slavery in the Colonies of the British Empire was passed in Parliament.

Earlier that year, on 9 March, Myers' wife Isabella died, aged thirty, giving birth to her third son. Myers took the tiny infant to his mother-in-law in Beverley to be cared for, but little George Patterson Myers lived only for five weeks. The child was buried beside his mother in the churchyard of Beverley Minster. Myers and his two remaining sons, five year old David Benson and two year old Joseph Patterson, moved to 3 Medley Street, Hull, one of the houses which he and Richard Wilson had built. The Directories of this date show that Myers

& Wilson now occupied property in Prospect Street as well as their building yards in Carr Lane and the wharf in Queen Street.

In 1837-8 two valuable contracts were undertaken both at a considerable distance from Hull. Myers & Wilson won the contract to build St Mary's Catholic Church in Derby. The architect was A.W.N. Pugin and within months of undertaking this commission they had also signed the contract to build a workhouse for 350 men, women and children for the Guardians of the Loughborough Union in the counties of Leicester and Nottingham. The Loughborough contract was signed on 1 May 1838.[19] George Gilbert Scott and W.B. Moffat of Carlton Chambers, Regent Street, in the City of Westminster were the architects. It is possible that Myers and Scott had met before as Scott's uncle, the Revd John Scott, was Vicar of St Mary's Church, Sculcoates in Hull where both David and Joseph Myers had been christened. At a later date the Revd Mr Scott acted as surety when Myers & Wilson borrowed money from The Hull Banking Company to finance the building of St Mark's Church in The Groves in 1843.[20]

The building of the Loughborough Workhouse proceeded uneventfully. Sir G.G. Scott refers to it in his *Recollections Personal and Professional* published after his death in 1879. He described Myers at that time as 'a strange rough mason from Hull who, as a boy, had been apprenticed to Comins at Beverley Minster'. He goes on to say that it was while Myers was working for him at Loughborough that Myers tendered for and got the contract to build St Mary's, Derby for Pugin, but Phoebe Stanton says that St Mary's was begun in December 1837, which was five months before the signing of the Loughborough contract.[21] The foundation stone of St Mary's was laid on 28 June 1838[22] and, since the laying of the foundation stone would normally take place some months after the signing of the contract, it would seem that Myers & Wilson started the St Mary's contract before Loughborough. The gaining of the Derby contract was to be of momentous significance to Myers. From then onwards he was 'Pugin's Builder'.

II

London - Craftsmen and the Lambeth
Workshops: 1842-75

The story which relates how Myers won the Derby contract is given in Benjamin Ferrey's biography of Pugin, published in 1861. Ferrey describes the first meeting of Myers and the boy Pugin in Beverley Minster and adds: ... 'but there their acquaintance for a time ended'. He continues the story: 'Myers and other builders were invited a few years afterwards to tender for the erection of a Roman Catholic church in Derby ...'. Pugin recognised in Myers the enthusiastic mason who had taken such an interest in what he was doing in Beverley and had there rendered his help. Rushing to him he clasped him in his arms exclaiming 'My good fellow, you are the very man I want, you shall execute all my buildings'.

The architect Talbot Bury, who disapproved of Ferrey's book, wrote a critical letter to *The Builder* accusing the author of dragging in anecdotes 'many of them inventions of the most palpable kind'. An unruffled Ferrey replied a week later saying that he had reliable authority for everything that did not come within his own personal knowledge, but 'it was not to be supposed that any biography had ever been written in which some of the incidents might not be open to a different version'.[1]

But whatever the circumstances and conditions of their meeting Myers was in every way the man the young Pugin needed. He was an artist and craftsman of considerable skill. He had spent his formative years working in Beverley Minster, one of the most glorious of medieval Gothic churches, and he had worked too on the restoration of Holy Trinity, Hull, another beautiful medieval church. He had also had eight years of building and contracting experience. Up to this time, Pugin had built only one church, in Reading, of which he was not proud, and his own rather strange 'Gothic' house near Salisbury. Pugin had found a man who was to be more than a contractor, he was to be a friend and collaborator. The understanding between the two men was to be such that detailed drawings would be unnecessary. This was due also to the element of traditional building still present, when the dividing line between architect and builder was blurred. Pugin did not have an office full of draughtsmen and, in future years, without Myers' involvement he could not have accomplished such an enormous amount of work as he did during his short life. His comment: 'Clerk, my dear Sir, clerk? I never employ one. I should kill him in a week.' is well-known.[2] He was able to manage without one because on Myers he could rely absolutely.

Pugin was a prolific letter writer and many of his letters to his friends and patrons survive. These letters often refer to Myers and from them we can learn much of his personality. When writing to his patrons, Pugin always extolled Myers' virtues, but in writing to colleagues who had complained of his behaviour his reaction was different: Myers was 'the greatest pig in Christendom',[3] and in answer to another complaint, Pugin described how he once 'made a sketch of a man ordering a thing of Myers ... quite a young man ... and receiving it when he was decrepit with age'.[4] But of Pugin's devotion to Myers there is no doubt. These remarks were addressed to Crace, the interior decorator, who was often irritated by Myers' self-assured behaviour.

Pugin and his builder were soon inundated with work. The passing of the Catholic Emancipation Act of 1829 meant that Catholics could now build churches and worship freely. Pugin's mission in life was to ensure that these churches were beautiful, dignified and liturgically correct. He had a difficult task before him. The old Catholic aristocratic families had their private chapels, but many of them were insular and uneducated. The Universities had long been closed to them. The Irish navvies, nearly all of them Catholic, who flooded into the country to build the roads and railways, were illiterate. Pugin's energy and writings were directed at the middle class Catholics to persuade them to his way of thinking. He had many zealous friends not only amongst his co-religionists but also among High-Church Anglicans, members of the Cambridge Camden Society and of the Oxford Movement. He had generous Catholic patrons such as Lord Shrewsbury and Ambrose Phillipps de Lisle who contributed towards the building of the new churches, schools and colleges. During these years Pugin was writing, designing and travelling. He wrote and drew in trains and in boats and he travelled to Ireland to build churches and to the Continent to sketch. He was often ill, but the indefatigable Myers was always there to 'execute' his buildings.

In 1841, Pugin moved to London. He had decided that the riverside situation of his house near Salisbury was unhealthy, and he took a house in Chelsea, 42 Cheyne Walk, (demolished and now rebuilt) as a temporary residence for his family. He longed to live by the sea and determined to build a house at Ramsgate where he had spent happy holidays at the home of his aunt, Selina Welby. He wrote to Mr Bloxam of Magdalen College, Oxford, describing his plans:

> I have bought about an acre of land facing the sea at Ramsgate. I shall not erect a green villa but a substantial Catholic home, not very large but solid ... the delight of the sea with Catholic architecture and a library, (not a circulating one). When it is finished I shall hope to induce you to come to me.[5]

Myers moved to London the next year.[6] While still living in Hull, on 18 March 1841, he married for the second time. His new wife was thirty year old Judith Ruddock, second daughter of David Ruddock, clothier and weaver of Horbury, Yorkshire, and of Mary Armitage, his wife. David Ruddock had died aged forty-four in 1830 and his widow and numerous children went to live with the eldest daughter, Elizabeth, who was married to Edward Jackson, goldsmith, of York. It was from the Jacksons' house, next door to the Church of St Martin le Grand in Coney Street, that Judith was married. Her brother, Richard Martin Ruddock, and Edward Jackson were witnesses.

By the end of 1842, Myers and his wife were settled in London. They had taken one of a row of new houses opposite the site of St George's Cathedral. Their address was 9 Laurie Terrace, St George's Road, Southwark. The terrace was built by W. G. Glasier & Thomas Crawley and named after Sir Peter Laurie, the President of the Bethlem & Bridewell Hospitals 1833-61. These houses still stand, mostly converted into flats. It was here that Judith gave birth to her first child, George Ruddock Myers. He was carried across the road to be baptised in the unfinished Cathedral three weeks later.[7] It was a Sunday, so the mallets and chisels of the stonemasons were silent. Between January 1843 and April 1850, Judith gave birth to six children, three boys and three girls. The two surviving sons of Myers' first marriage, David aged fourteen and Joseph who was eleven in 1843, completed the family. The Myers lived at Laurie Terrace for the next ten years.

In 1840, Myers had undertaken in London one of his biggest and most important early contracts, St George's Catholic Cathedral, Southwark, with its associated buildings.[8] Richard Wilson remained in Hull and all contracts continued to be signed 'Myers & Wilson of Hull', until Friday 21 June 1844 when notices appeared on the front page of the *Hull Packet and East Riding Times* announcing: 'Partnership dissolved ...'. The partnership subsisting between Myers and Richard Wilson was to be dissolved by 'mutual consent' and Wilson was to carry on business as before from the establishment in Paragon Street. Another notice in the *Hull Advertiser* announced that henceforth Myers would reside in London where 'he intended carrying on Business in all its branches'.

The firm of Myers & Wilson had been carrying out a great deal of work in the north of England. Myers was to continue working at St Mary's, Beverley for years, and there was much to be done at Ushaw College in County Durham;

St Mary's, Newcastle upon Tyne was almost finished.   There was work in progress in Liverpool and Winwick, Cheshire, in addition to the flax and cotton mills and the public baths both in Hull.[9]   There were also large contracts in the Midlands, but perhaps it was easier to travel to that part of the country from London, as the rapidly expanding railway network, whose branches stretched to all areas of the country, was centred on the metropolis.   Even so, one would have thought that Myers could have found it useful to have a partner and a base in Hull. But the partnership was dissolved.

There is a letter concerning church finances, dated 9 December 1844, from Mr H.R. Bagshawe, a prominent Catholic barrister and friend of the future Cardinal Wiseman, to a Dr Essingham, which says: '... I happen to know that his (Myers') late partner has let him into the necessity of making large and unexpected payments ...'.[10]

The facts of the matter appear to have been as follows. In the spring of 1843, Myers & Wilson won the contract to build the sub-workhouse and schools at Kirkdale, Liverpool. There had been thirty tenders and theirs had been £3,000 less than their nearest rival. The *Liverpool Mail* of 15 April 1843 mentioned that the successful candidates had built the Catholic Chapel in Wavertree and were 'now engaged in erecting the extraordinary structure that attracts so much attention in Catherine Street'.   The year before, thirty-nine architects had entered the competition to design the schools.   Allom and Lockwood were the winners with whom Myers & Wilson had worked on several occasions.

These schools were one attempt to assuage the appalling problem created by refugees from Europe and by the influx of starving peasants from Ireland.   Most of them had no possessions and nowhere to live.   Many of them died of cholera and other diseases, and large numbers of these desperate people ended up in the Law Courts charged with larceny and other crimes for which the punishment was transportation.   Orphans and children whose mothers were waiting to begin their sentences were housed in the sub-workhouse and were to be given the rudiments of an education in the Kirkdale Industrial Schools.[11]

The foundation stone was laid on 25 May 1843, but three months later the architects announced that the wrong materials had been used and ordered the contractors to demolish the building and rebuild it at their own expense. The firm of Myers & Wilson had undertaken the contract, so each partner was fully liable to the employer, irrespective of whether it was Myers or Wilson who had done the work. At that time Myers was building four cathedrals and was busy establishing himself in London and it is clear that Wilson had the conduct of the Kirkdale contract. This is borne out by the fact that the Liverpool newspapers, when reporting the matter, refer to Messrs Wilson and make no mention of Myers. But Myers had to bear the cost - presumably the large and 'unexpected payments' referred to by Mr Bagshawe. It was after this episode that Myers decided that he would be better off on his own than with a partner who could not be relied on.

Wilson continued to work at Holy Trinity, Hull and it was he who built most of the ill-fated vaults. In December 1845, when the church was reopened, the local newspaper described the pulpit and lectern as 'exquisitely designed by Mr Lockwood and executed by Mr Wilson'.[12] The Hull Banking Company employed him to make alterations and improvements to their premises, but before many years had passed he was in financial trouble. In the days when Myers & Wilson had done business with the Bank their credit had been good. In March 1843 they had been allowed to borrow £2,200, a considerable sum in those days. As security they had deposited the agreement for the purchase of ground in Carr Lane on which they had erected cottages and tenements. But on 11 June 1847, when Wilson had been on his own for three years, the Bank Manager was instructed to inform him that 'unless the small balance of £5. 4s. 10d. due from him be discharged within 14 days the Company solicitor would be instructed to adopt measures to enforce the same'. Wilson managed to produce the small balance and struggled on for two more years, but on 8 May 1849, the Court of Bankruptcy in Leeds declared Richard Wilson bankrupt. The fact was advertised in the *London Gazette* on 10 May 1849.[13] It appears from what followed that debts incurred by Myers & Wilson due to the Kirkdale Schools

Figure 6 A view of York from the River Ouse, showing the Church of
St Martin le Grand, Coney Street, where George Myers married Judith Ruddock in 1841.
Courtesy of City of York Art Gallery, Archives Department.

Figure 7   Interior view of Holy Trinity Church, Hull showing
the pulpit 'exquisitely . . . executed by Mr Wilson'.
Courtesy of the Hull Daily Mail.

fiasco, had not been paid. Myers had a friend in Hull, one John Ranson, a retired builder, who kept him informed of what was going on and acted on his behalf. On 4 May 1850, a year after the bankruptcy had been announced, Ranson wrote a long letter to Myers in London concerning the Kirkdale Industrial Schools, various money transactions and Richard Wilson who had 'made wrong statements about several people and these amounts, which you know has been a common practice for a long time with him'. Myers replied by return of post saying that he had already paid 'to and for Mr Wilson for the Kirkdale Schools £8,045. 10s. 9d., the sum is truly awful ... as well as a great deal of money at different times since that transaction'.[14] A few days later, at a meeting of the directors of The Hull Banking Company held on 17 May 1850, relative to the securities held by the Bank for the balance of Messrs Myers' & Wilson's account, the Bank's solicitor was instructed to

> cause a writ to be issued against Myers of London
> in respect of the said balance and also that a case
> be drawn up and submitted for Counsel's opinion
> with reference to the Bank's securities against the
> late firm of Myers & Wilson ...[15]

Myers' solicitors, at that time Messrs Palmer and Nettleship of London, corresponded with Mr Lee, The Hull Banking Company's solicitor, for years. Eventually, on 18 May 1855, Myers wrote offering to pay the Bank £100 on account of the balance due to them from Richard Wilson of Hull if the Bank would give up 'all and any claims they may have on the ground and premises in Carr Lane and Paragon Street'. The manager was instructed to accept this offer 'if he found it impracticable to arrange the matter on better terms'. But on 22 June there was a letter from Myers offering to pay £250 which was accepted.[16] One wonders what the manager said to get more than twice Myers' previous offer out of him, but his property in Hull was now free of any claims. Myers continued to own property in Hull at least until 1863 but it is not known if this included his own builder's yards.

That Myers survived this episode is very much to his credit. The foundation stone of the Kirkdale Industrial Schools had been laid in May 1843, but it was not until May 1855 that the financial problems caused by this contract were finally resolved. It was at the time when Myers was establishing himself in the South and undertaking some of his biggest and most prestigious contracts. He thought that he had disposed of the inefficient and untrustworthy Richard Wilson in 1844, but he was still responsible for the debts of Myers & Wilson and so had handed over very large sums of money on account of his late partner. Richard Wilson had been Myers' friend for many years and was a witness at his first wedding. Was Wilson dishonest or just a hopeless muddler who could not manage without Myers at his elbow? Myers' integrity was never doubted, but these financial problems must have caused a serious reversal of his fortunes.

But it is important to return to the year 1843, when Myers and his family had just arrived in London. Pugin had chosen the suppliers and craftsmen who were to work with him until the end of his life. The four men he chose were very different in character. Myers, in his capacity as contractor and builder, had close dealings with them all. Pugin and Myers had worked together since 1837. Their relationship was that of true friends and withstood the inevitable crises connected with the building trade in all ages. Pugin was to rely on Myers more and more as the years went by.

Pugin met John Hardman (1812-67) in 1837, the year of his second meeting with Myers. Hardman was the only one of the group who changed his craft at Pugin's request. He abandoned his family button-making business to manufacture medieval-style metalwork for Pugin's Gothic buildings and in 1845 he also undertook the making of Pugin's stained glass in his Birmingham studios. Pugin had previously employed several stained glass makers, but none of them measured up to his requirements.

William Wailes of Newcastle, who produced much of the glass for Pugin's early churches, appears to have committed some dreadful misdemeanour and fallen out of favour. There is a clue in a letter written by Myers to Hardman on 16 October

1845, complaining that Sir Wm. Eden's 'brass' was a very long time finishing, and in a postscript he added: 'Don't become a Wailes'. Hardman's reply no longer exists, but he was obviously offended, because on 19 October Myers wrote again: 'I am sorry you do not take Wailes as a joke. You know I meant it so, as no man could think higher of you as gentleman and tradesman than I do. It was a joke and that is all about it'.[17] Eventually stained glass, metalwork, enamelling and embroidery of great beauty were all made in Hardman's studio. A devout Catholic and a serious church musician, he became one of Pugin's closest friends.

Pugin employed John Gregory Crace, (1809-89), of 14 Wigmore Street, London, to make material, wallpaper, carpets and furniture. He was the head of a well-known firm of decorators. His father, Frederick, had made the dragons and other decorations for the Royal Pavilion at Brighton in the early years of the century and so would have been known to Pugin, whose father also had a hand in the decorating of that Royal Palace. Crace was well aware of his position as the leading interior decorator of the day and was concerned that others, including Myers, should know it too.

Herbert Minton, (1793-1858), was a second generation pottery manufacturer. His father, Thomas Minton, had started the production of pottery and bone china tableware in Stoke-on-Trent in 1796. In 1836 Thomas Minton died which left his enterprising son Herbert in charge. It was he who started manufacturing encaustic floor tiles[18] many of them, such as those in the Palace of Westminster, to Pugin's designs. Minton revived and adapted the medieval techniques. Pugin used Minton's tiles in many of his churches.

Thomas Earley, an employee of Hardman's, was another skilful craftsman. He painted the intricate patterns on the walls and ceilings of the churches and in the House of Lords, where on at least one occasion he was so busy that he asked Myers to lend him a man to help.[19] Earley's letters to Hardman reporting the progress of his work give, incidentally, a vivid impression of the character of many of his employers.

This group of talented men who were united in their admiration, devotion and loyalty to Pugin and served him faithfully, were already well-established when they started to work for him. But when Myers moved to London, he moved to a new environment. His well-established workshops were in Hull. But, as the Myers & Wilson partnership had been dissolved in June 1844, with Wilson retaining both the work 'emanating' from Hull and the workshops there, it was imperative for Myers to find premises in London. When he first arrived in the metropolis his business letters were simply headed 'London' and then '9, Laurie Terrace'. His office was in his home and he probably used the mews area behind the house as a mason's yard. The terrace was incomplete and building was still in progress when the Myers moved into No. 9 and only seven houses had been finished and occupied.

It was not until the spring of 1845 that Myers found what he was looking for, a wharf and yards on the Pedlar's Acre Estate in Lambeth, just North of Westminster Bridge and now the site of County Hall, former headquarters of the Greater London Council. It is a strange coincidence that in 1860 Myers should have built offices in Spring Gardens for the Metropolitan Board of Works which was the predecessor of the London County Council and of the Greater London Council. It was here that the L.C.C. held its first meeting in 1888.

The wharf at 9 Belvedere Road was known as Ordnance Wharf and was a piece of ground with a road frontage of 45 ft, and was 145 ft long ending in a jetty stretching out into the Thames. Here was a group of wharfs occupied by other builders amongst whom were Grissell and Peto, currently building the new Houses of Parliament, the timber merchants Walter Cosser and Sons, and other tradesmen. The lease of Ordnance Wharf was owned by a Mr Spedding, a coal merchant whose business was not prospering and who wished to dispose of the eleven remaining years of his tenancy. In June 1845 letters passed between the solicitors of the parties concerned, Myers being described as 'a respectable man' who was willing to carry out improvements to the value of 'say £350.[20]

Myers took over Mr Spedding's lease which had been granted by the Trustees of the Estate at a rent of £100 per annum, and in June 1856 he applied for a renewal. He asked

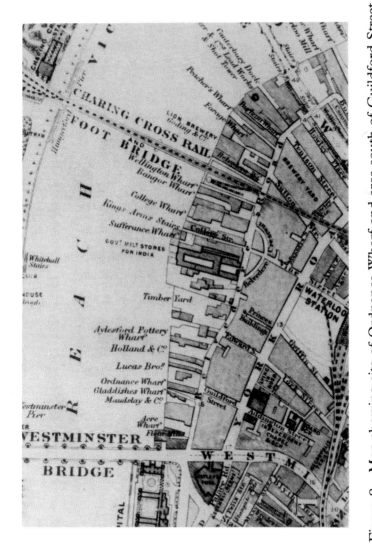

Figure 8 Map showing site of Ordnance Wharf and area south of Guildford Street where Myers had his wharf, office and workshops from 1847 until his death in 1875.

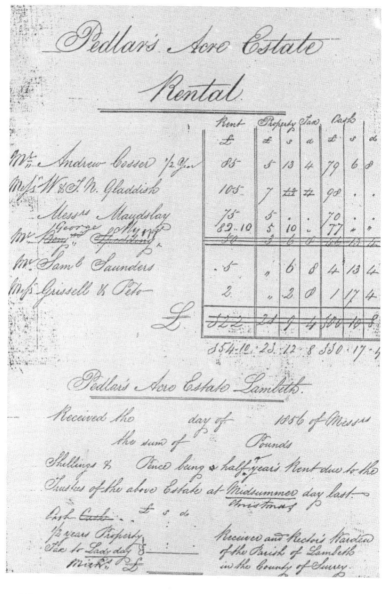

Figure 9   Page from Pedlar's Acre Estate Rent Book of
1856, the year George Myers took over the lease from Mr
Benjamin Spedding.
Courtesy of the London Borough of Lambeth.

that the draft of the fresh lease should be sent with as little delay as possible. But the Trustees of the Pedlar's Acre Estate, Lambeth, required Myers to undertake further repairs and stated their intention of increasing the rent by £30, to £130 p.a. In December 1858, two years and six months later, the Trustees received a letter from their solicitors, Messrs Waring & Blake of 42 Palace Street, Westminster, which said:

> Gentlemen,
> We beg to report that Mr. Myers has at length and after having given a great deal of trouble, completed the repairs of the Wharf in his occupation and that he is now entitled to a lease of the premises.[21]

It was from his Ordnance Wharf office that Myers was to conduct his business and write his letters, often late at night after returning from visits to his building sites all over the country. Now he was known as 'George Myers of Lambeth'.

Ordnance Wharf, half a mile distant from Myers' home, was a prime site on the main route from the South to Westminster and the Houses of Parliament. Waterloo Station was within a stone's throw, and the River Thames, in those days a busy waterway, provided access to the Port of London and world-wide trade. The canal system, especially the Grand Union Canal, north of the river, still provided the cheapest form of transport for building materials and heavy goods. The entrance to the wharf and office was in Belvedere Road and a footbridge across the road gave access to additional yards and buildings in Guildford Street and York Road, which Myers obtained under a separate lease, which was renewed from midsummer 1864 for a term of $59\frac{1}{2}$ years less fifteen days at £280. 11s. 10d. per annum.[22] The site of these workshops is now under the courtyard of County Hall. It is not clear from the evidence whether the freehold belonged to the Pedlar's Acre Estate, Messrs Grissell and Peto or to Messrs Nickels and Co., patent india rubber web manufacturers, who occupied some of the warehouses and factories on the site. The dwellings round about were inhabited by the craftsmen employed locally,

interspersed by two surgeons and a livery stable. Belvedere
Road and York Road can still be found on the South Bank they
are no longer muddy, rutted thoroughfares leading to industrial
sites, but modern streets leading to the townscaped Festival Hall
and Shell Building.

The five story building, on the other side of Belvedere
Road, was occupied on its upper floors by Messrs Nickels and
Co., and on its lower floors by Myers, who used them as
workshops and storerooms for joinery and machinery.[23] In the
yards outside the building the timber was stacked, much of it
rare and costly. Here too were the sawmills, the smithy and
other workshops, with stables for the horses and sheds for the
drays and carts. In the workshops worked Myers' craftsmen,
numbering at least 100 and acknowledged to be the best in
Europe.[24]

Myers sometimes undertook the training of young lads
recommended by his friends and many fine sculptors and
carvers first learned their skills under his watchful eye. We
know a little about one of these 'lads' because in the spring of
1849 Hardman asked Myers to take on a boy to train as a
glazier. On 11 April 'the lad' arrived and was set to work, but
Myers reported soon after that he did not look a 'very wide
awake boy', and that he would drive him a bit and see what that
would do. But on 21 July Myers wrote:

> I am sorry to have to inform you that the young
> man you sent me as a glazier has caused us such
> fun and games that I was obliged to discharge him
> for the sake of peace in the workshop. He seems
> to think more about fighting than working. We
> have lots of black eyes about. I am not sure where
> he has gone, but I thought it as well to inform you
> that he had left my works.[25]

In addition to the skilled craftsmen who applied to Myers for
employment, there were also many unskilled labourers who had
to take their chance in asking at the works for a job. Myers had
'thousands of recommendates'.[26]

Figure 10 Pugin's drawing of an oak seat made by Myers'
craftsmen for St Oswald's Church, Winwick.
Courtesy of the Revd D.A. Pankhurst, The Rectory, Winwick. WA2 8SZ.

Figure 11   A lion, the emblem of St Mark the Evangelist.

Soon after he arrived in London, Myers perfected a machine for 'cutting or carving wood, stone and other materials'. He decided to patent it. This was a lengthy process. He had to provide full-sized drawings and diagrams of his invention together with a description, which, including the archaic language in which it was written, amounted to over 2,700 words. These documents had to be delivered to the Patent Office at 25 Southampton Buildings, Holborn, where they were scrutinised by the Attorney General and where the inventor could be questioned. On 16 June 1845, Myers wrote to Hardman in Birmingham and said: 'On Saturday night I finished with the Attorney General ... I hope to get sealed in about ten days, though they say I must keep very quiet for a little while. I will tell you about it when I come ...'. But Myers had been too confident and another letter written on 21 June explained that he had another interview with the Attorney General and had been opposed 'in a very sharp way ...' but that he had cleared all opposition and hoped that there would be no more. He now expected to get his patent 'in a few days' time'. His patent was granted and on 14 July he wrote with delight: 'I got my patent the night before last'. It is Patent No. 10,756.

Much of the carving and sculpting was done in the workshops at Ordnance Wharf before being transported to the building sites. We know that the carving of the gateway for Magdalen College, Oxford, and the entrance to Viscount Midleton's estate at Peper Harow were both executed there. Pulpits, altars, windows and lecterns were made and dispatched. Birds of every feather came from the workshops including carved eagles, doves and two pelicans, for various clients. A triptych and a figure of the Blessed Virgin costing £20 were required for a London church and also a pulpit costing £16.

When Fr Robert William Willson[27] went to Tasmania in 1842, to be Bishop of Hobart, he took with him:

A gothic alphabet carved in stone,
4 head stones (for tombs),
2 flat stones,
2 crosses,
2 holy water stoops,

2 sacraria,
a font with pillars,
a top for an altar,
6 relic cases (like Liverpool),
a confessional,
3 model churches which took to pieces,

all of which were made in Myers' workshops. Pugin writing to
Lord Shrewsbury commented: 'it is quite delightful to start in
the good style in the antipodes. It is quite an honour'[28].

There were other orders for overseas: a double tomb was
required for two babies, John Henry Marie Louis Connelly
(aged 2½), and Marie Magdalene Eliza Julia Connelly, (only
seven weeks)[29] which was directed to:

St Charles College
Grand Coteau
Care of Monsr Vezian
Évêché
New Orleans.

A 6ft 9in. pillar was to be sent to:

Mr Pierce, builder
at St Peter's College
Wexford
Ireland.

It was to travel by the Wexford steamer from Liverpool. The
foundation stone of this collegiate church, the first of Pugin's
Irish churches, was laid on 18 June 1838,[30] when Myers'
workshops were still in Hull. The pillar was presumably
intended as a pattern which could be copied.

The carvings were created by Myers' craftsmen from
Pugin's working drawings, which were sketched on pieces of
paper seldom more than 9in. x 6in., sometimes smaller. Pugin
usually signed them, sometimes dated them and occasionally
wrote instructions, such as: 'keep as nearly as possible to one of
the early lions', or, on another occasion, beside a drawing of a

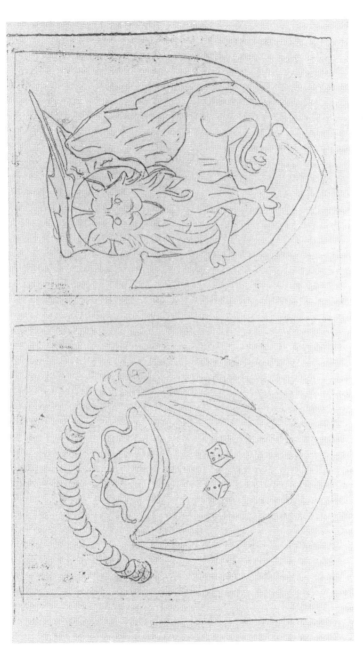

Figure 12 Judas' thirty pieces of silver and the dice used by the soldiers to cast lots for Christ's cloak without seam, and another lion emblem.

Figure 13   The Ox, the emblem of St Luke and the
emblem of St Matthew, both from two angles.

winged bull, the emblem of St Mark the Evangelist, he wrote: 'half the end of tail on the other side'. The destination, such as: 'Evangelists Nottingham' was often in Myers' hand. Sometimes drawings for two different churches were on the same piece of paper, Nottingham at the top and Southwark at the bottom.[31]

Myers travelled constantly to ensure the progress of his buildings and, with Pugin, to visit new sites and to discuss new projects. J.H. Powell in his manuscript *Pugin In His Home* describes how on these occasions Pugin was often embarrassed by Myers' enormous appetite because he was 'a maelstrom with which he (Pugin) was ashamed to travel', and that 'Myers caused a dearth of provisions wherever he went'.[32] Myers explained to Hardman that he had been to Nottingham 'yesterday' and that he would be 'in Ramsgate on Thursday', but that for the time being he would be at the Wharf as 'I have to be in the way to meet two or three important people'. He does not disclose who they were. He complained: 'I am not half my time at home'.

He was often abrupt with his correspondents. Writing to Hardman he pointed out: 'if you refer to our paper you will see that you have had the dimensions twice over'. If papers were lost the goods were not ready on the allotted day, and Myers' careful planning was upset. It was essential that the right craftsmen should be in the right place at the right time. There was much discussion as to when Thomas Earley would finish 'the painting' and where he was to proceed to next, and it was important that the stained glass windows should arrive as the masons reached the string course of the church being constructed, as the windows were built into the walls as the work proceeded.[33]

Of the many skilled jobs carried out in the workshops, one of the most demanding was the making of models or patterns for Hardman's metal work, both cast iron and brass. These patterns were a representation in wood, usually pine or mahogany, and were made from Pugin's drawings.

Myers, with his long experience of stone and wood carving, trained his men to the highest standards. When the patterns had been carved, they were dispatched to Hardman in

Birmingham who made the moulds.[34]   These were of sand, which may seem surprising but it was sand of a special consistency. The pattern was placed in the sand which was firmly compacted round it, then removed and the molten metal, either iron or brass, was poured into the space. Sometimes an awkwardly shaped object had to be made in separate parts which would be joined together later. Finally the casting would be smoothed and polished.

On 7 March 1851, Myers wrote to Hardman: 'I send you the models for the 2 Birds, 2 Shields, 2 Acorns and the Crown for the figure for Mr Pugin's B.V.—— I want you to get them done as soon as you can'. The work was done in such a hurry that the crown did not fit and Myers had to return it to Birmingham to be altered. The patterns for the brass lectern at Ushaw College near Durham were made by Myers' craftsmen in 1847.[35]   There was consternation when Pugin's drawing of it was lost. Myers wrote to Hardman: '... our people here are quite certain that it went off as I say, - (i.e. with the patterns when they were sent to Birmingham) - so let your people look round, I have no doubt it will turn up'. The letter was headed 'Monday Morning'. By Saturday morning it had turned up - in Myers' workshop. This lectern is a masterpiece of design and craftsmanship. Thomas Earley was working at Ushaw when it arrived in Durham. He took a wagon and went late at night on Tuesday 23 November 1847 to collect it and bring it to the College. He reported that it had arrived 'perfectly safely', and that he had 'fixed' it. He went on to say:

> it has caused quite a stir in the College. They were round me like a swarm of bees. Dr Newsham (President of Ushaw 1837-63) never left me for one instant while it was being fixed. I think that will be sufficient guarantee to you that it was carefully done. I cleaned it with new leathers. It is perfectly beautiful. Dr Newsham is in ecstasies about it ...[36]

They may have been rejoicing at Ushaw but at the Wharf, on 22 November 1847, Myers begged Hardman : 'do if

Figure 14   Lillies, the emblem of the Virgin Mary.
The Eagle, the emblem of St John.

Figure 15   The Pelican, the emblem of Mother Church.

you please get the brass done for Sir Willoughby Jones or I shall be shot in my wharf, for he was here again today, it is dreadful'. 'The brass' did not arrive until 20 June 1848, but when it did David Myers reported that 'it looked very well'. One can only hope that Sir Willoughby thought so too and that nobody was shot. He came from a family accustomed to firearms. His father, Sir John Thomas Jones of Norfolk, had a long and distinguished career in the service of the Duke of Wellington for which he was awarded a Baronetcy. Sir Willoughby's elder brother, Lawrence, succeeded to the title on the death of their father but was murdered by brigands in Greece on 7 November 1845. Perhaps 'the brass' was a memorial to Sir Lawrence.[37]

In May 1850, G. G. Scott employed Myers to make the lectern for the cathedral he was building in St John's, Newfoundland,[38] and a month later Myers wrote to Scott to ask for the tracing of the marble altar table also for Newfoundland, (and a cast for the Ely font: Scott was in charge of the restoration work at this Cathedral). The date on Myers' letter was 10 July 1850. By 22 July the goods for Newfoundland were packed, insured and ready to be dispatched to Canada aboard the 'good ship Bertha', whose Master was William Crowte.

A fireplace and other stone work went to Lismore Castle, the Duke of Devonshire's Irish home, which Sir Joseph Paxton was restoring. The fireplace had been intended for Horsted Place, Sussex but Mr Barchard, the owner of Horsted, did not like it and so, with the Duke's coat of arms added, it went to Lismore and looks magnificent in his Gothic Hall.[39] There were exhibits for the Dublin Exhibition of 1853 and at about the same time an altar was dispatched to Verviers in Belgium; in 1855 there is a reference to Myers' account with the Australian Benedictines. The Benedictines of Sydney had Pugin candlesticks and tabernacles in their church and much ecclesiastical furniture travelled to the Australian continent in those years.[40]

In the summer of 1851 Myers discussed with Hardman the possibility of having a separate workshop for Pugin's commissions, but nothing came of it as Pugin's health was deteriorating rapidly. But it is an indication of the amount of work Myers must have been doing for other people, as well as for Pugin, to make such an idea worth considering.

The craftsmen in the workshops were Myers' pride and joy, but working on the forecourt of the Wharf was a rough unruly body of labourers who loaded and unloaded the drays and barges, and packed the crates to be dispatched via Pickfords or other carriers. These men often packed the goods carelessly which resulted in breakages. In June 1847 a screen and the wings of an eagle were smashed in transit. Myers wrote to Hardman:

> I never saw the like of the fools to think of sending the things off without a case. Really I keep blowing up as hard as I can. The fact is I do believe all the men together are drunk half the time, I never saw such a year for drinking ... Really I could cry, I assure you, I don't know what to do with the beasts.

What a kingdom Myers had to rule over — the craftsmen in their shops, the carpenters, blacksmiths, glaziers and apprentices, and the great body of unruly labourers and packers. Past the Wharf flowed the malodorous Thames. In 1858 a debate in Parliament was cut short by the stench from the river, but the river odours were masked at the Wharf, at least to some extent, by the smell of the resins from the wood, the pungent smell of the blacksmiths' shop, of hot metal on stone and of horses and the smell of unwashed men.[41]

Here, very early in the morning of Thursday, 7 February 1850, fire broke out. Fires were common in the 19th century, but the *Illustrated London News* of 9 February described the fire at Ordnance Wharf and said that: 'in the extent of its ravages it exceeded any catastrophe of the kind with which the Metropolis has been visited for many years past'. The fire was said to have started in the blacksmiths' shop. There was a strong north-westerly wind blowing which fanned the flames so that before long, despite the efforts of the West of England Fire Office's fire brigade, Myers' whole premises were ablaze. Messrs Nickels' warehouse containing much valuable machinery and a large

Figure 16   An Angel.

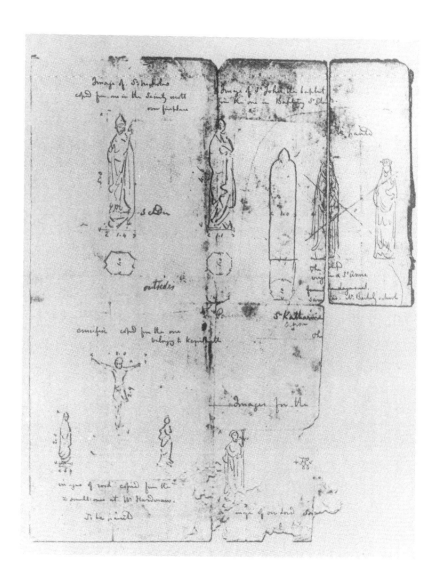

Figure 17   Drawings with dimensions, of statues from
various locations.

quantity of manufactured india rubber was destroyed. The houses in the adjoining streets where many of the craftsmen lived were gutted. Blocks of Portland stone lying in the yard, weighing several tons each, crumbled into fragments and were converted into lime by the heat of the fire. There appears to have been no night watchman on the premises to rescue four valuable horses which were burnt to death, and the fire caused the destruction of the entire carved stonework Myers was carrying out for 'Mr Pugin the eminent architect'.[42] Of all Myers' men not one managed to save a tool, and a large body of young women from the workshops in the area, which had been burnt to the ground, were thrown out of work. Myers was insured with The West of England and Phoenix Fire Offices. The other contractors and manufacturers with warehouses in the district were also insured but the inhabitants of the tenements were not. A few days later *The Times* appealed for donations to help the workmen and women to replace their tools and on 28 February the names of contributors were published. Heading the list was Mr Myers who gave £21. Workmen in his employ at Colney Hatch gave £18. 15s. 0d. and those at his other works gave £10. 16s. 6d. Messrs Gabriel, the timber merchants gave £10. Miss Burdett Coutts gave £2 and G.G. Scott, the architect gave £5. 5s. 0d. Many building firms made contributions. *The Times* noted that enough was collected to prevent the workmen's losses being seriously felt.

Pugin, writing to Crace the day after the fire, added a postscript to his letter:

> I have just heard that Myers' shops are burnt. I hope and trust it is not the workshops where all the pattern work is. He has been doing a deal of moulding work lately. I thought something would happen.[43]

Myers' premises were partly destroyed again in 1862 and, when a third disastrous fire occurred in July 1867, a lengthy article in *The Builder* pointed out that it was the terrified occupants of the nearby tenements who first raised the alarm, rather than the night watchman. The article asked a great many questions about the type of men who were employed as watchmen, what they were paid and also about the safety precautions insisted on in factories and stores. Shortly afterwards a Parliamentary Select Committee made recommendations concerning the protection of life and property against fire, the fireproofing of buildings and the storing of flammable oils, and in 1870 it was made obligatory for the water companies to supply their customers with water on Sundays, which had not been the case previously.[44]

The official report for insurance purposes concerning the 1850 fire, stated that Myers' offices, sawmills, workshops, including a very valuable and powerful steam engine and the stables with their contents, were wholly destroyed. Anyone but Myers would have been devastated, but two weeks later, on 20 February he was writing: '... we are all in a rough state at present, though I have all my works going on at full speed'. Nothing daunted him. The workshops were rebuilt, the stone was replaced, the patterns were remade and everything went on as before.

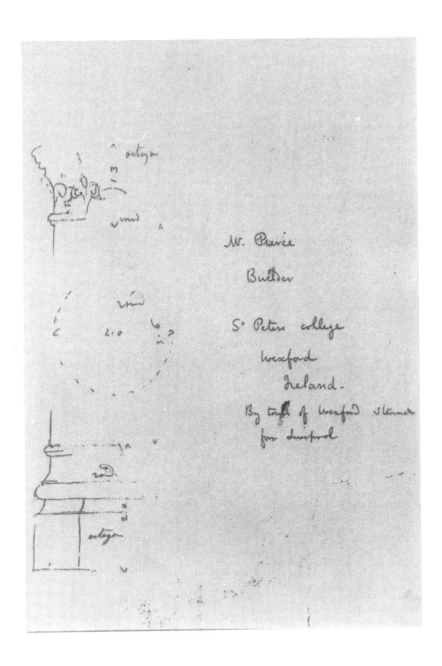

Figure 18   Pillar for Wexford.

Figure 19   Conflagration at Ordnance Wharf,
7 February 1850.

III

Perfect Gothic and the Great Exhibition: 1838-54

During the years 1840-1850 Myers carried out more work for
A.W.N.Pugin than for any other architect. There is no record
however that he had any official part in the most splendid of
Pugin's secular works, that is the decoration and furnishing of
the Houses of Parliament after the fire of 16th October 1834
nor was he called upon to tender, in 1838, for the first phase of
the rebuilding contract. At this time Myers' yards and
workshops were still in Hull where they were to remain for the
next eight or nine years. But in 1852, when tenders were
invited for the completion of the work (there had been
disagreement over prices and insurance with Grissell & Peto the
original contractors), Myers submitted a tender of £158,110.
14s. which was 4% higher than Jay's at £152,333. 6s.[1] Jay got
the contract, but the next year he was obliged to explain that he
had underestimated and had to ask for more money. Myers'
price had been more realistic. We know that on at least one
occasion Thomas Earley asked if he could borrow one of
Myers' men to help with the painting of the House of Lords.[2]
By 1847 Myers' yards and workshops were established at
Ordnance Wharf, the distance of Westminster Bridge from the
building site on the other side of the river, so it is unlikely that
this was the only occasion he was called upon for assistance.

     Pugin did not build great country houses but he did
enlarge and 'modernise' several well-known mansions. In 1837

he started work at Scarisbrick Hall in Lancashire for a wealthy bachelor, Charles Scarisbrick, and soon afterwards he began working for the Earl of Shrewsbury at Alton Towers in Staffordshire. There is no documentary evidence to show that Myers worked at Scarisbrick, but it is unlikely that Pugin would have undertaken this task if Myers had not been employed at least in a supervisory capacity. There are no documents showing the work Myers carried out at Alton Towers, but in a letter written by Lord Shrewsbury on 11 November 1848 in answer to Myers' request for a testimonial,[3] he refers to 'all the works you have executed for me ... '. There are also references to alterations (Gothicisation) at Chirk Castle for Colonel Middleton Biddulph in the 1840s and '50s in Myers' letters to Hardman and in Pugin's diaries.

In the 1840s Myers, with Pugin as architect, carried out work on two large estates near Guildford, at Albury Park for Henry Drummond and at Peper Harow for Viscount Midleton. As well as his park and farms in Surrey, Lord Midleton owned property in Ireland where Pugin had designed a model village for him with a Mr Pierce as Clerk of Works. Mr Pierce's fee was £1. 1s. 0d. a week, an amount Lord Midleton considered excessive, but Pugin assured him that this was a very moderate salary for good service, and he pointed out that it was a very different matter working with Irish builders compared with a man like Myers,[4] whom Pugin had had difficulty in persuading Lord Midleton to employ. Mr Moon was the local builder and His Lordship wanted him to do the work at Peper Harow, but Pugin wrote a lengthy letter explaining that he did not want to expend his time 'instructing modern Humbugs of builders'. He then listed Myers' many virtues - he was a man of tried skill and integrity who 'perfectly understands my principles of work and drawings'. Pugin objected to having to deal with a complete stranger who would require full-sized drawings, whereas Myers without such drawings could be relied upon to produce the most perfect work. For the future, Pugin insisted that he would decline any work for which he could not appoint his own builder.[5] Needless to say Lord Midleton objected to his builder being called a 'humbug', so Pugin wrote another long letter to explain that he had not applied the epithet to Mr Moon in

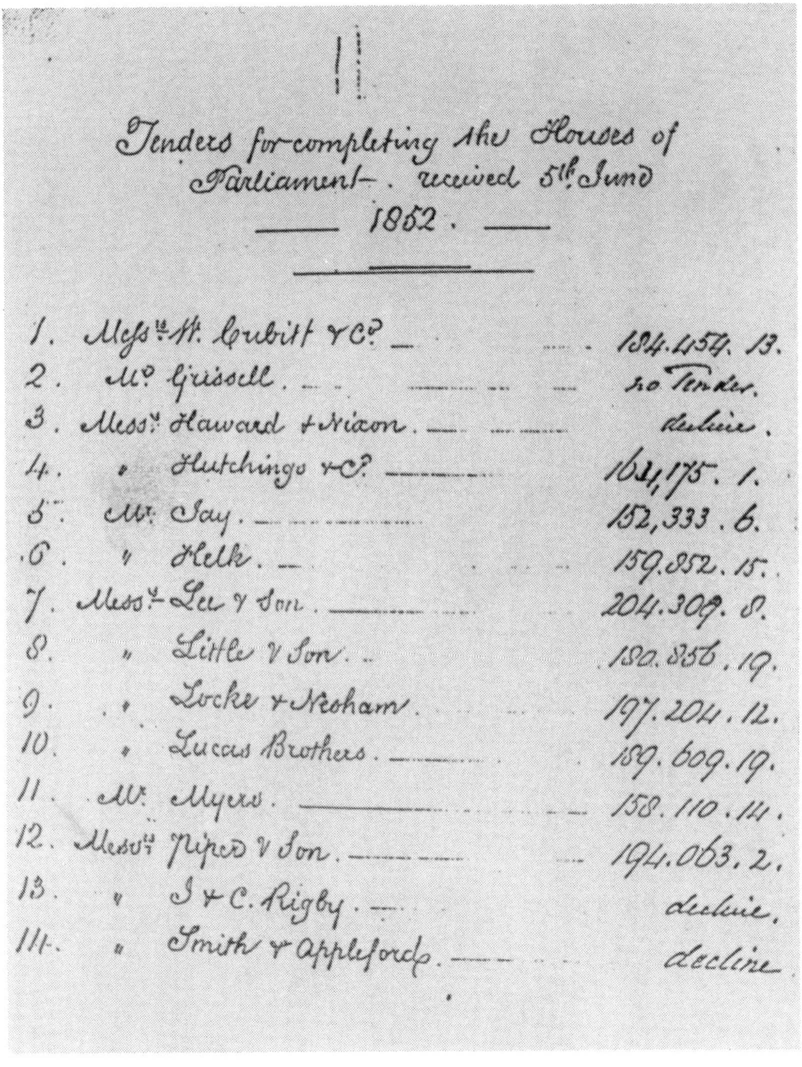

Tenders for completing the Houses of Parliament. received 5th June 1852.

1.	Messrs. W. Cubitt & Co.	184.454. 13.
2.	Mr. Grissell.	no Tender.
3.	Messrs. Haward & Nixon.	decline.
4.	„ Hutchings & Co.	164,175. 1.
5.	Mr. Jay.	152,333. 6.
6.	„ Kelk.	159.852. 15.
7.	Messrs. Lee & Son.	204.309. 8.
8.	„ Little & Son.	130.856. 19.
9.	„ Locke & Nesham.	197.204. 12.
10.	„ Lucas Brothers.	189.609.19.
11.	Mr. Myers.	158.110. 14.
12.	Messrs. Piper & Son.	194.063. 2.
13.	„ J & C. Rigby.	decline.
14.	„ Smith & Appleford.	decline

Figure 20   Tenders for the final stages of the rebuilding
of the Houses of Parliament, 1852.
PRO Works 11/6.
Courtesy of the Public Record Office.

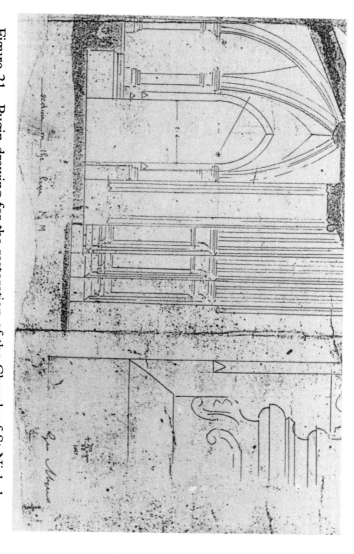

Figure 21   Pugin drawing for the restoration of the Church of St Nicholas,
Peper Harow, signed by Pugin and Myers 1842.
Courtesy of The Right Hon. Viscount Midleton.

person, but to the 'class to which he belongs, for modern builders build anything and everything that they think will pay and always work in a slightly unsatisfactory manner', an explanation which may not have improved matters. Mr Moon cannot have been very unsatisfactory as his name was still appearing in *The Builder's* list of tenders twenty years later. It appears that he was employed to build the cowfold and barn, with Pugin complaining that this caused him unnecessary trouble and anxiety.

There was plenty of work for Myers. In 1842 he built the Gate House at the Oxenford entrance to the estate at a cost of £2,052. Lord Midleton's coat of arms was carved on the inner boss of the arch, Myers having borrowed a shield so that it could be copied in his workshop. On the outer boss, was an ox crossing a ford with water-plant leaves round the edge. Both bosses were to be painted and gilded. There was also a turret with a weather vane. Pugin was delighted with it all and was very anxious that Lord Midleton should come to see it as soon as he returned to Peper Harow. Myers also carried out work on the estate at Mousehill House Parsonage for Lord Midleton where there was much discussion about the stone to be used. Myers rebuilt the romantic little spring house with its floor of tiles and its pond lined with lead. Lord Midleton wanted a rock garden and a fountain but Pugin hastened to write: 'the idea of the rock work gives me the horrors, already I seem at once transported from the Park to the back garden of a Brixton villa ...'. He was happy about the fountain until he discovered that it was to be made of Irish stone and that an Irishman was to be imported to erect it.[6] Once again Pugin wrote despairingly to point out that the Irishman would need two others to supervise him, presumably chosen by Pugin, in case he spoilt the stone by cutting it in the wrong place.

At about this time a letter arrived from Lord Midleton's cousin and heir, asking if he had found at Peper Harow the Pope's Plenary Indulgence for the sins of the Brodricks, (Lord Midleton's family name). Cousin Brodrick said that the last time he had seen it, it had been in one of the commodes between the library windows. He suggested that an inspection of it might raise him in Pugin's estimation.[7]

Myers built a Gothic 'ruin' in the garden and restored the 13th century parish church of St Nicholas which stands on the edge of the estate but there is no mention in the little guide book, to be found in the church, of Pugin, Myers or the restorations done in the early 1840s. The work done was extensive and the beautiful drawings, signed by both Pugin and Myers and dated 1842, can be seen in the Guildford Muniment Room.[8] The 'Irish' fountain was eventually carved in Myers' workshops by Myers' craftsmen, but it does not seem to have been a success, because on 9 May 1848, he wrote to remind Lord Midleton that his account had not been settled, that he had not been paid for three years and, even more distressing, Lord Midleton's secretary had desired Myers to remove the fountain 'forthwith'. Was this really His Lordship's requirement? But Lord Midleton was seriously ill both physically and mentally and was to die within a few months. He had no son and the title and estate passed to his cousin. One can only hope that eventually all debts were paid and that the fountain was appreciated.

Henry Drummond of Albury Park, who was a neighbour of Lord Midleton's, was a member of The Holy Catholic and Apostolic Church, which had been founded by Edward Irving who was the preacher much admired by Pugin's mother. Drummond contributed generously to the building of Irvingite churches, in particular the church in Gordon Square, London, which Myers was to build in 1851, and the church in Glasgow about which Myers was consulted. Drummond built a church of this denomination in the village of Albury and the new parish church in Western Street where most of the Albury villagers now lived. Drummond persuaded the Bishop of Winchester to declare redundant the old Saxon church which stood on the Albury estate, and then excluded the parishioners from both church and graveyard where their kin had been buried for generations. In 1844, Drummond had engaged Pugin to design the mortuary chapel in the old church for members of his family. Henry Drummond's three sons, all of whom died in early manhood, and a daughter are buried there, in addition to Drummond himself and his wife. The elder daughter married Lord Lovaine, later sixth Duke of Northumberland, and is not buried in the little church.[9] Myers did the masonry work in the chapel, which is in the transept of the Saxon ruin, Wailes of Newcastle made the eight armorial stained glass windows, Minton the tiles and, at a later date in 1847, Thomas Earley painted the walls and ceiling in glowing colours. Wailes charged £40 for the stained glass windows and £13. 4s. 0d., for their wrought iron frames. He wrote on 20 July 1844 and explained that it would be a most acceptable favour if he could be paid within the next two or three days as he was going abroad to copy 'ancient glass'.[10] After years of neglect the little church is once again being lovingly restored, services are held there several times a year and the parishioners have access at 'all reasonable hours'.

It was not until 1846 that Henry Drummond started to plan the alterations to his house with Pugin as architect. Pugin's reply to a letter of Drummond's on the subject was written by a scribe, as his eyes were so painful that he could not write himself. The letter was headed: 'Feast of the Holy Innocents' i.e. 28 December 1846. The letter discussed the question of a new roof and suggested that Myers 'who executes the greater part of my work ...' should be employed.[11] In a second letter, this time undated and written in his own hand, he explained that he was suffering from 'a dreadful nervous fever' brought on by anxiety and overwork, that he could not travel more than half a mile from his house and that he saw nobody. In a postscript he added: 'if you employ Myers in the alterations at your home, I will give him every benefit of my advice'.[12] Once again Mr Moon appeared on the scene quoting the price of 'coping and saddle stones in Bath Stone as per measurements ... at £6. 12s. 0d., each'. But Henry Drummond took Pugin's advice and Myers worked at Albury Park at least until the end of 1856.

Myers made many improvements inside the house. He sent in a detailed estimate, but pointed out that 'water closets were not included'. He made a new front entrance and replaced windows using the fashionable plate glass. He renewed the roof and built the forest of sixty-three 'Elizabethan' chimneys, each one different. He sculpted two magnificent eagles which stand sentinel on the roof holding metal vanes in their terrifying beaks.

He charged £15 for each one and described them as: 'splendid fellows - the finest eagles in the country'.[13] Anyone who visits Albury would agree.

Myers got on well with Henry Drummond, though he was domineering and often difficult, and continued to work for him after Pugin's death, but the work did not run so smoothly under the direction of Edward Pugin, A.W.N. Pugin's son. There were 'many attacks' and 'misunderstandings'.[14] This is not surprising as the very experienced Myers was nearly old enough to be the young architect's grandfather.

A.W.N. Pugin designed and Myers built the church of St Marie's near Rugby for Captain Washington Hibbert. They were also employed to enlarge and embellish Bilton Grange, which Capt. Hibbert had bought from Abraham Hume, Esq., some years before. Though he did not object to Pugin recommending his own builder, he was difficult to please. Myers complained that he was being 'ruled' by the autocratic Captain. Neither irate landowners nor striking masons perturbed Myers overmuch, but Pugin was more easily upset. On a visit to Bilton Grange in May 1848 he was so upset by Capt. Hibbert's 'running fire of abuse and sarcasm',[15] that he vowed never to return.

A letter from Myers to Hardman headed 'On the River Thames, Monday' and postmarked 12 September 1848, said: 'Capt. Hibbert wishes to see the Governor and yourself and your humble servant after 18th at Bilton Grange', the cause of the summons was not disclosed. Then in July 1849 'the Captain' desired Myers to inform Hardman that the dogs' heads on the grates in the drawing room and library wanted refiring and making straight. Myers advised Hardman: 'I think you had better send a smith, one who understands what to do'. Even so when asked to provide testimonials at the time of winning the contract to build Colney Hatch Asylum, he included Capt. Hibbert's name, but almost at the bottom of the list, just above that of two tradesmen.

The Revd Richard Waldo Sibthorpe, a Fellow of Magdalen College Oxford, who came of a Lincolnshire family, was in some ways even more difficult than Capt. Hibbert. He was a friend of Ambrose Phillipps and other Oxford Movement men. He had been born into the Church of England and had taken Holy Orders in 1815. In 1841 he had been one of the first of the Movement to convert to Catholicism and had been ordained a year later, but by 1843 he had reverted to the church of his birth.[16] Pugin was deeply shocked when he heard this 'scandalous story' and wrote an emotional letter to the Revd Mr Bloxam at Magdalen College saying that he hoped this news was not true. Apparently he had forgotten that Mr Bloxam, who was and always remained a loyal member of the Church of England, could not be expected to have the same ideas as himself on the correctness or otherwise of Mr Sibthorpe's behaviour. Waldo Sibthorpe became a Catholic again in 1865, though he decreed in his will that he was to be buried according to the rites of the Church of England, but by that time Pugin had been dead for ten years. Mr Sibthorpe must have known that his second change of religion had shocked Pugin greatly, but nevertheless he asked him to design the Bede Houses he intended to build and endow in Lincoln. Pugin did so but refused to supervise the building work and Myers built the very attractive little St Anne's Bede Houses from Pugin's drawings without supervision. After the work was finished Sibthorpe drew up a long list of complaints about the cost, the stone, the gutters and a great many other things and sent the list to Pugin. Despite his dissatisfaction in 1850 he asked Pugin to build a chapel, but stipulated that Myers was not to be employed. Pugin in a letter to Mr Bloxam explained:

> People imagine that anyone can execute church work but it is not so and it takes years to bring a man into it. Under these circumstances I have no hesitation in declining to have anything to do with the building.[17]

In the end it was Butterfield who built the church.

The old people who live in the Bede Houses are enjoined to pray (bede = pray) every day. It would be interesting to know if they pray for the repose of the soul of their restless founder.

In 1844 Myers built a new entrance to Magdalen College, Oxford. Many letters passed between Pugin and the Revd John Bloxam, Fellow of Magdalen, on this and other subjects. They were friends and their correspondence, which is kept at Magdalen, dates from 1840 and continued until the end of Pugin's life. Pugin was delighted to get the commission but the College authorities were not prepared to tolerate his unorthodox business methods and insisted on a formal contract. It pleased Pugin to work in medieval Oxford so he put up with this restraint on his normal practice, but he did insist on Myers being employed, exclaiming: 'how could I possibly execute such work with any but my own builder ...? I want it to be perfection'.[18]   The gate was dismantled in 1883 because it interfered with the College plans for expansion.

It was at this time, 1843-44, that Myers built the Grange at Ramsgate, Pugin's 'substantial home by the sea'.   Much of the furniture, made in his workshops in Lambeth, was acquired by English Heritage in the 1960s and is now in the Speaker's House in the Palace of Westminster.   Hardman made the stained glass windows and the metalwork, Minton the tiles and Crace the materials and wallpapers. The Grange, despite its pretentious name, was a comfortable family home, perhaps a bit chilly in winter, not large and only slightly Gothic.   It stood on the cliff and from its tower with his 'glass' Pugin could watch the sea and ships, and it was from here that he went to the rescue of many sailors, whose ships had been wrecked on the Goodwin Sands, carrying them up to his house to revive them. Those who did not survive are buried in the churchyard beside his house.   Their tombstones were carved in Myers' workshops and when the drowned sailors were French the inscriptions were in their own language.   It was here at the Grange that Pugin entertained his friends amongst whom he counted both Myers and Hardman.[19]   Myers sometimes came and stayed a day or two to collect urgent drawings and check plans.

Myers built The Glebe House at Rampsham in Dorset and restored the chancel of the church.   He declined to build the parsonage at Lanteglos by Camelford in Cornwall, (the living is in the gift of the Duchy of Cornwall).   He had been sent by Pugin to visit the site and to cost the materials, but

Figure 22   The Revd Waldo Sibthorpe's Alms Houses, Lincoln, 1848.
From the Local Studies Collection, Lincoln Central Library, by courtesy of Lincolnshire County Council Recreational Services.

Figure 23 Goods arriving at the Great Exhibition, 1851.
Courtesy of the Guildhall Library, Corporation of London.

Pugin decided that it was too far to travel for so small a work and Myers was unwilling to undertake the contract for the same reason. Eventually the plans and drawings were sent to the Rector and Pugin hoped that he would be able to manage with 'the builders on the spot ... (though) they do not take so many pains as Myers'.[20] In the event the local builder was successful and *The Gazetteer of Cornwall* dated 1885 p. 62 records that 'the rectorial mansion (at Camelford) is the largest and best in the County'.

It is difficult to think of work done by Pugin which is purely secular. The houses he enlarged and Gothicised all had chapels which needed restoring at the same time, or, as at Bilton Grange, he was engaged to build a church just a short distance away. Any commission to build a church included a presbytery or a priest's house as well: often schools and colleges were also required. The great expansion at Ushaw College in County Durham occurred at this time; work was also carried out at St Edmond's, Ware, Hertfordshire and there are also references to Oscott in Myers' letters to Hardman. These were all colleges run by priests. Myers was responsible for the building at Ushaw and St Edmond's during Pugin's lifetime, but whether he did any significant work at Oscott is not clear.

Then, in 1851, occurred the Great Exhibition which stirred and excited the imagination of the civilised world to an extent that is difficult to realise today and which gave Pugin's craftsmen a spectacular chance to exhibit their skills and artistry. It was the first to be international in scope. Before 1851 foreign governments had promoted their own national exhibitions but on a much smaller scale. This one was to be open to the whole world, much of which, at that time, was mysterious and unknown. It is said that the first seeds of the idea grew from a chance meeting of Francis Fuller and Thomas Cubitt. Fuller was a member of the Society of Arts, whose President was Prince Albert. Returning by train from the Paris Exhibition of 1849, Fuller met Thomas Cubitt who was on his way back from Osborne, in the Isle of Wight, where he had been working for the Prince. Fuller suggested that 'a much grander work' could be staged in London by inviting other nations to participate. Cubitt was enthusiastic and undertook to bring the idea to

Prince Albert's notice. When he did so, the Prince in his turn was filled with enthusiasm and with his encouragement and zeal the success of the project was assured.[21]

'The World' was invited to exhibit her goods, but the Hyde Park location was not decided on until June 1850, and it was not until 15 July that Joseph Paxton's design for the building was chosen. The decision to open the exhibition on 1 May 1851, just eleven months away, had already been taken and the exhibits themselves were to be in place by the end of March.

Joseph Paxton, the designer of The Crystal Palace, as the Exhibition Hall came to be known, had been the Duke of Devonshire's head gardener at Chatsworth in Derbyshire. He had experimented in glasshouse design and built the Chatsworth Conservatory. He had rebuilt Edensor village for the Duke, so that it no longer obstructed the view from the house, and had designed public parks in Liverpool and Birkenhead and a cemetery in Coventry. In 1848 he was appointed Agent for the Chatsworth Estate. He had been born in Bedfordshire in 1803, the same year as George Myers.

That part of the Crystal Palace allocated to Pugin and his craftsmen was known as 'The Medieval Court'. There is no record of his designs or details of the way in which space was to be distributed, but in the PRO there is a floor plan of squares and rectangles showing the space allocated to each country and the different areas to be occupied by machinery, textiles, glass, etc.[22] The third square on the left from the South Entrance has five names on it: 'Pugin, Crace, Hardman, Minton, Myers'. It is the only square on the whole plan which is labelled with the names of individual persons. This was the place where Pugin and his craftsmen determined to display their beautiful Gothic furnishings to the best advantage. Thomas Earley did the decorative painting and as usual he kept Hardman informed of his own and everyone else's progress.

His first letter about the Exhibition is undated but has 'March 1851' written across the top in another hand. It describes how he and Pugin set off from Myers' Wharf for the Exhibition site, which he very aptly describes as: 'the Great Babel'. When they got there, it took them over an hour to find

Hardman's sixteen cases and four packages stowed away among a multitude of other goods. There were no porters to fetch and carry, only soldiers to ensure law and order. Earley gave a shilling to one of them who, with the help of his friends, moved the cases to a safe place. Earley reported that Myers' man had to wait upwards of five hours with his waggons before he could come in with a load of stone. The effigy of Dr Walsh (the recently deceased Catholic Bishop of Birmingham), which was destined for his tomb, and a great quantity of other stonework had to be fixed on site. Earley also reported that Minton's tiles for his great stove had arrived at Camden Town. They had come by canal from Stoke. Then on Monday 31 March, whatever semblance of order and system which had existed in the Exhibition Hall was totally disrupted. The joiners and painters struck because they had not been paid. Earley reported that there was a fearful uproar: 'More than 1400 men rowing like madmen in the Colonial part of the building until they were driven out by the police and soldiers'. This must have made the exhibitors very nervous. Pugin refers to the episode in his diary but, as so often on other occasions, his date was incorrect.[23] Poor Earley finished his letter by asking that his scrawl should be excused as his hand was not very steady after 'mauling' heavy boxes about.

The confusion continued. Goods belonging to the different exhibitors were left in immense heaps. The Coalbrook Founders were fixing iron fenders and other ferrous objects which were about to overspill into the area allotted to the Medieval Court and an adjacent exhibitor complained bitterly that light was being excluded from his area by Gothic tapestries. Earley himself was in despair because as soon as he finished his painting or gilding it was entirely spoilt by the clouds of dust raised by the carts, trucks and barrows which filled the whole building.

In the Medieval Court there was still much to be done, besides the problem of Burns and Lambert's piano which had been decorated by Pugin and Crace. It was not only that the panels had yet to be gilded, but the manufacturers wanted it to be played at the Exhibition. Crace would have to fulfil this commission. Pugin explained in a letter[24] that he could not play the piano 'nor Myers either - and I don't think Minton would be very brilliant, so it falls on you to delight the entranced circle of admirers . . . with occasional selections from Rossini'.

Suddenly the authorities were appalled by the chaos and confusion. The Exhibition was by now due to open in less than a fortnight. Earley reported that an edict had been issued that all packages, wrappers and baskets must be unpacked and the cases removed by Saturday night next or they would be unpacked at the exhibitor's own risk. But Earley's letters did not contain only complaints about dust and masons. He tells how on 15 April he was painting away and when he looked up whom should he see but the Queen herself, paying one of several private visits to the Exhibition site before it was open to the public. She spent five minutes or more talking to him and expressed her pleasure at the beautiful things on the stand.

It is extraordinary that Earley had the time and energy to write such lengthy letters. He wrote not only about his own trials and tribulations, but his kind heart also prompted him to write about poor 'Seadon', presumably one of the apprentices, who had to be lent some money to buy clothes 'as he is a very good lad and his wages are small and so short he cannot get enough to buy himself anything'.[25]

At last the dust settled. Everybody put on their best clothes, as The Great Day, Thursday 1 May 1851, had arrived, and it was sunny and warm. The Queen, accompanied by Prince Albert, the Royal children and many of her German relations, declared the Exhibition open. The streets were thronged with foreigners and immense crowds were everywhere, with, it was said, 300,000 people converging on Hyde Park.[26] The Medieval Court was declared a great success. The *Illustrated London News* reported that: 'amongst all the admirably arranged treasures of the Great Exhibition the Medieval Court we may say, on mature reflection, presents the most unique (*sic*), and best harmonised display of art and skill'.

One would have thought that everyone would have been happy, but Crace was not. George Myers had upset him. We know all about it because Pugin wrote a long conciliatory letter to Crace which said:

My Dear Sir,
Both myself and Hardman are greatly distressed at the annoyance you experienced from Myers' absurd conduct and we are willing to do anything to meet your wishes and put an end to it. Hardman says he will move his lectern to the other side and make room for the cabinet by the cross if that would be more satisfactory to Myers. It is most distressing for him to create difficulties when everything is so satisfactory. I assure you we both feel how extremely kindly & generously you have acted on this occasion & how very very valuable your co-operation has been in the results achieved. It is to us very painful that you should have suffered the least annoyance on such unaccountable grounds & as I said before we will do anything in conjunction with you to put an end to it. We feel that it was exceedingly kind of you to allow the cabinet to be exhibited amongst your things — indeed I only asked it as a favour & you have met with a very unsuitable return. Myers is a man of most unfortunate temper & obstinate on some matters to a dreadful degree. However if we cannot bring him to reason I would really advise the removal of it to the other side & Hardman says he will move anything to suit the occasion. I hear on all sides the highest opinion on the Court — even it is the talk in the carriage in which I came down, I sitting as a perfect stranger.

A W Pugin[27]

It really must have been a dreadful fuss, because Hardman also had written a letter of 'condolence'. This letter, as far as is known, no longer exists, but Crace's reply does. He wrote from Wigmore Street on 7 May 1851:-

My Dear Sir,
I thank you and Mr Pugin very much for your kindly expressed notes in reference to Mr Myers

> of whom I had hoped better things - I do not wish his cabinet ruined but trust he will see the propriety of not nailing cards on the front of it - which does not look well independent of any objection to it.[28]

The clue to this distressing incident is possibly to be found in an article which appeared in the *Illustrated London News* describing how on

> the same side as Mr Crace's furniture (in the Medieval Court) there was an oak cabinet of very elaborate design, executed by Mr Myers as a present for his son. The panels contained various tools used in masonry, ornamentally disposed with foliage. The hinges, locks, etc., were of wrought brass.

It is not clear why Myers' cabinet was placed with Crace's furniture seemingly as a special favour, but as it was, of course Myers put a card on it. He did not want everyone to think that it was Crace who had created this beautiful work of art.

The journals and newspapers gave much space in praise of the Medieval Court, and called on the public to honour Pugin's artistry and the skill of his craftsmen. The *Illustrated London News* admired the medieval detail and design of the piano which would prevent this 'modern' instrument from looking out of place in a 'Gothic' room.

The exhibition Catalogue listed the awards. Myers won a medal for his exhibits which consisted of:

1. Font and cover in the style of the 15th century, the four carved panels showing: 'The Fall of Man', 'The Baptism of our Lord', 'St John Preaching in the Wilderness' and 'The Crucifixion'. (Now at St Augustine's, Ramsgate.)

2. A canopied tomb with effigy to be erected in St Chad's Cathedral, Birmingham for the late Dr Walsh.

3. Reredos and altar.
4. A stone tabernacle.
5. The Great Rood for the Chapel of St Edmond's College, Ware.
6. A screen for a church in oak. (St. Augustine's Ramsgate.)
7. A stone altar for a church.
8. A stone fireplace (Mr Barchard - Duke of Devonshire).
9. Compartment of a staircase (Horsted Place).
10. An oak cabinet in the style of the 15th century.
11. A copper casement for a Lunatic Asylum.

It was pointed out that all the stonework designed by Pugin had been executed in Myers' workshops and that he was the inventor of a patented machine for cutting Gothic tracery and mouldings and any circular form in wood or stone.

There had been those who doubted the wisdom of holding such an exhibition. Colonel Charles Sibthorpe M.P., the brother of the Revd Waldo Sibthorpe, deplored the whole enterprise on the grounds that it would tempt foreigners to come to these shores,[29] and Princess Lieven had considered it a 'bold, rash experiment' and 'apprehended a horrible explosion'.[30] But the huge crowd arriving in Hyde Park day after day throughout the summer behaved with the greatest decorum. People were fascinated and overawed by the strange vast engines and other machinery, and by the wealth of goods from all corners of the world. A visitor described the interior of the Crystal Palace as 'beyond the dreams of the Arabian romances'.

Myers' business had been well-established for many years but the success and publicity arising from the Exhibition (he had ordered 10,000 business cards for the occasion) had added to his renown.

A watercolour painting of the Medieval Court, painted by this versatile man, was exhibited at the Royal Academy Exhibition of 1853.[31]

After Pugin's death, when the Crystal Palace was moved to Sydenham (1852-4) to be used as a giant educational centre and amusement park, Myers was responsible for building the roads and for the masonry work. He also enlarged and improved Rockhill, the house which Sir Joseph Paxton bought for himself at Sydenham and it was under his direction that Myers altered and enlarged 'The Wood', now 16 Sydenham Hill and a Grade II listed building, for the Duke of Devonshire at a cost of £3,730. 2s. 8d.

The celebrations for the opening of the Sydenham Crystal Palace were almost as elaborate as those on the occasion of the inauguration of the Great Exhibition itself. Once again the ceremony was honoured by the presence of the Queen accompanied by Prince Albert, members of the Royal Family, foreign royalty and other distinguished guests who, after various presentations, formed a grand procession to tour the building. The procession was led by the Superintendents of Works and Principal Employees, followed by the Contractors amongst whom was George Myers, Principal Officers and Heads of Departments, the Directors of the Crystal Palace Company and finally the Queen, her family and guests. The Press[32] reported that:

> the whole spectacle ... could hardly fail to impress all who witnessed it with a sense of gratitude to the Almighty who permits England, while descending into the arena as the champion of Western Civilisation, thus to display what that civilisation means.

Figure 24   Sir Joseph Paxton (1803-65). Probably a
sketch study by Henry Wyndham Phillips for his painting
The Royal Commissioners for the Exhibition of 1851
(Victoria and Albert Museum).
Courtesy of John Kenworthy-Browne.

IV

Pugin Churches: 1838-54

It has been said that London, at the beginning of the 19th century, was a place of ungodliness, profligacy, intemperance, filth, riot, desperation and disease, which resulted in the destruction of physical, mental, moral and spiritual health. This state of affairs was greatly exacerbated by the Industrial Revolution and the enormous growth of the urban population. Very few of the governing class were compassionate but many of them were frightened. They feared that England would suffer the same fate as her European neighbours and came to the conclusion that one way to prevent revolution was to build churches. The result was the Church Building Act of 1818, which provided £1,000,000 for the building of Church of England churches in newly populous areas with another £1,000,000 voted a few years later. The fears remained very real, because of the unsettled political climate on the Continent and when, on 20 May 1848, Archdeacon Sinclair launched his appeal for funds to build Christchurch, Victoria Road, Kensington, he wrote:

> Recent events, both at home and abroad, have
> demonstrated, by evidence too plain to be
> mistaken, and too fearful to be overlooked, that
> the only real security for the peace and happiness
> of a country is the attachment of the people to its

civil and religious institutions. It is a duty which
every motive that can influence reasonable beings
- self-preservation, natural affection, patriotism,
brotherly love, and above all, Christian principle,
requires us to discharge.

The Catholics were almost destitute of churches as those
in which they had worshipped before the Reformation had been
taken over by the Established Church. There were a few
private chapels in the houses of the 'Old Catholics' and since
the Relief Act of 1778 there had been Mission Centres in some
towns. Owing to the penal laws under which recusants had
existed for so long, there were few Catholics able to pay for the
building of churches. Pugin's patron, the Earl of Shrewsbury,
was a wealthy man, however, and determined to contribute as
much as he was able towards the construction of churches for
his co-religionists. To this end he with his family spent much
of each year in Italy, where living was cheaper and where he
was not expected to entertain as much as when at home on his
estates in England.[1] The money he saved went towards the
building of Catholic churches. His favourite architect was
Pugin, and, as we know, Pugin had promised that George
Myers should 'execute' all his buildings.
    The first Pugin/Myers church to be built was St Mary's,
Derby, acknowledged by contemporary critics to be beautiful.
Wiseman, the future Cardinal Archbishop of Westminster, in a
letter to his mother said: '... it is without exception the most
magnificent thing the Catholics have yet done in modern times
in this country, and it is worthy of ancient days'.[2] It was built
of white stone and stands on a hill overlooking the main road
into the town.
    The foundation stone was laid on 28 June 1838, with
Myers bearing a ceremonial silver trowel on a crimson cushion.
Pugin was not there, having returned to London to see the
coronation of Queen Victoria. He was absent again on 9
October, 1839, when the church was consecrated. Pugin, the
Earl of Shrewsbury, and Ambrose Phillipps de Lisle, a convert
friend of both Pugin and Lord Shrewsbury, had arrived for the
ceremony, but when they discovered that instead of Gregorian

plain-chant there was to be a full orchestra and a choir including 'Women', they drove away in high dudgeon, the Earl 'pausing only to forbid the wearing of the cloth of gold vestments which he had given and Pugin had designed'.[3]

On the 12 January 1840, Mr Bagshawe, who was a member of the Building Committee, wrote to Bishop Walsh of Birmingham to report that: '... these bills ... will discharge every farthing owing on account of Derby except a balance of £1,300 to Mr Myers', presumably for building the presbytery as Catholic churches are not consecrated until all building debts have been paid.

The church has recently been restored and in October 1989, Cardinal Basil Hume of Westminster, wearing gold vestments, went to Derby to lead the celebrations in honour of the consecration of St Mary's one hundred and fifty years before.

Before St Mary's was finished Pugin had been commissioned to build St Chad's in Birmingham, the first Catholic Cathedral to be constructed in England since the Reformation. Myers was to build five Catholic cathedrals during his working life. Only St Chad's was built as such, the others being elevated to that status later. They will all be referred to here as 'Cathedrals' to make identification easier. Four of these very large churches, all designed by Pugin, were constructed simultaneously.

In January 1834 the Catholics of Birmingham had decided that it was 'desirable that a commodious and splendid church be erected in the town'. Thomas Rickman was chosen as architect, but there were differences of opinion over the site and other matters until finally, in 1839, Bishop Walsh, without consulting anyone, decided to build the Cathedral on the site of his church.[4] He asked Pugin to submit designs, which he did just one week later. Pugin's diary for 4 March 1839, says: 'Mr Myers at Birmingham & London', so presumably Myers had been consulted. It was agreed that Myers and Wilson should construct the Cathedral which was to be brick built. The foundation stone was laid on 29 October, just three weeks after the consecration of St Mary's, Derby. From a legacy, Dr Walsh provided £14,000 of the £20,000 total cost. Myers' bills were settled on time and he was able to pay his men, so that the commotions and disagreements inevitably caused by the Bishop's high-handed action affected Myers hardly at all. John Hardman presented the organ and was the first choir master. Bishop Wiseman preached at the opening ceremony. Five years later, Pugin's second wife Louisa died and was buried there and when Bishop Walsh died in 1848, the monument on his tomb in the north aisle was designed by Pugin and carved by Myers with his own hand. It was exhibited at the Great Exhibition in 1851. The Bishop's house, designed by Pugin, was erected nearby, but this has since been demolished to make way for a ring road.

Myers built eleven churches in the Archdiocese of Birmingham, all except one to Pugin's design. The church of St Barnabas, Nottingham, now a cathedral, was begun in 1841 and finished in 1844. A presbytery and a convent were also built by Myers, who made furniture for both.[5] Fr Robert William Willson had been parish priest in Nottingham when the building work started, but had been sent to Hobart, as Bishop of Tasmania, before the completion of the church.[6]

Myers was building so many churches in the Archdiocese of Birmingham at this time that there was confusion over the accounts. A letter from a Mr Searle, whose address was St Mary's College, Oscott, says: 'The times when the bill was paid are not easily determined as Myers' bills included Nottingham, Birmingham and Brewood and he was paid by instalments on account ...'. And the fact that the Revd Robert Richmond, parish priest at Brewood, died while his church was in the process of construction, added to the financial confusion. Kind Dr Walsh wrote soothing letters and Myers seems to have been paid all he was owed in the end.

St Mary's, Newcastle, was the last of the four Pugin cathedrals to be commissioned,[7] but was finished the same year as St Barnabas, and several years before St George's, Southwark, which was started in 1840. By the time Pugin was commissioned to build St Mary's, his reputation as a great designer was well-established and his ideas on Christian architecture were well-known.

Pugin visited Newcastle in August 1840. He inspected the site which was rather restricted and on a slope, and made a

Figure 25   Evangelists for Nottingham.   Top, an eagle for
St John, bottom, a lion for St Mark, 'keep as nearly as
possible to one of the early lions'.
Working drawings, *Courtesy of the Myers Family Trust.*

Figure 26   Drawings for Newcastle signed by Pugin, 1842.
Courtesy of the Myers Family Trust.

rough plan. Letters that passed between Pugin and Fr Riddell, the parish priest, and Mr William Dunn, secretary of the Building Committee, have survived. It is clear from the very first of these letters that Pugin expected to be acknowledged as the authority on church design. He explained that he would design a church capable of seating '1,200 persons on the floor, as galleries are utterly inadmissible in a Catholic church'.

The Committee did not appear to understand Pugin's determination concerning the rightness of his designs and, as usual, wanted a large and beautiful church for very little money. Pugin insisted on more than one occasion: 'it will be a vast building and (will) swallow up an immense deal of material'. He went on to explain that the materials to build large churches cost money even without decorations and furnishings and on 23 July 1842 he wrote:

> if the Committee will neither consent to diminish the length of the building nor increase their proposed outlay, I would rather decline the business, in which case I shall not expect any remuneration for my drawings or estimates, but merely the travelling expenses coming over.

But by 20 August of the same year Pugin had promised to send 'the draft for the contract etc.,' so presumably agreement had been reached. Less than a week later however the situation had deteriorated once again. Pugin's exasperation is obvious in his next letter when he exclaims:

> Regarding the matter of excavations and concrete, I thought I had gone into the explanation at length when I had the pleasure of meeting the Committee. The contract of course includes all excavations and all foundations to a depth of 6' 6" below the floor of (the) church, below that it is put in at measurement.

(This was a system of charging by measurement when the cost of the work was difficult to ascertain beforehand. The work was

then checked by an independent surveyor.) Pugin then went on
to say:

> Mr Myers will furnish you with a list of prices if
> you choose to do the work by measure and value,
> but such matters have always hitherto been
> referred to me, and before any extra work has
> been done I have furnished an account of its cost
> and all deductions have been determined by me.
> I see no reason for departing from this system on
> the present occasion for I need hardly observe,
> that work done by measure and value is very
> expensive and I think I am so well deserving of
> the confidence of the Committee that I could
> settle all these matters. The clause has only been
> inserted as a matter of form for I do not expect a
> shilling of extra work will be done in the
> superstructure. Everything has been provided for
> in the design even to the minutest detail and the
> building has been estimated ready for divine
> service.

There is a cheerful postscript which says:

> I have just procured from Lincoln Minster the
> most glorious authority for carving I have ever
> seen. I think I shall make the corbels of (the)
> nave roof a succession of angels playing on
> various musical instruments. They will form a
> beautiful variety from the shields that have been
> usually intended. I have got 16.

The next set-back was when, having been sent the
contract to sign, the Building Committee inserted a clause to say
that Myers should complete the building not only to the
satisfaction 'of Mr Pugin, but also to such other architect as the
Committee might think fit to appoint ...'. This really was an
extraordinary idea and Pugin hastened to point out that this
could only be allowed in case of his death. On 15 July 1843,

Figure 27   Newcastle.   Pugin drawing with Myers' superscription
concerning the base of the two crosses.
Courtesy of the Myers Family Trust.

Figure 28   St Anne for Newcastle on Tyne. Pugin drawing
Courtesy of the Myers Family Trust.

Pugin had to write to assure them that 'the mortar was of the very best quality ... that 12 inches of lead on each side of the gutters is quite sufficient ... and that the work is proceeding in a very satisfactory manner'. The laying of the floor tiles had also 'become a source of unpleasant feelings'. The Committee came to the conclusion that Myers' men were laying the tiles in an extravagant manner and complained to Pugin. But by now Pugin had had enough. The reason he selected Myers, he wrote, was to secure the interests of the building because he, Pugin, had 'full experience of his (Myers') integrity and zeal'. He went on to point out that until now he had always been treated as the friend and adviser of his employers and not ordered about like 'a pork contractor in a workhouse'. Another extraordinary fact which comes to light in this letter is that although by this time, July 1844, the church was due to be opened in just over a month, Myers had still not signed the contract to build it. The reason for this was that he hesitated to do so for fear of a law suit if he departed in the smallest degree from the drawings, and, as happened not infrequently, he had not been paid for a very long time.[7] It is not known whether Myers ever signed the contract but it is presumed that he was paid, as on 14 November Mr Dunn wrote to Pugin: '... the money will be paid to the credit of Mr Myers according to your order ...'.

The stained glass windows were made by Wailes whose workshops were in Newcastle and the spire, designed by Joseph Hansom, was added at a later date.

St George's, Southwark, together with the numerous buildings associated with it was an important contract, the first large Catholic church to be built in the London area since Emancipation, but it was to cause Myers much trouble.

Until this time the Catholics of Southwark had used a chapel, in Bandyleg Lane, which was too small. The parish priest, the Revd Thomas Doyle, was determined to build a great church capable of seating 3,000 people. He set about collecting funds and by 1838 decided that he had enough to start. A special Act of Parliament was passed to enable the Mayor and Commonalty of the Citizens of the City of London to sell to Dr Doyle a piece of land in St George's Fields, which had been one of the principal sites of the Gordon Riots in 1780. One condition of the sale was that the church should be completed in six years and another was that no 'image whatever, or emblem of a religious nature should be exhibited on the outside of the building'. Presumably the authorities feared renewed riots. *The Tablet* of 12 September 1840, reported that the site had been well-chosen, as it was within five minutes drive of Whitehall (the Editor must have had a very swift horse) and very near to the Bethlehem Hospital, which was certainly true. Pugin was asked to submit plans. But the drawings he produced were for a large and beautiful Cathedral, the cost of which would have far exceeded any sum that Fr Doyle had contemplated. When the Building Committee, consisting of three clergymen and thirteen laymen with Mr Michael Forristall as secretary, asked Pugin how much the church would cost, he refused to answer. Instead he asked them who had ever heard of a Cathedral being built in the lifetime of one man (never mind six years) and, saying that costs were impossible to estimate, he took up his hat and left the room.[8] He was eventually persuaded to produce simpler plans which were accepted, but lack of money continued to be a problem from start to finish.

Myers signed the contract to build the church, clergy houses and schools without decoration, for £20,000. This included the stone altars but not the tower and spire. The cost of the internal decoration and furnishing of the church was estimated at £2,995. 10*s*. 0*d*. On 25 October 1840, Myers wrote to Dr Doyle to ask him to have everything ready as within a few days he and Pugin would be arriving to peg out the site. The official laying of the foundation stone was to take place on Wednesday, 26 May 1841. Myers was concerned that all should go smoothly, and, in another letter to Fr Doyle,[9] he said 'you may rely on me being in Town by 5 o'clock Wednesday morning, (Myers was still living in Hull at this time) when the stone will be ready as I have ordered this day, but you must produce a silver trowel - as for the rest, I am prepared'. Myers had plenty of experience of laying foundation stones, while Fr Doyle had not. The stone was laid at 7.00 a.m. The early hour was chosen for fear of anti-Catholic demonstrations. Pugin was not present as he was in Macclesfield attending the opening

Figure 29   Drawings for St George's Cathedral, Southwark.
Courtesy of the Myers Family Trust.

Figure 30   Drawings of Cornice Bosses for St George's Cathedral, Southwark.
Courtesy of the Myers Family Trust.

ceremonies at St Alban's Church which was built by Smith of Haxley.

It is said that the wealthy Catholics were not forthcoming with large donations for the building of this church and that it was built with the pennies of the poor, which did not go far. Perhaps Fr Doyle's too persistent 'jokey' appeals for money in the Catholic press irritated those who might otherwise have been more generous.[10] Myers' letters to the Building Committee reminding them that payment was overdue, were frequent and show his anxiety in never knowing whether he would be provided with 'the needful' with which to pay his masons at the end of the week or if he would have to pay them out of his own pocket.[11]

Despite financial problems, work at St George's progressed. The High Altar screen, the sedilia, choir seats, the great screen, the rood with its carving, the font cover, the seats in the nave and the seats in the aisles, the four confessionals, the almeries for the vestments in the sacristy and much else, were made in Myers' workshops and, notwithstanding the shortage of money, the building programme continued. Myers must have known that there was no money in the bank, but in May 1843 he agreed to proceed with the building of 'the house, convent and school adjoining St George's Catholic Church in St George's Road, Southwark for the sum of £6,000'. He agreed to receive his fee by instalments at the rate of £250 per month. Provision was made for failure to pay by which it was agreed that he would get interest at the rate of 3% per annum on any instalments that remained outstanding.

On 12 November 1843 Myers wrote to Mr Forristall, secretary to the Building Committee, to ask if he had made plans for the 'roofing over' supper, as it was, and still is, the custom to have a celebration when a building got to this stage. Myers pointed out that they had not yet had a treat for the church and that this would suffice for the other buildings as well. He reminded Mr Forristall that it helped to keep the men in good heart, which was essential in 'a great work of this sort'. He went into the practical details of the entertainment. It was time to pickle the beef since the supper should take place that week as he would be laying off some of the men very soon. He explained that on other occasions he had paid one third of the cost and the Committee had paid two thirds and that for 90 men this would not be far short of £20. In fact it cost £22. 5s. 6d. He suggested:

> that the supper be at Mrs Lane's, the adjoining neighbour, as having to borrow part light from a quarter which she, if so disposed, could take from us - it is only for this, and this alone that I mention this at all, thinking it would create a good feeling - but will be guided by your better judgement.

He was presumably referring to the possibility of Mrs Lane interrupting light to one of the new buildings. This is not the only time that Myers' good sense and tact smoothed the way for his employers.

Perhaps the masons could be kept in good heart by a roofing over supper, but Myers had other problems which could not be resolved so easily. Messrs Wailes had not finished the windows by the allotted time and the snow was getting into the building. Myers heard of this when he was away in Hull, visiting his mother who was very ill. He wrote to Mr Forristall to tell him of his mother's illness and added: 'last Sunday she departed this life of vanity and yesterday I saw her buried'. He assured Mr Forristall that he had written to Mr Pugin and Mr Wailes many times about the windows, and that as he was going to Newcastle himself in a week or two he would see what he could do. In the meanwhile, he would be back in London on the morrow and would take good care to prevent the snow getting in. It seems strange that the clerk of the works could not have arranged to have something done about the snow, but perhaps he was the individual whose pay Pugin said would be much better spent on three altars and who was fit only to show ladies about the building. A few months later there was another distressing incident which necessitated Myers hurrying from one end of the country to the other. The foreman in charge of the building work at Ushaw College absconded with £42 which had

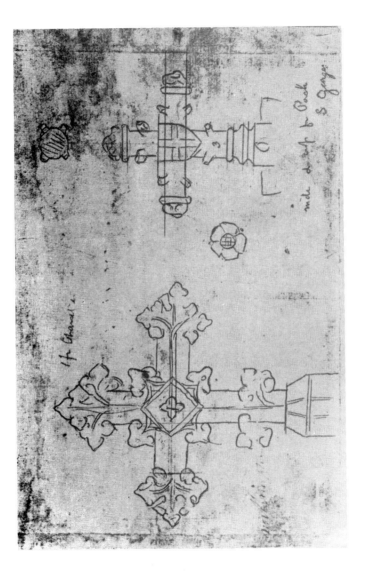

Figure 31   Drawings of crosses for St. Barnabas, Nottingham and St George's, Southwark.
Courtesy of the Myers Family Trust.

Figure 32   Altar of the Blessed Sacrament,
St George's Southwark. Pugin drawing.
Courtesy of the Myers Family Trust.

been intended for the men's wages and it was a week before Myers discovered what had happened. The masons had been idle all that time and Myers was obliged to make a special journey to Durham with a new foreman and to explain the work all over again when he got there. The 'scoundrel' was caught and tried but was found 'not guilty', much to Myers' fury.[12]

But all was not gloom and despondency, and Myers' letter to Mr Forristall telling him of the misfortunes at Ushaw ended by saying:

> I am glad to inform you that I hope we shall commence fixing Mr Knill's altar in about a fortnight and we shall also make a good show shortly of the Dr's reredos &c. Your screen is also nearly finished which shall be fixed as soon as pos.

In 1849, a second chantry designed by Pugin, and carved in Myers' workshops, was installed in the Cathedral - that of the Petre family.

On 4 July 1848, the Cathedral was opened in the presence of the Duke of Norfolk, the Earl of Shrewsbury, all the prominent Catholics in the land and 260 clergy. It appears that quite large sums of money, probably in the region of £11,000,[13] were still owed to Myers who threatened to disrupt the ceremonies if his account was not settled, but the proceedings seem to have taken place uneventfully.

Whether it was that inevitably, at this time, the Catholic Church was short of money and Myers foresaw continuing financial problems or for some other reason, it was over twenty years before he undertook the building of another Catholic church. That was in 1869-73 when he built Arundel Cathedral for the Duke of Norfolk. The extent of the debts at St George's is underlined by the fact that the church was not consecrated till 1894, and the spire was never built.

The design for the spire was used with slight alterations for the Highland Tolbooth Church on Castle Hill in Edinburgh. At this time, 1839-44, Pugin was helping Gillespie Graham with drawings. Myers was not the builder; it was David Lind, one of the six 'respectable' Edinburgh contractors invited to tender, who carried out the work. Lind also built the Sir Walter Scott Memorial in Edinburgh.[14]

Southwark Cathedral was bombed in 1941 and rebuilt in 1958, still without a spire. Not much of the original Pugin/Myers building remains except the beautiful Knill and Petre chantries.

Myers built not only these great Cathedrals but also enchanting village churches which Pugin visualised standing on the green in his dearly loved Gothic Age. There are many of these dotted about the countryside and they must have entailed a great deal of travelling for Myers. In most cases the church and presbytery were paid for by one generous donor. The church of Our Lady and St Wilfred at Warwick Bridge, Cumbria, built in 1841 of the local pink sandstone was paid for by Henry Howard of Corby Castle. It, too, has recently been restored and the inside glows like a medieval jewel while the outside of the church, the comfortable-looking presbytery and the peaceful churchyard fit unobtrusively into the northern landscape. St Austin's Church, Beehive Hill, built of brick on the outskirts of Kenilworth, was paid for by Mrs Amherst, a kinswoman of the Earl of Shrewsbury. It has been enlarged since Myers built it, but it remains small and rural with its grassy graveyard. Myers built the chapel at Ackworth Grange, Pontefract, for the Tempest family and St Marie's, Rugby, for Captain Washington Hibbert whose wife was a Catholic. She also was a connection of Lord Shrewsbury's and it was through him that Pugin and the bewhiskered Captain had become acquainted. Pugin and Myers were to work for him from 1841 to 1851, but it was not a happy relationship, something always seemed to go wrong: even the stained glass windows leaked and 'the Captain was wild'.[15]

Mrs Bowden was the patron of the church of St Thomas of Canterbury in Fulham where she and Pugin disagreed about screens, and the Scott Murray family were responsible for St Peter's, Marlow, a very pretty church which has been cleverly and unobtrusively enlarged. It was while he was visiting the Scott Murrays, in November 1852, that young Edward Pugin lost a roll of drawings. Myers who arrived the next day,

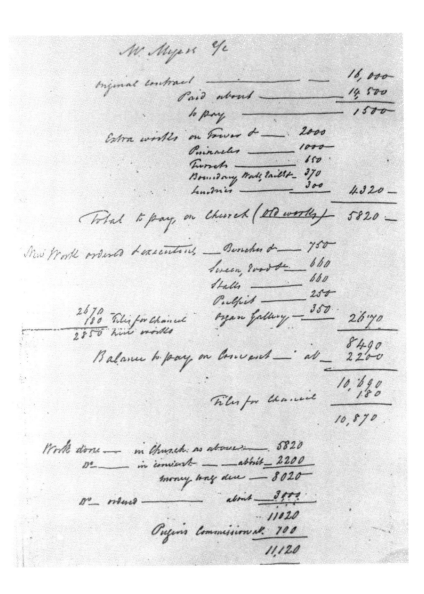

Figure 33   George Myers' account with St George's,
Southwark Building Committee.
Southwark Archdiocesan Archives.

Figure 34   Pugin's design for a spire for St George's,
Southwark, subsequently used by James Gillespie Graham for
St John's Tolbooth Church, Castlehill, Edinburgh.
Courtesy of the Royal Incorporation of Architects in Scotland.

remarked that: '... it is likely he has left them at the station or on the train'.[16]

Myers worked at Mount St Bernard, Leicestershire, for Pugin's very Gothic friend, Ambrose Phillipps de Lisle . The little churches at Whitwick and Shepshed, built by Myers, were commissioned by this ardent and generous man. St Winifred's, Shepshed, was built in 1842 and was planned to cost £300, but probably cost nearly £500. Pugin described it as 'a miracle'. Despite this, in 1928 it was abandoned by the parish which had increased in size and was in need of a bigger church. The altar and other carvings were removed to the new church, but the little Pugin building itself was allowed to become a ruin. In the 1980s it was bought by a discerning consultant engineer and is now a cherished home and office with what remains of the Italian wall paintings preserved behind glass.

Pugin built a church beside his house in Ramsgate and dedicated it to St Augustine, who, in A.D. 597, had been sent to convert England to Christianity by Pope Gregory the Great. It was near this site that St Augustine and his forty companions had landed.

Once again Myers was the builder and he, Hardman, Crace and Minton produced some of their finest work to adorn the church. The carving, done in Myers' workshops, is superb. The stone font with its elaborate oak cover was the centrepiece of the Medieval Court at the Great Exhibition and Myers' carving of the Virgin and Child from this church was also exhibited. His craftsmen carved the screens and choir stalls and much else besides. The detail is amazing: it is possible to discern the dowelling of the roof of the gothic stable in the nativity scene decorating a side altar.

This church should be visited on a fine day when the light coming through Hardman's stained glass dapples Myers' carving. In fact the church was sited so that the early morning sun would shine through the east window onto the High Altar, but a neighbour, a Mr Habershone, also an architect and an author who had crossed swords with Pugin on more than one occasion, built his house next door, so that instead of the morning sun a shadow fell on the High Altar.

Pugin and Myers were not asked to build the fashionable Jesuit Church of the Immaculate Conception in Farm Street, Mayfair. There is a letter in the Farm Street archives, written on 10 August 1844 by the Revd Randal Lythgoe to Lord Shrewsbury who had suggested that Pugin should be engaged as architect to build the Jesuits' new church. Fr Lythgoe wrote as tactfully as he could, (the Jesuits were anxious to get as large a donation as possible from Lord Shrewsbury), explaining that he, personally, would not object to employing Pugin, but that the work had already been half promised to Scoles, and that 'there are many who object to Mr Pugin that he is expensive and that he will not allow any competition. I know it is more convenient for him to employ one builder but people generally do not like it'. Then, perhaps thinking that he sounded a bit rude, he added: 'of Pugin's great talents there can be no doubt, especially for everything connected with decoration'. The 'one builder' was, of course, Myers. It is interesting to speculate whether there were many occasions when Pugin's insistence on employing Myers cost him a commission. Pugin usually got his way, but there was certainly one occasion when the Revd Waldo Sibthorpe wanted Pugin to design a chapel for his alms houses in Lincoln, but refused to allow Myers to carry out the work. Pugin turned down the commission.

Miss Monica Tempest, a member of the Yorkshire family for whom Pugin had recently designed a chapel, donated the reredos and High Altar at Farm Street, which were designed by Pugin and carved in Myers' workshops in the 1840s.[17] The date inscribed on the altar is '1888'. So far extensive research has not revealed the reason for this. The most obvious explanation is a mistake when restoration work was carried out. The date should be '1848'. By 1888 both Myers and Pugin had long been dead. Myers was disappointed not to have been allowed to build this very prestigious church, as his irate replies to Hardman's questions about the opening date suggest. On 14 July 1849 he wrote of Farm Street: 'I have so little to do with it, I can't get to know when the opening will be, but I can't think it will be open for some time yet'; and in answer to a further question as to when the steps would be finished he said: 'ask the Builder of the Church not I'.

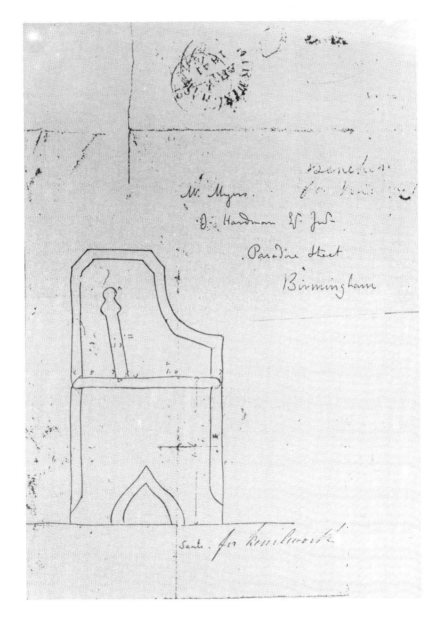

Figure 35   Pugin's drawing of seats for St Austin's Church,
Kenilworth.
Courtesy of the Myers Family Trust.

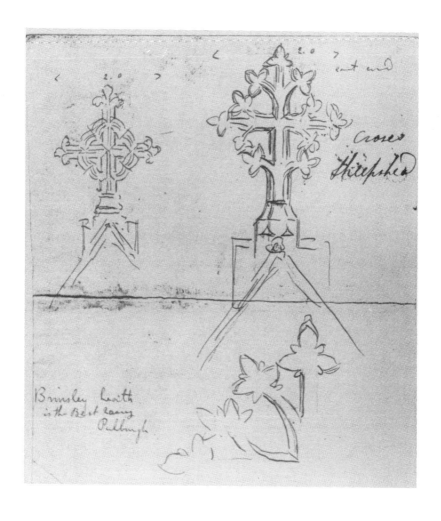

Figure 36   Crosses for St Winifred's Church, Shepshed
and a drawing for another church not located.

Most of the churches Pugin designed were for his Catholic friends and patrons, but some of his most successful work was for the Established Church. He designed the little church of St Lawrence at Tubney, which was built by Myers in 1844 for his friend the Revd Mr John Bloxam of Magdalen College, Oxford.

Once again Pugin had been unwell and Mr Bloxam and Myers went together to stake out the position of the church without him. Pugin had been anxious that Myers and the learned Oxford Don might not be the most ideal companions, and so he explained in a letter that Myers was 'a rough diamond, but a real diamond, for he is thoroughly acquainted with my branch of ancient construction and detail and a most honourable person in his transactions'.[18] But Pugin need not have worried. George Myers could be tactful when the situation required.

Then in 1846 the Revd James Hornby, Rector of St Oswald's, Winwick, near Warrington, asked Pugin to enlarge the chancel and vestry of his church. The parish of St Oswald's had always been large, but, by 1841, the population in the area had expanded so much that the parish was divided into fifteen small ones by act of Parliament at the instigation of the Rector. The combined stipends from the many parishes brought in a considerable income and the Rector lived in great style in the palatial Winwick Hall.

Pugin was ill again in the autumn of 1846 but he managed to write to Mr Hornby on 5 November to explain that he had produced some plans. His letter said: 'I have drawn out your specifications and agreement and written you a long letter on various details all of which will be brought to you by Mr Myers himself on Monday ...'.[19] Myers arrived with a long letter and some beautiful drawings. The letter containing the 'various details' explained that Myers would be prepared to sign the contract and commence work.

He and Mr Hornby inspected the site and discussed building materials but when Mr Hornby looked at the agreement he noticed that there were 'neither bondsmen nor penalties', both of which had formed part of all his previous building contracts. Myers assured him that neither were 'requisite'. Mr Hornby wrote to Pugin and asked him to confirm this, but there was another matter which concerned him even more and it is strange that he had not already raised it. His letter went on: 'You are aware of my resolution not to shock my congregation by any supposed approach towards the arrangements of the Church of Rome ... my chancel must be strictly Anglo-Catholic ...'. Mr Hornby went on to describe a long list of worries and then ended his letter: 'Now my dear Sir, I have honestly told you my whole mind ... therefore shrink not from telling me yours'. If Pugin felt he could not produce a truly Anglo-Catholic building, he must say so, and they would part, but part the best of friends. Pugin replied reassuringly that no penalty clauses were required where Myers was concerned and reminded Mr Hornby that he, Pugin, was both an artist and an architect and that 'in the former capacity I enumerate certain principles and write for the world, in the latter I act for my individual employer' and that 'we certainly hold enough in common to make a very magnificent chancel'.

It was agreed that work should go ahead. Pugin paid a visit to Winwick and stayed in the very large rectory where, although Mr Hornby was away, he had every attention from the butler. He brought with him the full-sized templates for the windows which were to be made by Hardman. The carving of the new oak pews and the screen as well as the altar table and reredos and the new vestry furniture were all to be made in Myers' workshops. The tiles, to be supplied by Minton, had to be settled without delay as they took so long to make.

The new chancel needed foundations and Myers' men started to dig in May 1847, but Matthew the foreman was concerned because there was so much earth to be moved that he did not know how he could dispose of it. He appealed to Myers who wrote to Mr Hornby:

> you are most likely aware that the earth should not
> be taken out of the consecrated ground as I have at
> times seen such things done which has caused a
> great noise ... you will please excuse me in this as I
> am sure you will know better what to do than I can
> tell you - but sometimes things slip through ...

(He added that a dray of stones would leave that day and that he had just returned from the Isle of Wight where he had gone to do a little work.) This was surely a very tactful and amiable letter to have been written by a busy contractor. On another occasion he assured Mr Hornby that never in his life before had he seen Mr Pugin so particular to make a fine job. In letters to Pugin, Mr Hornby expressed his great satisfaction with the workmen and the work. Then when everything had been going so well, something went seriously wrong. The East window, when it arrived from Hardman's Birmingham studio, did not fit. This seems strange as Pugin had brought the full-sized template with him when he had visited Winwick earlier in the year, probably in February 1847. To make it fit, the emblems of the Evangelists had to be removed, spoiling the general beauty of the window. Pugin was distraught, and wrote letters implying that Myers was to blame. Myers was upset, and could not think how the mistake could have occurred. He pointed out that the figuring on the plan was not his, and that anyway measuring windows was not his job and that in future someone else could take the 'dimensions'. He added that this was not the first time something of the sort had occurred - the dining room windows at Bilton Grange had had to be altered and that had nothing to do with him either. Finally Pugin admitted:

> it is difficult to say certainly with whom the error originated. On the papers Mr Myers sent me, 7ft to the spring is distinctly marked (in Pugin's previous letter he had said 7ft 2in) so I worked to my dimensions, but this was figured by Jackson from a paper sent by Piddock, which paper is not forthcoming ... so we cannot verify it ...

No wonder.

The Winwick windows were altered and tempers had been calmed when Mr Whittington, the curate who was in charge of the parish in the absence of Mr Hornby, made another unfortunate discovery and decided to write directly to Mr Hardman in Birmingham. His letter said:

Sir,

The tables of Commandments arrived safely last Monday, and have been fixed by Mr Thomas Pennington, we think them very handsome, but on reading them over, find mistakes, about which I have thought it advisable to communicate with you before I write again to Mr Hornby on the subject. The first mistake occurs in the second Commandment - 'under the waters' - The whole of the Fourth Commandment is omitted with the exception of the words 'Remember that thou keep holy the Sabbath Day'. In The Lord's Prayer another mistake occurs: 'Deliver us from all evil'. And in the relief the word 'conceived' is spelled 'concieved'. Possibly there may be others which as yet have escaped my notice ...

But despite these problems Mr Hornby, his architect and his contractor remained on the best of terms and when Myers tendered for the contract to build Colney Hatch Asylum and was asked for testimonials, the Revd Mr Hornby, at Myers' request, provided a very satisfactory reference. So it is not surprising that in January 1850, when Myers sent a receipt for the final payment for the work at Winwick, he wrote to thank him for 'past favours and also for your kind wishes towards me, which I assure you Revd Sir, is a great comfort to my mind'.

Another very pretty church restored by Pugin and Myers at about this time was St Mary's, Wymeswold, in Leicestershire. In 1835 Henry Alford accepted the Living, which was in the gift of Trinity College, Cambridge. He had been interested in the Romantic Movement and the Gothic Revival when he was a student at Cambridge and so determined to have Pugin as his architect, though 'he had been a very early casualty to the Vatican'.[20] As Mr Alford was the first vicar to live in the parish for many years, both church and vicarage were in a sad state of disrepair. Since he had recently married his young cousin Fanny Alford, he decided the more pressing need was for a vicarage fit to live in, and it was not till 1844 that he turned his attention to the church which, by that time, had deteriorated still further.

To attract subscriptions for the building fund, a *History and Description of the Parish Church of St Mary's, Wymeswold*, was published in 1846, the authorship of which is uncertain. The church is described as being 'embosomed' in the little town and there are lovely illustrations of both the inside and outside of the church. The book tells us that 'the pulpit, font and sedilia were executed by Mr George Myers of Lambeth who was the contractor for the whole works'. Pugin designed new pews and a new screen so it is probable that these also were carved in Myers' workshops.

The stained glass windows were made by Wailes of Newcastle, the metalwork and binding of the Great Bible by Hardman of Birmingham and the inscription and painted decorations by Mr Ferriman of Wymeswold. Myers' men worked so quickly that the new roof for the nave was completed in the interval between two Sundays, so that the services did not need to be interrupted.

A less satisfactory commission was Lord Rolle's tomb at Bicton, Devon. Pugin's diary entry for 1 March 1850 says: 'Exeter, Lady Rolle and London'. A note on page 98 in Alexandra Wedgwood's edition of Pugin's diaries records: 'Lady Rolle commissioned Pugin to build a Chantry Chapel for her husband at the South-East corner of the ruined medieval church at Bicton. The tomb and elaborate carving were executed by Myers'. This sounds a straightforward undertaking in an enchanting rural setting. Lady Rolle had at first wanted an Oriental design, but Pugin persuaded her that Gothic would be more in keeping with the ruin. Myers was the builder and the carving was done in his workshops. The stained glass windows were made by Hardman and his man Thomas Earley did the painting.

It is to Thomas Earley that we owe the information that there was disharmony at Bicton. On 15 April 1851, when preparations for the Great Exhibition were nearing completion, Earley wrote to Hardman from London to describe Queen Victoria's visit to the Medieval Court. He added: 'we had also (a visit from) the Redoubtable Harpy of Exeter. She desired me to thank Mr Pugin for his great artistic talents in designing that beautiful tomb'.[21] Earley's uncomplimentary language about

Lady Rolle is the first intimation that all was not going smoothly at Bicton and by March the following year, the relations between her and the craftsmen working for her had obviously deteriorated still further. There is a despairing letter from Earley to Hardman[22] bewailing the fact that Mr Myers had been expected the day before and had not arrived. There had been a tremendous row between 'Lady Rolle and Mr Chinnock (the foreman) about the centre of the slab that covers the tomb'. He goes on:

> when her Ladyship, I am sorry to say, spoke in the most disgraceful manner of poor Mr Pugin and all parties engaged in this job. She said she regrets the day she ever saw Mr Pugin or any of his lot and further stated her determination to lock up the place and bundle all hands off when she goes to London in a fortnight's time, or else when she comes back, she will find the place covered in Crucifixes, Angels, Saints and Virgins. I had hard work to control myself from giving her a first-rate blowing up, in a respectable manner. But I remained silent.

He adds that 'she is the most Refined Black' he ever heard in his life and that he is wretched striving to please a 'disgusting old frump' and that he cannot do it. Two days later Hardman received another letter, this time from David Myers to say that his father was on his way to Bicton.[23]

Some time before, when another, undisclosed, mishap had taken place, Myers had written to Hardman: 'you should be like me, take things coolly'.[24] One can only hope that on this occasion Myers managed to take things coolly himself. He arrived with a carver, 'but Lady Rolle treated him in a most disgraceful manner'.[25] Unfortunately the tact which Myers had employed in his dealings with the Revd Mr Hornby did not work with Lady Rolle. Earley's next letter relates that she was compelled to acknowledge the beauty of the ceiling, but still she abused the painter (Earley) like a pickpocket and said that she would certainly lock up the chapel and take away the key.

Earley said that: 'all hope of now soothing her down had gone'. He hoped that he would: 'never again fall in with such a specimen of the Aristocracy'.

Lady Rolle clearly had second thoughts about employing Pugin and 'his lot' to design and build her chantry, being nervous of Pugin's Catholicism. The booklet describing Bicton Church in the Parish of East Budleigh with Bicton, reprinted in 1981, makes no mention of Pugin in its pages. So perhaps its anonymous author shared, or at least sympathised with, Lady Rolle's misgivings.

There are many references in Myers' letters to John Hardman concerning the work carried out for St David's Church, in North Wales, at Pantasaph, a place name they all had difficulty in spelling. The altar, tabernacle, screens, other sacristy furnishings and the font were all made in Myers' workshops.[26] This church has a strange history. The Earl of Denbigh's heir, Viscount Feilding, married Louisa Pennant, an heiress whose father owned property in Flintshire including Pantasaph, a bleak little village surrounded by lead mines and quarries. It was here that Lord and Lady Feilding decided to build a church (architect T.H. Wyatt) as a thank-offering for the joy of their marriage.

The foundation stone was laid by Lady Feilding on 16 August 1849. The Venerable Archdeacon Manning of Chichester preached. The following year when the church was nearing completion, Lord and Lady Feilding were received into the Catholic Church, and so wanted their church to be devoted to Catholic worship. This led to litigation with the Bishop of St Asaph, who claimed that the church had already been given to the Established Church. But the Courts decided that transfer of ownership could not take place until the building had been completed. This decision distressed the villagers, a public subscription was raised and two Anglican churches were built in the neighbourhood. Lord Feilding then called upon Pugin and Myers to adapt St David's for Catholic use. Some of the carving done by Myers' craftsmen was exhibited at the Great Exhibition. A few years later, in 1857, a Franciscan Priory was built adjoining the church. On this occasion the architect was J.Hansom.[27]

During the 1840s and 1850s, Myers was engaged on a very special contract - the restoration of St Mary's, Beverley. It must have given him great pleasure to return to work in this town which he had known and loved since childhood. In the early 1840s Pugin was asked to restore St Mary's, which had been built in 1120 as a chapel of ease to the Minster but which was now suffering from long neglect. In his reply to the churchwardens Pugin said he would arrive 'early in the morning of Thursday the 19th' (as usual his letter was undated), and that he would bring Myers with him. He added that he would be in a hurry as he was obliged to leave by the Great Northern at half past one. When Pugin left, Myers remained behind to make a more thorough inspection of the building. Pugin's subsequent letters to the churchwardens reported that buttresses were needed to support the south transept, repairs were essential to the east end of the church, the safety of which would be endangered by delay, and there was an ominous postscript to one of these letters saying: 'Myers tells me that the water rises in the crypt, this will occasion some trouble, but it can be effectively remedied'. New doors and three ornamental oak benches were ordered but the benches were an extravagance to be regretted later. Among the vestry papers is a bill from Myers for drawing out 'windows, doors, chimney piece, quatrefoils for crypt per Mr Pugin's orders', for which he charged 15*s*. 0*d*. There were other urgent and unexpected repairs which were to engage Myers' attention until 1854, two years after Pugin's death.

As happened so often, payments to Myers were once more in arrears. By 1 April 1846, he had done work to the value of £1,005. 5*s*. 1*d*. and had only been paid £200. Eventually the churchwardens held a meeting and after much deliberation came to the unanimous decision to ask Myers to send in an exact account of all monies owing to him as early as possible.

Myers produced a detailed bill the next morning, but it was two months before another meeting was called to discuss it. No objection appears to have been taken to the sums of money Myers paid to 'Mr Wobble, Mr Wombler, Capt. Beaumont and Capt. Leddham' for undisclosed services, but when it came to

Figure 37   St Mary's Church, Wymeswold, west view from the Chancel showing the restoration work carried out by Myers' craftsmen. From - A History and Description of the Restored Parish Church of St Mary, Wymeswold, Leicestershire. Shelfmark G.A. Fol.A. 69.

Courtesy of the Bodleian Library.

Figure 38 St Mary's Church, Beverley.
Courtesy of Humberside Archives Services, ref. DDX 378/4.

the rest of Myers' account the wardens wanted to know why the foreman was paid 3*d.* a day more than the masons; they queried the amount of stone used; they asked to have the tradesmen's 'vouchers' handed over to them and considered Myers' travelling expenses of £15 excessive - they claimed that the travelling expenses should have been included in the original estimate for the cost of the work. Finally, without saying anything to Myers, they packed up the three ornamental oak benches which had been in use in the church for some months and directed The General Steam Navigation Company to deliver them to Myers' home address in Lambeth. Myers refused to accept delivery of this 'very large package' on the grounds that it was not his property.

Myers' letters to Frederic Hobson, the Clerk to the Vestry, were restrained until on 10 September 1846 he finally lost patience and wrote: 'I cannot help thinking that the delay arises from vexatious neglect ... I therefore feel it my duty to put the matter in the hands of my solicitor'. Only then was it agreed to pay Myers by half yearly instalments of £200 plus 5% interest on the amount undischarged. Myers pointed out that this would put off the final payment for nearly two years and that he was 'a poor man'. He asked them to give him four promissory notes. They refused. Pugin was only to be paid as and when parish funds permitted. This was hard on him as the not infrequent entries in his diary: 'borrowed £5 from Mr Myers' show that he was often short of cash. Myers too was short of money at this time. Out of eight contracts which he had in hand in 1846, he was not being paid for two of them - St George's, Southwark and St Mary's, Beverley, and he was building Pugin's house in Ramsgate, where he would not have cared to press for money. Whether his bills were met or not, he had to provide all building materials and equipment as well as pay his men at the end of the week. He was owed a great deal of money and the threat of bankruptcy must have been real. But salvation came from an unexpected quarter - from Mr Forristall, the secretary of the Southwark Cathedral Building Committee. Myers wrote to the churchwardens at Beverley referring to him as 'a friend ... who has kindly consented to assist me ... on receiving a letter from you that the four orders

now enclosed will be paid at the time hereunder mentioned ...'.
Myers had written to the churchwardens on 4 November 1846,
and this letter was followed on 11 December by one from Mr
Forristall which said:

> 13 West Square
> Southwark
>
> Sir,
> Will you have the goodness to procure from the
> churchwardens of Beverley a cheque payable
> through some London Bank for the sum of £227
> 3s. 0d. on account of work done by Mr Myers. I
> have his order for me to receive the amount and
> on receiving a Letter stating to which Bank I am
> to apply for the money I will call and give a
> receipt for the same.
> I am Sir, Your Obt Servant
> M.Forristall

Perhaps the fact that a third party was involved on this occasion
persuaded the churchwardens to pay up promptly and regularly.
They evidently did so as on 24 June 1848 Mr Forristall wrote to
Mr Hobson:

> Sir,
> I have to crave your pardon for not answering
> your letter before, which I certainly would have
> done had I not been out of Town. I have now
> the great pleasure in enclosing you a receipt for
> the balance and take this opportunity of thanking
> you for the prompt and satisfactory manner you
> have transacted this business.
> I am Sir, Your Obt Servant
> M.Forristall

During this time work at St Mary's had gone on as usual. The
churchwardens were impatient because the church doors which
had been ordered in July 1845, had not arrived. It was now
April 1847 and Myers assured them that the doors were 'in a

very forward state'. Mr Sands, the Vicar of St Mary's from 1834-56, decided this would be a good time to have his servants' pew repaired and extended, because when they were all at church they could not fit in the pew 'as seating is at present arranged'. He undertook to pay any part of the expense the churchwardens thought proper. The new buttresses were finished and Myers wrote to Mr Sands to suggest that they should go and admire them together as they were 'a nice piece of work and very appropriate for the purpose'.

But the churchwardens continued to be short of money and once again payments to Myers fell behind. In 1847 work eventually came to a halt through lack of funds and did not start again until 1849.[28] Then in January 1854, Myers received a letter from Mr Hobson informing him that the foreman Mr James and a man called George Gawan had been arrested on a charge of felony. They were said to have sold Caen and Tadcaster stone, sand, lead, iron cramps and other building materials, the property of the churchwardens, to their friends in the town and pocketed the money. A man called Boswell had worked some of the stone for chimney pieces. The wardens were particularly hurt 'in consequence of remarks having been made by some of the Parishioners that the masons were not half looked after by the churchwardens'. Mr Hobson assured Myers that the wardens 'regretted that they should have been driven to a course which was very painful and unpleasant'. Myers replied that he had already received this information from another quarter and that he would be in Beverley 'on Monday morning'.

John James, a Londoner, and George Gawan, a Beverley carter, were both brought to trial and indicted, the former for stealing a quantity of stone and sand, the property of the churchwardens of St Mary's, Beverley, and the latter with having received it knowing it to have been stolen. There seems to have been an organised system of petty robbery going on for years, with the dividing line between this and what the masons regarded as their customary 'perquisites' becoming vaguer as the years went by, until a church pinnacle ended up in the garden of Mr Churchwarden Shepherd, which was said to have been sold to him by James.

Many witnesses vouched for Gawan's good character and George Myers told the Court that John James had worked for him for seventeen years and had always proved trustworthy. Mr Ireland, a churchwarden in the Minster Parish, said that far more pilfering went on from that 'edifice' than from St Mary's. The Chairman of the Court summed up: Gawan was found 'not guilty' but James was sentenced to three months' imprisonment - but without hard labour.

By this time Myers' work at Beverley was drawing to an end and there is a letter dated 5 August 1854 addressed to Mr Hobson which says:

Sir,
I received your letter of 3rd inst setting forth the Churchwardens' offer of £1,250.0.0 in balance of my account for work done at St Marie's church, Beverley. In answer I need hardly say that this is a most serious deduction from the account now delivered, as the percentage I have charged is certainly below average and having charged nothing for travelling expenses and finding the money for carrying on the works, I can't but say it is not what I expected - the view I take of the matter is peculiar to myself in as much as I have been a workman in Beverley for several years, and other matters closely connected, all of which have a tendency to induce me to accept the offer made by the Vicar and Churchwardens who on all occasions have shown great kindness to me. Therefore I beg to say I accept the offer namely that I receive the £1,250.0.0 within one week as set forth in your letter.
I am dear Sir,
etc.
George Myers

To Mr F.Hobson
Vestry Clerk
St Marie's Church
Beverley[29]

The money did not arrive within the week, but perhaps by then it did not matter so much. The address at the top of Myers' letter was 'Mentmore'.

V

1852: A Sad Year

Pugin was forty when he died, at his home in Ramsgate, on 14 September 1852, but this was not an unusually early age to die in the mid-19th century. Even at the beginning of the 20th century the average marriage lasted a mere eleven years (as a result of the death of one of the partners), and the average child had lost one parent by the age of nine. Pugin had been a delicate child and his health did not improve as he reached manhood. In a letter to Lord Shrewsbury written in 1840[1] he said: 'I feel quite well again and my eyes are better'. Yet the next year he told Lord Shrewsbury that he was taking three grains of mercury every four hours. This is a dose certain to produce severe mercury poisoning. It was prescribed for his iritis and would have killed him if prolonged. He complained of 'dreadful nervous fevers' when he wrote to Henry Drummond[2] in the early 1840s, saying that his eyes were so bad that he could not see to write. Going abroad does on at least one occasion appear to have done him good. Myers in a letter to Hardman reported that: 'the Governor' had returned 'as fat as a seal'. Had he forgotten to take his mercury with him? If he had not had Myers as his builder, who understood his work and could always be relied on, and his devoted third wife, Jane, who looked after him for the last four years of his life, it is unlikely that he would have achieved so much building or lived as long as he did.

By the beginning of 1852, it was clear that Pugin's health was failing. On 7 February Jane Pugin wrote to Mr Bloxam at Magdalen College:[3] 'my husband is far from well'. Different doctors and different remedies were tried. J.H.Powell[4] described the last months of Pugin's life, and how the family doctor, James Daniel, considered that if Pugin could go to London 'a change of thought could do him good'. So it was arranged for him to spend two or three days with Myers at Laurie Terrace, 'seeing all that remained of Medieval London which he knew so well, St Bartholomew's, the Charter House, St Etheldreda's and streets and alleys known to few'. But this did him no lasting good. He was admitted to a private asylum, Kensington House, on 27 February and transferred to the Royal Bethlem Hospital (Bedlam, now the Imperial War Museum) on 21 June. He was diagnosed as suffering from 'Mania'. The 'supposed cause of his insanity', as his clinical report puts it, was 'over labour and study in his profession'.[5] When the news got abroad there was a public outcry and to the embarrassment of his family, the Editor of *The Builder* suggested that a subscription should be raised to enable him to be sent to a private asylum. Bedlam was a pauper lunatic asylum which housed not only the harmlessly mad but, until 1863, when Broadmoor was built, the criminally insane as well. But Jane Pugin must have been desperate. Of Pugin's eight children she had six under her care, the youngest only one year old, and the Bethlem Hospital had certain advantages not known to the general public. It stood among fields and trees just up the road from Laurie Terrace. St George's, Southwark, where Pugin and Jane had been married, could be seen from the hospital windows, and the public would not have known that on 12 June 1852, the enlightened Dr William Charles Hood had been appointed resident Physician Superintendent of the Hospital by the Commissioners in Lunacy. This would be the first time a resident doctor had been put in charge of the Bethlem Hospital. Dr Hood did not take up his appointment until November of that year. He was the physician at Colney Hatch Lunatic Asylum and time was required to find someone to replace him. But the alterations to the buildings and improvements in the management of the patients instigated by Dr Hood had already started. Myers had won the contract drawn up in May 1852, and was working on the building to provide more space and larger windows without the iron bars that 'darkened and disfigured the bedroom windows'. He was to replace them with windows of a lighter and more cheerful appearance, and there were many other alterations as well.[6] But the outcry was such that Pugin was moved to The Grove in Hammersmith where it was possible for his family to be with him. He stayed there for some weeks until 11 September, when, as he seemed better, he returned home to Ramsgate in Jane's care, but he died there three days later. Pugin's funeral took place as he would have wished, in St Augustine's, Ramsgate, the church which he had built. The Vespers of the Office of the Dead were recited and the coffin was carried to the church in procession with candles. The next day Bishop Grant of Southwark celebrated the Requiem Mass in the presence of a great crowd. The cantors were John Hardman and John Lambert, a friend since his Salisbury days (who was later knighted and Mayor of Salisbury). Myers was a pall bearer. Pugin was buried in St Augustine's. The chantry and his effigy in stone were probably designed by his son Edward Pugin and carved by Myers.[7] Queen Victoria granted Jane Pugin a pension from the Civil List. Pugin's library of historical, topographical, antiquarian and ecclesiastical books was sold in January of the next year by the auctioneers S.Leigh Sotheby and John Wilkinson of 3 Wellington Street, Strand. The sale lasted three days. This remarkable collection of books, some of which dated from the 16th century, was sold for what seem, from a distance of nearly a century and a half, to be derisory prices, and it is a tragedy that the library was dispersed. Myers bought thirty-one books covering a variety of subjects, several written in Latin or French.

He paid 10s. 0d. for the biography *Vie de la Princesse Borghese, née G.Talbot* who had died in 1840. Myers must have known her. She was the younger daughter of the Earl of Shrewsbury who had married an Italian nobleman and died soon after. He bought *The Baronage of England* in three volumes for which he paid £7 and which would have been useful in describing the ramifications of the families of his aristocratic patrons. This book had been published in 1675. He bought *British Topography* in two volumes and *A Dictionary of the Lives and Writings of the Most Eminent Persons in Every Nation*. He paid £11. 12s. 0d. for four volumes of the Household Books of the Earl of Northumberland, Henry VIII, Elizabeth of York and of the Princess Mary. Hardman and Crace both bought a number of books. Minton was practical and bought a *History of Staffordshire* with a large map and a map of England and Wales.

Other familiar names occur amongst those who made purchases. Knill appeared frequently and Jones was there. Could this have been Owen Jones who wrote *The Grammar of Ornament*? There were two further sales in February and April of Pugin's Medieval and European carvings. Myers made further purchases at these, including a German wrought iron birdcage.[8] It was a sad time for Pugin's family and friends.

The death of Pugin was not the only reason why the year 1852 was a tragic one for Myers. On 20 February, Polly, the eldest of his three little daughters, fell from the swing while playing with her brothers, fractured her skull and died a week later. Pugin's friend and patron, Lord Shrewsbury, died of malaria in Naples on 9 November just two months after Pugin. Myers himself had been ill in May.[9] The two new workhouses he was building for the City of Westminster were finished four months late. There seems also to have been some difficulties concerning the alterations he was making at Bedlam. He had started working there in May 1852, but a paragraph in the 1854 contract reads:

> from divers causes and difficulties it has been found impracticable for the said George Myers to complete and finish the said works so specified in the time limit ... the same has by mutual consent of both parties ... been extended to the 5th day of July next (i.e. July 1854).[10]

There is no clue as to what the difficulties were and the penalty clause of £10 per day does not appear to have been invoked.

On 24 October 1851, Myers had signed a contract to build a mansion at Mentmore for Baron Mayer de Rothschild. The finishing date was to have been 1 July 1853 with a penalty clause on this occasion of £20 per day. But work did not start there until the end of 1852, the first payment being made on 25 January 1853.[11]   The building of the mansion was not finished by 1 July 1853, yet no penalty clause was invoked in this case either.

One wonders what had happened. Whatever it was the employers seem to have been sympathetic. Could Myers have been more involved than is realized in settling the affairs of Pugin, who died intestate ? There is a letter written by Myers to Hardman on 1 October 1852 which says: 'We better have all these accounts done when you come to London - for I don't like to have them talked over so much - every line brings up poor Mr Pugin to my feelings. I think this will be the best way ...'.

It was in the same month that the Myers family moved from Laurie Terrace to 143 Clapham Road, Lambeth, leaving behind them the scene of Polly's death (Myers gave his wife a mourning ring and brooch in memory of their little girl) and the view of the Bethlem Asylum which evoked memories of Pugin's last illness. It had been a dreadful year.

In the autumn of 1852 there was still Pugin work to finish. At Beverley, Edward Pugin took over as architect. Contracts at Albury, Ushaw, Marlow, Pantasaph and West Tofts were unfinished beside other, minor Pugin commissions. But Pugin's commissions had diminished during the last years of his life and so the amount of work being carried out for him by Myers at that time was small. Pugin's death did not greatly affect him financially.

Myers and Hardman continued to work together, but this was mostly completing work which had been commissioned when Pugin was alive. When Myers built Mentmore, it was Hardman, in 1856, who made the balusters,[12] and, in 1870, when building Arundel Cathedral, once again the stained glass windows were made by Hardman's firm. Hardman's stained glass had nearly always been destined for Catholic churches, but, during the eighteen years prior to 1870, Myers had not been involved in the construction of any of them.

Figure 39   The Bethlem Hospital in the 1850s,
now the Imperial War Museum.

Courtesy of Patricia Allderidge, Archivist and Curator, The Bethlem Royal Hospital.

Figure 40   The sea off Ramsgate.   Drawing by J.W.M. Turner, R.A. Engraved by Robert Wallis.
Courtesy of the Guildhall Library, Corporation of London.

Crace continued to collaborate with Myers. When Myers improved and modernised grand houses, Crace was often called upon to decorate the new rooms. And when pavilions required for the balls and receptions which took place during the London season were constructed by Myers, Crace frequently supplied the 'tasteful ornamentation'.

Myers had been known as 'Pugin's builder'. It has been said that without Myers, Pugin's buildings would never have stood up. Without Myers Pugin's buildings would certainly not have been so beautiful. The carving done in Myers' workshops was superb, as any visitor to the churches at Wymeswold, Winwick and especially Pugin's own church in Ramsgate, can see.

It is a biographer's tragedy that none of Myers' letters to Pugin or Pugin's to Myers have survived. It was Pugin's habit to answer letters at once and then burn them. This was not Myers' practice but his letters suffered the same fate when they were destroyed in the years when so many Victorian manuscripts were disposed of as they were not thought to be worth the cupboard space which they occupied.

One note from Pugin to Myers has survived in the RIBA drawings collection. It is a scratched message beneath a drawing of the Virgin and Child. It says:

> Mr Myers,
> I don't think the sketch I sent you for the B. Virgin for Mrs Petre's altar was late enough in style. I now send you a better one - of course the whole front will be carved in bas relief - the carving should be strictly of the same date as the Chantry.
> Yours Truly
> + A Welby Pugin

There must have been hundreds of these messages, altering instructions, adding to and countermanding. He must have found it easy to communicate with Myers who, from years of working in Gothic churches in Yorkshire, knew as much about the dates and style of Gothic architecture as Pugin himself. Their consultations were frequent. Myers visited Ramsgate when plans were being drawn up and Pugin called at the Wharf when he came to London. If he travelled to Waterloo by train the Wharf was only a few minutes' walk along York Road and if he chose a more leisurely mode of transport, Captain Warman of the *Resolution*, sailing from Ramsgate to London, would doubtless deposit him at Myers' jetty and their consultations continued.

Myers was nine years older than Pugin and was mature enough to tolerate his eccentricities. He understood and appreciated his genius and their love of Gothic Art united them. Jane Pugin also relied on and trusted Myers. We have seen how Pugin's doctor, desperate to find some possible palliative for his patient's illness, had suggested the age old remedy of a change of air: it was decided that he should stay with the Myers where 'a change of thought might do him good'.

This tells us a great deal about the relationship between the Myers and Pugin families. Jane knew and loved the Myers so well that she felt she could ask this great favour of them - that they would welcome and care for her husband whose bouts of insanity were becoming ever more frequent and violent. Jane had six children in her care at Ramsgate. Judith Myers had five aged between nine and two years. We do not know the exact date of Pugin's stay at Laurie Terrace, but it must have been in the spring of 1852. It was in February 1852 that the Myers' little daughter Polly was killed falling off the swing. Surely only one's dearest friends would ask for help from grieving parents at such a time.

VI

Business Methods

At this point in the story, following the death of Pugin, it is well to pause and consider what is known of Myers' business methods and workforce. In 1852 he was in his fiftieth year and was known to most of the eminent architects of the day. During his working life he is recorded as having undertaken contracts for ninety architects. For thirty-eight of these he worked once only, while for Pugin he carried out fifty-five major contracts, four times as many as for Sir G.G.Scott, the next on the list. Myers first worked for these two men in 1838.

He worked on seven large contracts for Sir Joseph Paxton which included much work for the Rothschilds. Myers and Paxton had known each other for several years having first worked together at Burton Closes in 1847-48. For Clutton also, seven contracts are recorded and, in 1849, Myers introduced Clutton to Hardman, a useful introduction for them both.[1] Myers worked for Daukes on six occasions, including two great lunatic asylum contracts, and was to give him valuable support in the action against him known as *Skaife v. Daukes*. Myers worked for Anthony Salvin and Sydney Smirke, and many others, but the list is too long to pursue here (see Architect List in the Appendix). Two notable names not included in the list are those of Sir Charles Barry and Alfred Waterhouse. Myers worked for Edward W. Pugin, but mainly finishing work started for A.W.N. Pugin.

Myers' business was established and he was well-placed to take a leading part in the great building boom of the 1850s and 60s. According to the 1861 census, slightly more than 10% of the adult male population of London described themselves as 'builder'.[2] But there were only a small number of firms (about ten) capable of carrying out more than one contract worth more than £10,000, in a year.[3] Amongst these firms were: Mansfield, Lucas, Dove Bros, Grissell and Peto, Kelk, Holland and Hannen, and — Myers.

Mansfield's base was in Henry Street, Gray's Inn Lane, Dove's in Islington and Kelk's in Commercial Road, Pimlico, but the other three were near to, or next door neighbours of Myers in Belvedere Road. Though some of these firms are still active today, Sir John Summerson described them as 'historically speaking, a lost tribe, their biographies and business methods having by now become almost impenetrably obscure'.[4] These words emphasise the difficulty which hampers investigation into the business concerns of these contractors, but the obscurity which surrounds Myers' business methods, though impenetrable in places, is not completely so. Information can sometimes be found in the archives of those for whom he worked and in the newspapers of the day. Myers' wife, Judith, had three scrap books, covering important events of the 1850s and 60s, as well as incidents affecting George Myers & Sons which shed light on the running of the business. In addition, about three hundred letters have been found, in various archive libraries, written by Myers to his employers and colleagues, which tell of what took place in the office and workshops and on the forecourt at Ordnance Wharf. Ordnance Wharf was in an industrial area of yards, wharfs and jetties stretching along the south bank of the river Thames to the Pool of London, to the docks and beyond.

The firm of George Myers & Sons provided employment for several members of the family. David, the eldest of Myers' five sons, worked as a clerk in the office. He attended business meetings and went to official dinners on behalf of the firm but he does not appear to have worked on the building sites. The second son, Joseph, spent a short time as a student at Christchurch College, Cambridge, but did not graduate for unknown reasons. When he returned home he helped his father overseeing the sites. We hear nothing of the three younger sons born in 1843, 1845 and 1848 until 1871 when, in George Myers' Will, they are recorded as owning the River Lea Iron Works in Canning Town. They had an office at 57 Gracechurch Street in the City.

Myers employed his brother-in-law, Richard Martin Ruddock, as his cashier. C.W. Jackson, another clerk who sometimes illustrated his letters with skilfully executed technical drawings, was Judith Myers' nephew. From 1851 onwards there were always at least three clerks working in the office at Ordnance Wharf and apart from the work involved in the day to day running of as many as ten building sites and the wages of, sometimes, thousands of men, they also calculated, under Myers' supervision, the prices for the tenders, the means by which a continuous flow of work was maintained. It would appear that more than half Myers' work was obtained by public tender. These contracts were advertised in the press and those seeking information would be given the name and address of the project architect and the time at which the plans could be viewed in his office. No reputable builder would tender for a contract unless the quantities were supplied by a recognised quantity surveyor and working drawings were available for scrutiny.

The builder was usually expected to provide against the event of his bankruptcy or failure to perform under the contract. He would be required either to put forward two or three 'respectable' people who would stand surety for him up to a given sum, or he would be required to deposit money as a bond. The bond put up by Myers when he contracted to construct a new roof and execute other work at the Guildhall in the City, in 1863, was £3,463 which was 20% of the value of the contract sum. The bond was released to Myers when the work was completed.[5]

Tendering was an endless task in the Ordnance Wharf office and it is possible to get some idea of the work which this entailed from the lists of tenders which were published every week in *The Builder*. These lists do not include all the tenders which were submitted by Myers and the figures which are quoted below are an underestimate of the true situation. Between 1846 and 1874, 727 tenders by Myers' firm are recorded in this journal, and the clerks averaged one every two weeks over the twenty-eight year period. During the quinquennium 1860-64 the average increased to one every eight and a half days. The sum of the lowest bids for all these tenders, that is their overall value, was £8,540,146. Myers' share of this was 16%, both in terms of value (£1,332,818), and also by number of projects (116). The median value of rival lowest bids was £4,500, while Myers' corresponding median value stood 67% higher, at £7,536. In 18% of tenders he was the highest bidder .

Of the six firms listed on page 82, other than Myers, Dove Bros had the largest number of lowest bids with a 'score' of fifteen (value £103,000) while Holland & Hannen were next with twelve (value £181,000). Of the others, Kelk's 'score' was five (value £386,000), Mansfield's two (value £9,088), and Lucas's two (value (£94,482). The value of the lowest bids made by these 'big' firms was only £729,000, less than 10% of the global value of all lowest bids. The evidence provided by the list of tenders suggests that the really serious rivalry came not from the big firms but from the multitude of other firms, often with names now totally forgotten, which succeeded in gaining one contract (141 examples) or two contracts (37 examples). The cost of these contracts was £3,230,511, nearly 40% of the global value.

The number of firms which submitted tenders for individual contracts ranged from one to forty-five. The most frequent number of submissions for a contract was seven and the mean was nine. The number of competitors tended to rise with the value of the contract. Thus when there were ten or fewer firms tendering, the mean value of the contract was about £8,000; when there were between eleven and fifteen this value rose to £21,000 and when there were sixteen - twenty it reached £33,000, but when there were more than twenty bidders the value fell back to about £20,000. Such extravagant tendering was an expression of the fierce competition which beset the construction industry during George Myers' lifetime.

The largest of all the tenders for which Myers entered was that for the Thames Embankment at £495,000 which he missed by 8%; he missed St Thomas's Hospital (£332,000) by 2.5% and the 1863 tender for the Foreign Office by 1.5%. His bid for the Commercial Docks at Rotherhithe was closer still, only 0.5% above that of Kelk (£128,000). Myers undertook two small drainage projects in 1853 and then bid four times without success for major contracts concerned with the construction of London's great new drainage system. His tender was 57% above the successful bid in one case.

The list of 727 tenders brings out the very diverse nature of the buildings which Myers was prepared to execute. There were tenders for churches (137), mansions and houses (122), warehouses and docks and railways (115) amongst which was his construction in 1849 of the railway from the West India Docks to Camden Town Station where it joined the London-Birmingham line. His had been the lowest of forty-five tenders. Myers also tendered for banks and offices (76), schools and colleges (61), hospitals and alms houses, workhouses and similar buildings (24), hotels (12), and asylums (11). The list shows that amongst the great London teaching hospitals, apart from St Thomas's, he also tendered without success for the new King's College Hospital in Denmark Hill as well as for the considerable extensions at Guy's. But his was the lowest bid for the London Hospital Medical School in Whitechapel, which he built, as well as two related contracts involving extensions and alterations to the Hospital itself. Lastly there is a diverse group of buildings for which he tendered, some of them very costly, including gas works, theatres, great London markets, breweries and the coastal fortifications near Portsmouth.

It was not always the lowest tender which won the contract. There were occasions when Myers' was the lowest and yet he did not carry out the work. In 1860, his tender for a new iron conservatory in Kensington, for the Royal Horticultural Society, was the lowest of eleven bidders at £14,167, but the job went to Kelk (the ninth bidder) who had estimated 2.5% more than Myers. There were other times when his was not the lowest bid and yet he was offered the contract. For example, also in 1860, he tendered £12,229 to build the Assize Courts and Police Station in Reading, his price being higher (2%) than that of Woodroffe, a local man, who bid £11,974. There were ten tenders on this occasion, the most costly being that of Messrs Young and Co. of Oxford, at £15,000. The county surveyor's estimate had been £10,000.

In 1851, in open competition, Myers won the contract to build Mentmore (but excluding the foundations and fittings) for £15,472. On that occasion only two other contractors tendered. Grimsdell was prepared to carry out the work for £20,721 and Kelk's price was £16,470. Myers' working methods evidently pleased Baron Mayer de Rothschild and other members of the Rothschild family because, from then onward, until he retired, he was to carry out all their major building projects in England.

Myers carried out much work for the government. On these occasions selected contractors were invited to tender. Fifteen tenders were invited for the completion of the Houses of Parliament in 1854, three for the restoration work at the Tower of London and only two (Myers and Kelk) for the building of the Prince Consort's Library at Aldershot. Myers was the lowest bidder in the last two cases and undertook the work involved but in the case of the Houses of Parliament he was the 'underbidder'. Myers' work for Pugin was done without tendering and, apart from Mentmore, no record of tendering has been found in connection with his work for Paxton. But because none of Myers' business records survive, it is impossible to know how many of his contracts were awarded in this way without competition.

Several contracts signed by Myers exist. The basic details varied little over the years. There were two principal documents. The first contained the contract terms and the second the specification of work and plans to be carried out. Firms such as Myers & Sons contracted 'in gross', that is to say they quoted a single figure for all the work necessary to complete the building instead of itemising individual costs and prices. Sometimes separate contracts were awarded by the employer for such items as gas lighting, heating and ornamental carving. The heating of churches was often handed over to specialists such as Messrs Haden who installed the heating

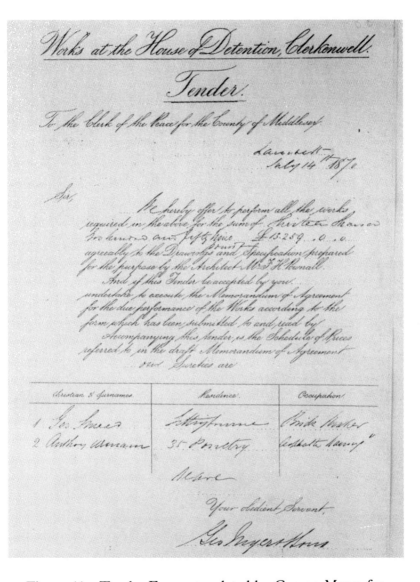

Figure 41   Tender Form completed by George Myers for
work at the House of Detention, Clerkenwell.
*Courtesy of the Corporation of London, Greater London Record
Office, ref. MA/G/CLE/3494.*

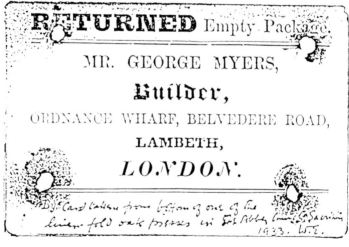

Figure 42   Two-sided package label found attached to one of
the linenfold oak presses in St Augustine's Church, Ramsgate.
*Courtesy of Dom Bede Millard, OSB, of St Augustine's Abbey,
Ramsgate.*

system at the Westminster Chapel and at Christchurch, Spitalfields, as well as other churches which Myers built. When lifts became fashionable the only name was that of Sir W. Armstrong. Ornamental carving was seldom subcontracted by Myers as he had his own highly skilled craftsmen, including another brother-in-law, Samuel Ruddock, who, with his son Oliver Ruddock, was a frequent exhibitor at the Royal Academy in the second half of the 19th century. When filling in his 1861 census return, Myers stated that he was a builder and then added gratuitously that he employed 100 men. He must have been referring to his permanent employees such as his artist-craftsmen and clerks. Beside these men, who formed the nucleus of his workforce, we know that, in his workshops, he had apprentices, and that, on the forecourt of the Wharf, he had those men who caused so much trouble when they were drunk. On the building sites, Myers sometimes employed several thousand men, but these numbers fluctuated as the occasion demanded. The recruitment of this army was the responsibility of the general foreman. He engaged the tradesmen, who worked under a foreman of their own trade. There were at least a dozen separate trades to be considered, bricklayers, carpenters, plumbers, paperhangers, etc., as well as carters with their waggons and horses.[6] The work done by each group of men was listed in great detail under separate headings in the work specification section of the contracts. These men were engaged individually, whereas the labourers who did the digging, and were sometimes employed instead of horses to drag heavy loads and do work which today is done by mechanical means, were often taken on in gangs without much scrutiny, though this was not likely to be admitted. The tradesmen and labourers were engaged at the beginning of each contract.

Some of the foremen worked for Myers for years. John James who was caught stealing stone in Beverley had worked for him for seventeen years; in 1861 Mr Lambert, Myers' agent in Box, had been employed by him for fourteen years.[7] The craftsmen and specialist workers required on site moved from contract to contract travelling by whatever form of transport was available. Many letters survive discussing the movements of these craftsmen and the progress of their work.[8]

The gangs of labourers were engaged locally whenever possible. In undertaking building work in London, the problem of housing the workforce did not arise. Many of Myers' craftsmen lived in houses or tenements in Belvedere Road and, in any case, men were prepared to walk for an hour or two to get to and from their work. Outside London, when a comparatively small number of men were involved, accommodation or lodging could be found with the local villagers but when accommodation for 1,000 men or more was needed, a subcontractor or agent was engaged. He would put up temporary huts on site and also provide two meals a day including a pint of beer at the main meal for each man.

As we have seen, much of the skilled work was done in the workshops at Ordnance Wharf. This applied not only to the sculpting and carving required in the churches but also to joinery, 'the doors, jambs, linings and architraves as well as windows, shutters and fittings to the same'. It was the carpenter who was responsible for the structural woodwork of a building and the joiner's work to make the wainscoting, doors, shutters, sashes and suchlike fittings. In a small undertaking the same man might carry out both jobs. If built-in furniture or other high grade furnishings were required, this would be carried out by a cabinet-maker.[9] These, as well as much else in the same line, were constructed at the Wharf for Sir Joseph Paxton's house in Sydenham. He ordered furniture as well, a table for the kitchen and one for the hall with two drawers. The long bill headed 'Sir Joseph Paxton, to preparing work at the Yard for Rockhill House' has survived.[10]

Myers, like Thomas Cubitt before him, had the latest equipment in his workshops. We know that he had a very powerful and valuable steam engine that had been destroyed in the great fire of 1850. It was insured and would have been replaced. Its use would have been to drive most of the machinery in the workshops by means of a system of shafts, pulleys and belts. With his 'modern' machinery it was more efficient and economical to carry out as much skilled work as possible at the Wharf and then transport the finished articles to the site. Water transport was cheap and nearly always available. The railway was less than half a mile from the workshops and was spreading rapidly over the country and the toll roads were good. Transport for George Myers was not a problem.

The main building materials, brick, stone, tiles and slates were chosen by the architect in consultation with the employer or building committee. There is a reference in the 1853 *Trade Directory* to a brickfield at Mount Farm in Ealing which belonged to George Myers. Until well into the 19th century brickworks were set up usually on a rather temporary basis on or near the building site. The equipment needed was very simple and could be moved to another location when no longer required. Presumably Myers' brickfarm at Ealing was of a more permanent nature to merit a mention in the local *Directory*. In 1848, when Myers was about to start building Colney Hatch Asylum, a Mr Smith, who had contracted to supply bricks, failed to do so and Myers was obliged to manufacture ten million bricks on site, using the clay dug out of the ground for the foundations. This was an old fashioned method which could cause serious subsidence problems. The tax on bricks, first imposed in 1784, had been withdrawn in 1850, so perhaps it was at this time that Myers decided to make his own. But within a few years the manufacture of bricks was mechanised which resulted in cheaper production methods, and with brickfields surrounding London Myers probably decided that it was not worth his while to continue. One would like to think that the reason he gave up making bricks was because of the appalling custom of employing very young children in brickyards. At this time boys of eight and girls between nine and ten years were used to carry 40-45lbs of clay on their heads to the brickmaker, for thirteen hours a day, often covering a distance of fourteen miles.[11] But George Myers was a man of his time and no doubt considered it a necessary evil if the children were not to starve.

When Myers was working on the Guildhall in the City of London, the bricks were supplied by George Smeed of Sittingbourne, Kent. (Myers gave Smeed's name as surety when he tendered for the contract to undertake works at the House of Detention in Clerkenwell in 1870.) When Myers was building Mentmore, the bricks came from Lawford and Sons of Leighton, Bedfordshire, a mere three or four miles away.

But Myers' favourite building material was stone. He was after all a stonemason by trade. It is known that in the 1850s and '60s he leased underground quarries in Wiltshire from the Northey family, those at Box and Kingsdown certainly belonging to them, possibly those at Farleigh and Pickwick also. The stone quarried in this area is Bath stone, the name used generically to denote the product of many Great Oolite quarries. Myers also leased from the Northeys and the Great Western Railway jointly, a stone yard and wharf (with a crane) which fronted onto the line. In the 1850s he was one of only two quarrymasters to have his own yards and wharves in the area. He also had his own rolling stock.[12]

The exact date of his arrival in the district is not known, but there are reasons to believe that he had arrived in the 1840s, probably about the time he was establishing himself in London.[13] It was a time of expansion in the quarrying business. The building of the Kennet and Avon Canal facilitated the transport of stone from Box and the other nearby quarries, and with the completion of the Box tunnel and the coming of the Great Western Railway in 1841, overland transport, which had been expensive, became much less so. From then on, the price of Bath stone in London was much reduced.

The Romans used Bath stone and in the Middle Ages it was used in the construction of many monasteries and churches. Much Bath stone was used in the construction of Victorian London. Myers may have used stone from the same quarries to build some of Pugin's 'Gothic' churches. Myers' first contract in the Metropolis, in 1840, was to build St George's Catholic Cathedral in Southwark and Pugin's specifications stated that 'the whole of the dressings, external and internal, moulds, string courses, water tables, jambs, arches, tracery, copings, pillars, arches, etc., to be worked in the best Bath stone'.

When he was building Magdalen College gateway, in Oxford, in 1844, Bath stone was again used. Pugin believed it to be the best that could be employed, 'that it was far superior to Caen stone and that when it was taken from the right quarry, it was of a very durable description'. And writing to the Revd Mr Bloxam at Magdalen he says: 'I now have all the Farleigh stone in London ...'.[14] Presumably he was referring to Ordnance

Wharf where Myers' craftsmen would have started to carve the Gateway.

Magdalen College still has Myers' account for 'rebuilding side wall of Gateway and new porch, door, etc'. There is a list of the wages due to the fourteen masons engaged on the work which ranged from 3s. 6d. to 6s. 6d. a day, and another list which shows the materials used and their cost:

	£	s.	d.
540 ft of Bath stone at 2s/	54	0	0
35 cube Caen stone at 3s/6	9	12	6
18 ft of York landing, 8 ins thick	2	10	0
40 ditto of York paving	3	10	0
Lime sand arches etc etc	5	0	0
Lead for Porch roof and flashing, labour included	8	0	0
1 Gothic snow box	0	6	0
Oak door for side entrance	21	0	0
Iron hooks, bans, lock, studs etc etc	31	0	0
Total:	267	17	3

Bath stone was used at St Marie's, the little church in Rugby built for Capt. Washington Hibbert in 1846, which was constructed entirely of Farleighdown stone. Some years later, the houses in Broad Sanctuary, Westminster and the Middle Temple Library were built of Bath stone from Myers' own quarries and we can be sure, when Combe Down or Box stone was stipulated for the restoration of the windows of St John's Chapel in the Tower of London, where Myers was the contractor, that he would have arranged for stone from his own quarries to be used.

The railway station at Box was built by Myers in 1849.[15] While the work was in progress the masons went on strike in sympathy with their fellow masons in London. A letter in the *Bath Journal* reported that the workmen had been demanding contributions to the 'strike fund' from the local residents and that 'some families, consisting of ladies, had given through fear of molestation'. Twelve years later, on 23 October, 1861, the *Bath Herald* reported that, since the start of the strikes in London, delegates from various places had visited Box to endeavour to persuade the quarrymen to stop work but that, due to the great esteem in which the masters of the various firms in the locality were held, the agitators had little success. The inhabitants of the village and neighbourhood of Box were so impressed and delighted with this state of affairs that they decided to give the men an 'invitation dinner' to which 120 sat down in a spacious tent in the grounds of the Northey Arms Hotel. The chair was taken by Mr Jacob Pocock of Sheylor's Farm. After the usual loyal toasts the chairman proposed the health of Mr Myers 'one of the principal employers'. Mr Lambert, Myers' agent, acknowledged the toast and in doing so said that he had now occupied this position for upwards of fourteen years. We have no record as to when George Myers bought his quarries, but if Lambert had been his agent from the beginning we can suggest that he acquired them not later than 1847. In 1866 Myers sold his quarries to the Bath Stone Company.

It is possible to visit one of Myers' quarries, Travellers' Rest, at Pickwick in West Wiltshire, which is no longer worked. It is spacious and lofty and very damp. The men, who worked in gangs of four under a foreman, were tough. They worked a ten hour day and were paid according to the cubic footage of trimmed stone produced at the quarry head. They provided their own tools and candles to light the underground chambers. The stone they quarried was freestone, that is stone which could be cut in any direction by means of the large square-ended saws which had to be kept wet with water. The great blocks of stone were then removed from the workface with a crane and lowered onto a trolley mounted on tramlines and towed by a horse to the quarry head. Young boys were used to get water from a well in the quarry and to fetch the beer for the men's meal which consisted of a loaf of bread. Many of the men were nonconformists and teetotal. The rats, much in evidence in George Myers' day, have now departed.[16]

Timber was supplied to George Myers & Sons by 'Thomas Gabriel & Sons' of New Barge House, Commercial

Road, Lambeth. Gabriel's wharf was less than a mile down stream from Ordnance Wharf. Myers gave Gabriel's name when he had been asked to produce testimonials, and in 1858 Myers had built granaries, warehouses and a dock at the Old Barge House Wharf in Commercial Road.[17] He would have known the wharfs and warehouses and their proprietors well. Gabriel was a merchant of some consequence. He was invited to the ball given in honour of the Sultan of Turkey in the Guildhall on 18 July 1867, one of only three timber importers so favoured. He owned creosote works in Rotherhythe and doubtless supplied Myers with this also. The wharf next to Gabriel's was occupied by Messrs Dawson, importers of mahogany, ebony and other rare woods. Soft wood used by the building trade frequently came from the Baltic. Fir from Danzig and Riga was imported in large quantities.

On site, apart from building materials, the contractor was required to provide all machinery 'wagons, carts, horses, staging planks, ladders and tools for the workmen', as well as 'all necessary tarpaulins, casing or other proper covering or protection for the building while the work was in progress'.[18]

The contractor had to ensure that men and equipment arrived at the site and was required to replace any broken or stolen machinery. Later contracts stipulated that an insurance policy should cover all damage to property or theft from the site. Insurance to cover injury was not considered until 1862 when a Bill was passed providing for compensation for servants and workers and for the families of men or women killed at work.

The contractor was paid in tranches on completion of stages in the contract as certified by the architect. He would receive only 80% of the contract sum by completion and the remainder was usually paid three or six months later when the architect had checked and certified that there were no defects. The workmen were paid weekly in cash. If the contractor was not paid promptly by the employer, as sometimes happened, this gave rise to serious problems which made the builder's business a hazardous enterprise. It was only those who were financially astute who survived.

From the 1850s onward there were many strikes. In the autumn of 1851, Pugin wrote a letter to the Bishop of Shrewsbury about the building of churches and said: '... this strike of Myers' men, above 2 thousand, I have no doubt it is a great scheme got up by some builders to ruin Myers by stirring up his men, for it was done in an hour ...' and he went on: 'I would not undertake (the building of) a gravestone at this moment'.[19]   There were doubtless unscrupulous builders who would have been delighted to have a chance to ruin Myers, but the workers were striking without any encouragement from employers. By 1851 the shorter working Saturday was the norm, but strikes to obtain the nine hour day continued for years. On the occasion of the great lockout in 1859, 24,000 workers were adrift in the London streets for eight weeks.

It was against this background of industrial unrest and financial uncertainty that George Myers carried on his business.

VII

More Churches and a Synagogue: 1842-73

During the course of his working life Myers constructed or restored over ninety churches in London and the Provinces. Although he had spent his youth restoring beautiful medieval Beverley Minster and Holy Trinity, Hull, it was not until 1837, when he won the contract for St Mary's, Derby, that we hear of him actually building a church. From then on he averaged three a year, taking about thirteen months to complete one of average size.[1] Each one of these churches has been identified in Appendix 1, with its date, site, architect, etc. In this chapter it is proposed to refer only to a few, that is, to those which are of special interest, as well as being well documented.

It will be remembered that in 1818 the Government granted £1,000,000 to encourage the 'Building and Promoting the Building of Additional Churches in (newly) Populous Parishes'. A similar grant was made a few years later. This money was made available only to the Established Church, the Church of England. As Government money was involved, the Church Commissioners set up a complex bureaucracy with detailed application forms. 'Commissioners' Churches' were sometimes said to be unimaginatively designed and cheaply built, but the contracts undertaken by George Myers cannot be included in this category.

The church of St Mark's in the Groves, Hull, was to be built in a desperately poor parish, surrounded by mills and factories. Of 1,178 houses, only 35 were rated at £20 a year and upwards.[2] It was to have 1,100 seats, 600 of them to be free. The Commissioners accepted from Mr George Liddell of Sutton, the gift of 800 square yards of land to be the site of the new church and churchyard, but they became anxious that foundation problems could arise. They consulted various authorities. This was the occasion when Myers wrote to them explaining that stable foundations could be ensured on the site by the use of wooden piles. The church wardens were reassured and Myers & Wilson subsequently won the contract to build this church. The foundation stone was laid by the Venerable Archdeacon Wilberforce on 9 June 1841 and it was opened on 3rd May 1843. It had cost £5,086. 16s. 0d.[2]

Soon after they began working at St Mark's, not far away in Great Thornton Street, Myers & Wilson also built a very large Wesleyan Chapel. The architects were Messrs Allom and Lockwood, the designers of St Mark's, but the two places of worship could not have been more different: whereas the style of St Mark's was 'Gothic', the Great Thornton Street Chapel was a strange mixture with classical columns flanked by wings which looked like Egyptian sarcophagi. One can only hope that Pugin never saw it.

Another Yorkshire church built by Myers, was St Michael's, Cherry Burton, near Beverley. It stands in the old part of the village which is as pretty as its name. It had been restored by the rector, Robert Darley Waddilove, in 1800 and had seating for 151 people including sixty-four free seats for the poor of the parish. By 1850 the Revd Robert Swann, who was rector at that time, decided that his dilapidated church was too small to accommodate his parishioners; he applied to the Incorporated Society for Promoting the Enlargement, Building and Repairing of Churches and Chapels for a grant to assist in the rebuilding of his church. He was promised £80 on condition that the work should be finished within five years. George Myers of Ordnance Wharf, Lambeth won the contract and on 5 August 1852, the foundation stone was laid by Miss Burton of Cherry Burton. The architects were Horace Jones of London and Charles Vickers. The Building Committee consisted of:

The Revd Mr Robert Swann
John F.Hicks
David Burton Esq
Lord Hotham

Myers had signed the specifications and agreement on 31 May 1852. He was to pull down the old church, erect and complete a new one and execute all other work to the entire satisfaction of Charles Vickers for the sum of £1,700 within seven months. The bells, font, communion table, stove and organ were to be moved to a place of safety and 'refixed in due course'. The tombstones were to be carefully removed and preserved until they could be reset as near as possible to their old positions. Myers was to provide a new pulpit of Caen stone with 'solid steps' and entry through a door from the chancel. He was to be paid £26 for the oak communion rails and table, £7 for the reading desk or lectern. The pews were to have low doors, bookboards and hat rails, and children's pews were to be provided. The work to be done by the painter and stainer, plumber and glazier, and the smith was all listed on Myers' specification and initialled by him. There is no indication as to whether or not these were local men. Myers still had men working at St Mary's, Beverley about five miles away so it is quite possible that the same group of craftsmen worked on both churches. The work was finished within the specified time and the church was consecrated on 24 October 1853 by the Archbishop of York. One wonders why Horace Jones was engaged to design a small village church in Yorkshire. His clerk did not know how to spell Beverley or Yorkshire. Ten years later Myers worked again for Horace Jones who, as the City of London Architect, designed the new roof for the Guildhall. Jones was still the City's Architect in 1887 when Myers' son-in-law, Sir John Jackson, built the foundations of Tower Bridge for the City Corporation.

In 1858, Myers built two churches in adjacent Yorkshire villages, both with the same architect, John Loughborough Pearson, in charge. One of these was St Leonard's Church, Scorborough which was paid for by James Hall Esq., Master of the Holderness Foxhounds. It cost upwards of £5,000. There is an elaborately carved oak roof and seats and stalls also of oak. The other was St Mary's, Dalton Holme, which is larger, costing £25,000 to build. The third Baron Hotham was the donor. He spent large sums of money on churches, it is said, so that he would have less to leave his heir, a nephew whom he disliked. Here too the seats, pulpit and choir stalls are carved in oak. This was the last time that Myers travelled so far north to build a church. It is of interest that Myers owned a picture of Lord Hotham's ancestor, Sir John Hotham, refusing King Charles I entry into Hull, of which town he was the Governor during the Civil War. Later, Sir John changed sides, was arrested by the Roundheads and beheaded on Tower Hill.

In Oxford, Joseph Hansom designed a church, dedicated to St Aloysius, whose foundation stone was laid on 20 May 1873. Messrs Myers were the builders. This church has a large presbytery beside it. Now, a hundred years after the death on 11 August 1890 of Cardinal Newman, a Catholic Oratory as a centre for prayer and study is to be set up in his memory in this church. Newman, a Fellow of Oriel College, was one of the founders of the Oxford Movement. His conversion to the Church of Rome, in 1845, caused a sensation.[3]

As, apart from St Aloysius, Myers had built eleven churches in the diocese of Birmingham, the strange story concerning the church of St Joseph in Avon Dassett, Warwickshire, is not to be wondered at. This church is said to have had George Myers as architect. This is not so. The confusion arose owing to the fact that when it was built in 1854, *The Builder* reported that 'Mr Myers' was the architect. As George Myers was the best known Mr Myers in the construction industry other journals and newspapers copied the report as 'Mr Myers of London' and so it was presumed that it was he, when in fact the architect was Thomas Meyer.[4]

Myers built many churches in the home counties. By 1844, the ancient parish church of St Thomas and St Clement in Winchester had become 'decayed and dilapidated' and too small for the expanding congregation,[5] so it was agreed that a new church should be built on a plot of land bought for that purpose in what is now Southgate Street. The old church had been in St Thomas' Street. Myers won the contract and was

Figure 43   The Great Thornton Street Chapel, Hull.
Courtesy of Hull City Record Office.

Figure 44   St. Mary's Church, Dalton Holme, Yorkshire,
Photograph held on deposit at the Humberside County Record Office, ref. P.E. 54/11.

described as 'of Laurie Terrace, St George's Fields, Southwark in the County of Surrey'. The address is interesting as it shows that at this date he was still conducting his business from Laurie Terrace where the houses were not yet numerous enough to require numbering, and the area was still known as 'St George's Fields'.

The Rector of the parish was the Revd George James Cubitt and his Building Committee of seventeen local residents consisted of a cross-section of the community, including five lawyers. The church was to cost £5,170 without a tower or spire, £5,630 with a tower and £6,230 with both tower and spire. The main part of the church was completed in 1847 having been started in 1845, but it was not until 1855 on the death of Mr Cubitt that it was decided to build the tower and spire as a memorial to him.

This church is now the Hampshire County Record Office where the papers concerning the building and conversion of the church are kept. On the top floor, where the reading room is, the roof beams and carving can be closely examined without the aid of 'ladders and scaffolding'.

Between May 1847 and August 1848 Myers built St Mary the Virgin, the parish church of Ewell in Surrey, which replaced a much older one. The Vicar, the Revd Sir George Glyn Bt., was to be the third name on George Myers' list of testimonials which he provided when he won the Colney Hatch contract. In about 1850 he restored another church in this region, the flint and stone 13th century church of St Mary's, Beddington, where the Vicar, Mr Hamilton, was the tenth on the same list. He re-roofed it, installing strange little dormer windows, perhaps as an insurance against dry rot. He made new arches and piers for the nave, the galleries were removed and the chancel arch was rebuilt. The description of the restoration work says that earth to a depth of six inches was removed from the floor. Did the old church have a mud floor or was it the result of hundreds of years of worshippers who did not wipe their feet before entering the church? The mud was replaced with smart red and black tiles. New pews were carved in the Ordnance Wharf workshops, each bench end being decorated with a different plant motif. There was a new reading desk and the old font and pulpit were restored. At about this time a new rectory, schools and almshouses for the aged poor were also constructed. George Myers may have built these too.

In Norfolk, George Myers was working on another medieval church at this time, the church of St Mary's, West Tofts, for the Sutton family. The restoration plans, including the designs for the church furniture, had been drawn out by Pugin before his death in 1852, but most of the work was carried out at a later date under the supervision of Edward Pugin. The specifications for the new chancel and sacristy were agreed in November 1853, but Myers' letter consenting to undertake the work for £2,900 0s.0d. is dated 5 February 1855.[6] Very little of the 14th century walls of the old church remained. The new walls were to be built of the same knapped flint; Farleydown stone ashlar was to be used for the inside of the church, for the window jambs, and weathering cornices, and the best Caen stone, a soft stone, for the capitals, hood moulds and other carving. The stalls, screen doors, etc. were to be worked according to the plans furnished, and done in 'the most workmanlike manner'. An oak ambry was to be provided for the sacristy and an oak lectern for the sanctuary. A pulpit and font were also required and the organ loft was to be worked in the best foreign oak.

The Suttons were a wealthy family and no expense was spared. Phoebe Stanton who visited this church says: 'it was serious, respectful and evocative ... it was brilliant'.[7] The stained glass windows were made by Hardman, the tiles by Minton and Thomas Earley painted the ceiling in muted colours and decorated the walls of the sanctuary with musical angels. The reredos was the work of Lane & Lewis of Birmingham. The lace-like screens were the work of Myers' craftsmen who also made the lectern, the pulpit and font and the substantial pews which they decorated with birds and beasts of the forest. The external carvings are of a very high standard including a hauntingly lovely girl's head which personifies the peace of this church which has now been deserted for half a century.

In 1942 the village of West Tofts, its church and three neighbouring villages with their churches were requisitioned by the Army as a battle training ground. The area has been closed to the public ever since. There is no sign of the villages but the churches remain surrounded by lush grass and forest. Wild flowers and animals proliferate. In recent years, a candle-lit carol service has been held each Christmas at St Mary's, to which many from the surrounding villages come to worship once again in the church of their ancestors.

Most of the furniture was moved for safe keeping and Myers' pews, benches and the pulpit are in the Garrison Church in Colchester. This unusual clapboard church was built in 1856, at the same time as the hutted camp. It was here, at the end of the Crimean War, that fifty-six German Legionnaires, who had come to Colchester to be disbanded, married fifty-six local girls preparatory to emigrating to South Africa. It was not until they were on the high seas that the authorities realised that the Garrison Church was not licensed for marriages and so the Germans and their 'spouses' were 'living in sin'. A special Act had to be passed by the South African Parliament to regularise their union.[8]

In Berkshire, Myers built several churches including a chapel for Wellington College and a parish church for Eton where the townspeople had always used the College chapel, until eventually their numbers became too great. The Provost and Fellows of the College gave the site and £500 so that the town could have a church of its own. Benjamin Ferrey was chosen as architect and Myers won the tender to construct the new church of St John the Evangelist. Prince Albert laid the foundation stone on 25 October 1852. The building which was completed in 1854 was large, seating 728 with a tower and spire.[9] It stands back from the road and those wishing to enter pass through a small garden. When the trees and shrubs grew the church was not immediately visible. As time passed the congregation dwindled and eventually it was declared redundant and the vandals took over. But the exterior of the building was comparatively unharmed. The girl's head to the left of the principal entrance still enchants, and must have been carved by the same craftsman as the head at St Mary's, West Tofts, and the buttresses are ornamented with a strange breed of cat with demons' tails, trying desperately not to slide head first down the masonry.   Recently, (1991), the church has been adapted for secular use for the community.   The largest area of the building is now a sanatorium for Eton College, and there is a health centre on the ground floor.   On the upper floors are flats for members of staff and a chapel.   Almost the whole of the east side of the chapel is filled by the great stained glass window of the old church.   The brightness and colour of this window is stunningly effective.   Once again the building is used to capacity.

It is well to pause here and say something of ecclesiastical finance, a subject that in the 19th century would have been understood by all those whom it concerned, such as the parishioners.

Private donors were not uncommon.   Catholic and other non-conforming churches were built entirely by voluntary subscription as no government grants came their way. Generous donors contributed towards the construction of many Church of England churches, and money was raised by subscriptions, loans and occasionally mortgages.   The Church Commissioners usually contributed a small amount, sometimes as little as £10, to give them authority to fix the seat rents.[10] Christ Church, Craven Hill, Kensington, cost £14,500 to build, the Commissioners making a grant of £10.   A scale of rents had been fixed for this church, by an Instrument dated 29 December 1855.   The gross amount came to £1,789. 11*s*. 6*d* and was assigned to the Minister less £20 to the clerk.   St Barnabas, in Kennington, cost £5,360 to build and £200 was accepted from the Commissioners.   There were 900 pew and rented sittings and 526 free seats for the poor of the parish. The seat rents amounted to £851. 2*s*. 0*d*., all of which was assigned to the Minister less £15 to the clerk.

At Stoke Newington the old parish church had had an endowment of £350 since the reign of King Charles I.   As well as this, the income from the seat rents was vested in the churchwardens and the people of the parish.   Considerable distress was caused when the new Vicar, the Revd Mr George Jackson, decided that the expanding population in the district needed a new and larger church and that the old church should be pulled down.   This meant that the endowment would be assigned to the new church and that, by some sleight of hand, the seat rents would be assigned to Mr Jackson. The Lord Bishop of London became heavily involved in this parochial affair and decreed that the new church was to be the parish church and that the old one would not be pulled down but that it should act as a chapel of ease. George Myers built a beautiful new church with a spire, which at that time, was the tallest in London.[11]

Seat rents could produce a considerable income for the Minister. This induced some of them to do all in their power to prevent the building of new churches on their boundaries for fear that the 'carriage folk' might desert the old church for the new. At St James the Less in Garden Street, Westminster, as it was a very poor district, all the seats were free. To compensate for this, the Commissioners endowed the church with the sum of £250 a year, to be charged on the eight houses in Broad Sanctuary, Westminster, (houses built by Myers) near the west front of the Abbey. Myers built this church which was paid for by the Misses Monk in memory of their father who had been Bishop of Gloucester. It was the architect G.E. Street's first London church and is built of red and black bricks with slate roofing and impressively ornate railings. Inside are to be found multicoloured marble pillars and patterned floor tiles. Over the chancel arch is a mosaic designed by G.F. Watts. The *Illustrated London News* of 1 February 1862, described the church as: 'a lily among weeds ... rising from the poverty and squalor surrounding it'.

Of churches built by Myers in London itself, one of the first was St Andrews, Wells Street (1845). This interesting church is famous as a monument to early Victorian Anglo-Catholicism. The architect was S.W. Daukes. Other architects involved were G.E. Street who designed the metal chancel screen, metal pulpit and the reredos, John Loughborough Pearson who designed the font cover and W. Butterfield who was responsible for the lectern. The east window was designed by Pugin and made by Hardman. Most of the other windows were made by Clayton and Bell and an Irishman, Michael O'Connor (1801-67), who worked in London for a time and

then returned to Dublin. There is an undated letter written by
Myers to Hardman, probably in 1846, which says:

> The glass is at Wells Street and the Rector likes it
> very much indeed. There is something rather
> curious about O'Connor getting it. The fact is
> there is no doubt that he agreed to have it - or he
> would never have troubled about it at all. He
> wanted to get all he could out of it. The mistake
> appears to be this - it is put in the top light
> instead of the bottom, but it can't be altered now -
> and looks very well.[12]

£9,000 was given by the Incorporated Church Building Society
towards the costs of this church. Myers was paid £7,000
exclusive of extras. At a later date, in 1934, St Andrews was
taken down and re-erected in Kingsbury, Middlesex.

Myers built churches in the old squalid streets of
Westminster and for the inhabitants of the smart new terrace
houses of Kensington. He built St Matthew's in Great Peter
Street, at that time one of the very poorest districts in the
metropolis, and St Peter's, Windmill Street (in the parish of St
James's, Piccadilly) which was reported to be the 'most
dissipated of the whole metropolis being the headquarters of the
Great Social Evil. Adult intemperance, juvenile disorder and
Sunday trading with a total disregard for the Sabbath prevailed'.

In 1853 a new Rector, the Revd John E. Kemp was
appointed and he decided that the only way to cure these evils
was to build two new churches, where most of the seats would
be free for the poorer members of the parish (he planned for a
congregation of 4,000), and to build schools. No grant was
forthcoming so all the money had to be raised by voluntary
subscription. *The Builder* published the list of donors headed by
the Queen with a donation of £125. Her example was followed
by notable churchmen and Peers of the Realm, rather a large
number of whom had 'since deceased'. Very few of the wealthy
shopkeepers in the district had contributed as most of them now
lived in suburban villas and presumably supported local charities
and had no wish to be reminded of the spiritual needs of the

badly paid workers who supplied the goods sold in their shops. Of the sixteen West End Clubs in the parish not one contributed even a shilling. In the end only St Peter's was built and it has now been demolished.[13]

In 1864 Myers rebuilt one of Westminster's most fashionable churches, the Queen's Chapel of the Savoy. This ancient Chapel had been one of three serving almshouses founded by Henry VII.[14] The land on which it was built had once belonged to Peter of Savoy, uncle of Henry III's Queen, Eleanor of Provence. When the almshouses ceased to exist the chapel was used by the military and then from 1702 onwards by the inhabitants of the area, but the Sovereign has always been responsible for defraying all expenses connected with it. There is a little graveyard beside the church but it has not been used since 1853. In 1860 the Chapel was extensively restored and modernised. 'The hideous gallery' at the south end was removed and high pews replaced with open seats. But four years later the Chapel was burnt to the ground leaving only the walls standing. With Sydney Smirke as architect and George Myers as builder the Church was rapidly returned to use. This church is now the Chapel of the Order of the Commanders of St Michael and St George.

Also built by Myers was the Non-Conformist New Westminster Chapel in James Street. It has always been carefully maintained and, apart from war damage, restoration work has never been required. There are 2,500 seats. Billy Graham preached here to a capacity congregation in 1981.

Another well-cared for and important place of worship built by Myers was in Upper Berkeley Street, for the West London Synagogue of British Jews who wished to establish a place of worship to which Jews of this country, irrespective of origin, might come and where a revised Service would be performed. To this end, in November 1866, a building committee was appointed. By January 1867, a donation list of £8,602. 10*s*. 0*d*. had been collected. Once the site in Upper Berkeley Street had been acquired, Messrs Davis and Emanuel were appointed architects and Myers tendered for and was engaged to build the Synagogue, for £9,532. He also erected the entrance at a cost of £3,198. The memorial stone was laid on 23 June 1870 and the Consecration Service took place on 22 September 1870. Ever since that time a thriving community has worshipped in this beautiful Synagogue.[15]

The area now known as the Royal Borough of Kensington and Chelsea boasted five complete Myers churches, as well as a spire and chancel in two others. They are:

All Saints',   Kensington Park
St George's,   Campden Hill
St Jude's,   Collingham Gardens
St Augustine's,   Queen's Gate
Congregational Church,   Markham Square,
                            Chelsea, now demolished.

In this part of London the parishioners lived in houses with gardens, most had carriages and some of them kept cows. The churches were under the jurisdiction of the Venerable Archdeacon John Sinclair, whose nephew was to marry George Myers' granddaughter on 4 July 1905 in St Mary Abbott's Church - which was not built by Myers. In a district such as Kensington there cannot have been any serious difficulty in obtaining money to build churches from the prosperous residents, in the days when it was fashionable to attend Matins, smartly dressed on Sunday morning. But to find a site in an area where gardens were large and developers were rapacious, was much more difficult. On 8 December 1862, a letter headed 'Vicarage Kensington W' and signed 'John Sinclair' complained:

> Lady Holland is willing that I should have a site in the Eastern portion of Holland Park, but to this arrangement the contractor for the villas, Messrs Radford object. On the other hand Messrs Radford would readily allow me to have a site on the Western portion of the Park, but to this proposal Lady Holland objects.[16]

Eventually a site was found on Campden Hill, which was paid for by Mr John Bennet of Westbourne Villas, and the church was constructed by Myers. On a corner stone where all can see, are two inscriptions which explain that:

Figure 45   St John the Evangelist, Eton.
Reproduced by permission of the Provost and Fellows of Eton College.

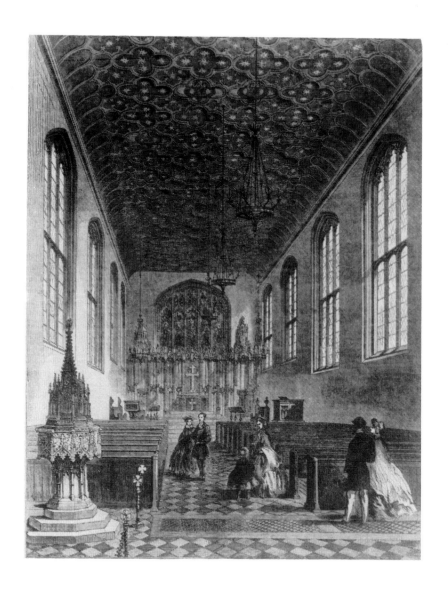

Figure 46   The Queen's Chapel of the Savoy.

This stone was laid by
The Venerable Archdeacon Sinclair
On Saturday the sixth day of February A.D.1864
Except the Lord build the House,
They labour in Vain that Build it

On the other face it says:

Church of St George's
Campden Hill
Kensington

E. Bassett Keeling
Architect

G. Myers & Sons
Builders

In later years, Sir James Barrie and the children for whom he wrote *Peter Pan* worshipped in this church. They all lived in Campden Square.

In 1866, Myers returned to a less salubrious area to carry out extensive restorations at Christchurch, Spitalfields.[17] Ewan Christian, architect to the Ecclesiastical Commissioners, was in charge. The church had been built by Hawksmoor in 1714. The churchwardens' appeal for money to do the work explained:

> Christchurch, Spitalfields, the noblest and stateliest
> in East London excessively needs repair, though
> surrounded by a Poor population, provides for
> them but little accommodation and that both
> unsuitable and repulsive.

Myers remedied this by renewing the floor and by altering and repairing the pulpit and desk. In addition the galleries were taken down and re-erected at a lower level, the side windows were lengthened and the roof and drains repaired. Once again (1990), Christchurch is undergoing extensive repairs and the many corpses discovered in the bricked up vaults under the church have been removed, so that no doubt its 'repulsive' character has been eliminated.

This account of some of the churches built by Myers over the years is in a geographical order of a sort and has now been almost completed. The final church is that of St Philip Neri at Arundel in Sussex, which Myers built for the Duke of Norfolk in 1870-3. It is now the Cathedral of Our Lady and St Philip Howard. Joseph Hansom, the inventor of the Hansom cab, was the architect. This was the first Catholic church to be built by Myers for twenty years and it is said that he did so at the request of the Duke himself. Perhaps he liked the idea of signing the architectural drawings 'Geo. Myers and Sons' below 'Norfolk E.M.', the Duke's signature. On 23 July 1870 *The Builder* reported that the foundation stone was laid by the aged Bishop of Troy in the presence of the Duke of Norfolk and thousands of spectators. It is interesting to remember that thirty years before, the foundation stone of the Catholic Cathedral at Southwark had been laid very early in the morning, in secret for fear of anti-Popery riots.

Work started on 27 December 1869. Here again difficulties were encountered with the foundations,[18] but instead of wooden piles 20ft deep as had been used at St Mark's and the Wilberforce Memorial in Hull, it was necessary to sink concrete supports 57 ft deep. The church was built of Myers' favourite Bath stone and though Messrs Hardman of Birmingham made the stained glass windows, John Hardman, the old friend of Myers and Pugin, had died in 1867.

This beautiful Cathedral, Myers' fifth, stands on the hill at the top of the town, close to the Castle entrance. The *East Sussex Gazette*, in its account of the opening ceremony, described him as: 'The Great Builder'.

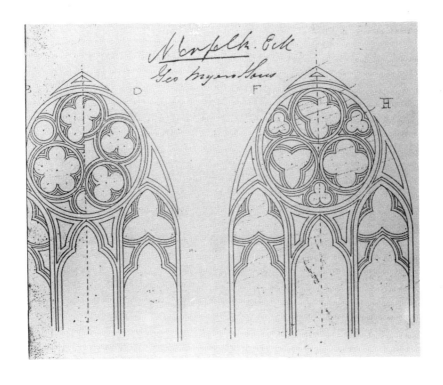

Figure 47   Joseph Aloysius Hansom's architectural drawings for
Arundel Cathedral signed by the Duke of Norfolk
and George Myers.
Reproduced by kind permission of His Grace the Duke of Norfolk.

Figure 48   Arundel Cathedral.

VIII

Asylums and Scandal at Colney Hatch: 1847-58[1]

In 1845 the Shaftesbury Lunacy Act for the Care and Treatment of Lunatics (4 August 1845) obliged every County in England and Wales to build an 'asylum' for the humane treatment of the mentally ill. Victorian lunatic asylums were intended to be places of sanctuary for those unfortunate individuals who were thought to be affected by the waxing and waning of the moon. Doctors were appointed to the staff and, for almost the first time since the dissolution of the monasteries, the mentally ill were to be regarded as patients and not as wild beasts. The Society of Friends had established an asylum in York in 1786 for the humane treatment of lunatics which, under the direction of Dr Tuke, enjoyed considerable success and set an example for others to follow. These new asylums were regulated by Commissioners in Lunacy, (the Earl of Shaftesbury was chairman of the Metropolitan Commissioners for fifty-seven years), and Justices of the Peace or Magistrates. They were responsible for the provision of asylums and for ensuring their smooth running by the appointment of a committee of visitors for each asylum chosen from amongst the magistrates and appointed by the Crown. The involvement of the Crown in the running of these hospitals foreshadowed the setting up of the National Health Service almost exactly one hundred years later.

Myers built three county asylums: Colney Hatch, the Middlesex County Asylum, the Lincolnshire Asylum in

Bracebridge and the Essex County Asylum at Brentwood. He also enlarged and modernised the Bethlem Hospital in Southwark, which is now the Imperial War Museum, as well as building Broadmoor, the asylum for criminal lunatics in Berkshire.

Criminal lunatics were transferred to Broadmoor from asylums all over the country, except when humanitarian reasons rendered their removal inexpedient. The Commissioners in Lunacy emphasised that although Broadmoor was a place of detention and safe custody for the criminally insane, some of whom were very violent, it was to be conducted as a hospital. There are letters in the Public Record Office which reveal some facts about the construction of this place.

On 23 April 1858, Major General Sir Joshua Jebb, the senior Civil Servant in charge of the Prison Service, replied to a letter from R. Gordon Esq. enquiring, on behalf of the Commissioners in Lunacy, what progress had been made towards the erection of the proposed Criminal Lunatic Asylum, subsequent to the purchase of the land on Bagshot Heath. The Major General replied:

> ... I have the satisfaction of informing the Commissioners that a contract on favourable terms has been entered into with Mr Myers, ... he has already purchased a large quantity of bricks and is now making arrangements for laying down a railway to convey them to the site.

But although Myers was waiting to start, the plans had not been agreed. Evidently none of the Commissioners in Lunacy had time to go and inspect them. Sir Joshua pointed out that if only 'the general disposition of the building could be determined then the drains and other heavy work could be commenced'.[2]

The work on the main building did begin in 1858, but there were delays due to strikes. 1859 was the year of the Great Lockout, when the strikes were at their height. The female wing was eventually opened in 1863 and the male wing a year later.

The building of county asylums, which began about a decade before Broadmoor, is well-documented in bound minute books which record the frequent deliberations of the Visiting Justices and of other Committees concerned both with the buildings themselves and with the administration necessary to run them.

In January 1847 advertisements appeared in the press concerning the purchase of one hundred acres of land for the building of the Middlesex County Lunatic Asylum, which was required to be in an airy, healthy situation, well supplied with water. Chalky, gravely or rock subsoil was preferred and the area was to be easily accessible by public conveyance. Unlike the Essex Committee of Visitors at a later date, the Middlesex Visitors did not stipulate that the site should be 'distant from any gentleman's residence'. Particulars were to be sent to Charles Wright, Clerk to the Committee of Visitors. The land which was purchased from Sir William Curtis was not as specified in the advertisement but was of clay. A station was provided by the Great Northern Railway. *The Builder* pointed out that the asylum[3] was required to accommodate 1,000 patients and that this made it a work of difficulty as well as of magnitude ... and that it would probably influence the construction and arrangement of all those that would be erected in the future. It also reported that thirty-nine architects sent in plans for Colney Hatch, and that the estimates varied from £40,000 to £150,000 but that some of the architects had 'disgraced themselves' by showing plans privately to their friends amongst the magistrates before submitting them officially. The Committee first chose twelve designs from which they selected three, namely those of S.W. Daukes, George Godwin & Harris and Allom & Crosse. The plans of S.W. Daukes were eventually chosen and it was estimated that they would cost £83,930 to execute. In January 1847, seventeen contractors were invited to tender for the work, but after widespread interest only three did so. They were Jackson at £225,000, Jay at £198,000 and Myers offering to do the work for £165,000. Even so the Magistrates refused to accept Myers tender as it was almost double Daukes' original estimate. Myers was requested to make economies and a sum of £138,000 was eventually agreed. A draft contract was drawn up on 8 November 1847 and Myers was asked to produce sureties and testimonials. His list of fifteen people willing to give testimonials is headed by the Earl of Shrewsbury, followed by Pugin,[4] G.G. Scott, and other patrons, whose names have provided clues to works carried out by Myers. Myers put forward three sureties:

Mr Robert Peck of Wright St., Leeds	£5,000
Mr Richard Wilson of Hull, stonemason	£2,500
Mr Matthew Smith of Potternewton, Leeds	£2,500

There is a note in the Colney Hatch minute book that the persons named all appeared to be respectable and fit to be accepted as sureties. The inclusion of Richard Wilson's name is strange as he was to be declared bankrupt five months later and he had recently had a request from The Hull Banking Company for repayment of £5. 4s. 10d. which he owed them. Perhaps the Colney Hatch Building Committee had not thoroughly checked the background of the sureties or perhaps Myers, needing a third name, gave Wilson some form of counterindemnity so that the bank could give Wilson a sound reference. In any event the contract was completed and so the Committee was spared the embarrassment of calling upon Wilson after he had become bankrupt.

On 10 January 1849 the contract was finally signed. The completion date for this vast undertaking was to be 1 March 1850, less than one year and two months later. The hospital which was to care for 1,004 patients, was 1,884 ft long and was to include washhouses, kitchens, offices, laundries, workshops, airing courts (where the patients could take exercise), etc. But - there were no bricks. The Committee had entered into a contract with a Mr Smith to make the bricks for the asylum, but he had not produced any. This was embarrassing for the Committee so Myers took the opportunity to demand an interview and insisted that the completion date be postponed until 31 July 1850 and offered to make the ten million bricks on site, from the clay dug out of the foundations. His offer was accepted and Mr Smith's contract was terminated.

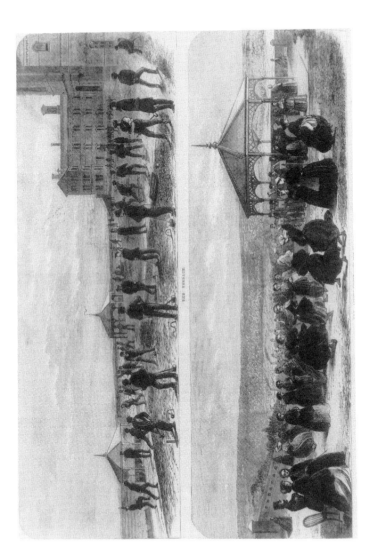

Figure 49   Broadmoor Asylum.
Courtesy of the Guildhall Library, Corporation of London.

Figure 50   Colney Hatch Lunatic Asylum.
Courtesy of the Guildhall Library, Corporation of London.

At last the work began. Thomas Ingham, of Battle Bridge, contracted to erect accommodation on site for the 1,300 men employed by Myers and to provide them with breakfast, dinner and one pint of beer each a day. The work progressed rapidly and plans were made for the laying of the foundation stone by Prince Albert in early May 1849. Daukes designed an ornate silver trowel and Myers built a platform for the ceremony. Refreshments were to be provided for the Prince and his suite and for the Lord Lieutenant and members of the Committee, but there were to be no refreshments for the Justices of the County or their friends. They were told that they could get their sustenance from the Orange Tree Inn in the village. Twenty constables attended the ceremony to ensure law and order. On 8 May the foundation stone was laid in the presence of an august assembly of noblemen and gentlemen. The inscription on it declared that it had been laid by His Royal Highness Prince Albert in the presence of the Committee whose names were listed, that Samuel Daukes was the architect, George Myers the builder and C. J. Shoppee, the Clerk of Works. The Committee noted that the foundation stone would be an 'improving feature' in the entrance hall.

Myers' progress was so much ahead of schedule that payment became due before the money was available and it was necessary to borrow £24,000 to discharge the debt. The authorities felt in honour bound to pay him immediately instead of making him wait as did some of his other employers. At Colney Hatch he was always paid on time. Many extras were needed such as a supply of hot water and baths costing £2,398. It seems strange that this was considered an 'extra'. The Chaplain needed a house, and cottages, farm buildings, sheds and a gas works were also required. The asylum, like any big estate in those days, was expected to be self-supporting. The farm produced food for staff and patients, who baked their own bread and brewed their own beer. The male patients worked on the farm and some were trained as cobblers and the women sewed and laundered. The Committee stocked the farm and Myers was required to lay out the gardens. He sold to the Committee £100 worth of manure which had been produced by the horses working on the site. He built roads and a wall to surround the whole estate. He was asked to supply furniture and fittings for all the buildings but the Committee took so long 'in deciding upon ... the best description of fittings such as locks and water closets, etc ...' that Myers had to request another extension of the completion date, which was granted.

Though much remained to be done, on 1 November 1850 the contractor delivered up possession of the asylum to the Committee. But there was something which the Committee had overlooked and that was that the tax on bricks had been abolished on 27 March of that year. This raised the question of their new price and 'it was ordered that the architect do ascertain what quantity of bricks have been used by Mr Myers in the works since 27 March under contracts entered into before 17 May last ...'.

The tax problem was sorted out and at the meeting held on 15 January 1851 the Committee agreed the draft of a speech to be delivered by the Chairman announcing the completion of the asylum

> exactly one year, five months and twenty three days from the laying of the foundation stone by H.R.H. Prince Albert, thus exhibiting a specimen of English enterprise, energy and exertion which may vie with any yet on record and of which the County of Middlesex may well be proud ...

In fact so proud were they of their asylum that there was consternation when they realized that the building was hidden from view by the high brick wall which they had just paid Myers £800 to build. He was hastily instructed to substitute 'iron railings for so much of the boundary wall as will give a view of the asylum coming over the bridge from Hornsey'. This he did, and by mid-summer 1851 all was finished. It was possible to get a train from King's Cross to the new station at Colney Hatch, the journey taking 18 minutes and costing 4*d*., 6*d*., or 8*d*. according to class. Many visitors both English and foreign who had travelled to London to see The Great

Exhibition availed themselves of the opportunity to visit the famous lunatic asylum, the most costly ever built.

At a Committee meeting on 21 April 1852, 'J. Wilson Esq seconded by C. H. Warner Esq' moved that Mr Daukes had built a magnificent asylum for the County of Middlesex. The Committee of Visitors had much pleasure in stating their great satisfaction at the manner in which the whole works had been executed.

> They also desired to express their sense of the zeal, energy and punctuality displayed by Mr Myers in all his dealings with them, the original contract having been completed to the entire satisfaction of the Committee without any extra charge whatever.

Future events make it important to remember this citation. The committee room, which was 'fitted up very sumptuously and splendidly', had been presented to the Committee by Mr Myers.[5]

Lunatic asylums were required in other parts of the country and, as we have seen, Myers was to build two more of these. Before he had finished Colney Hatch he was engaged to build the asylum at Bracebridge, Lincolnshire.

In 1847 the Poor Law Guardians of Lincolnshire had started to plan the building of a pauper lunatic asylum for 250 patients. A site was chosen at Bracebridge, $1^{1}/_{2}$ miles south of Lincoln. The project was advertised in the press and thirty-two architects submitted plans, twenty-five of which were discarded as 'defective'. Some of the 'architects' had not read the specifications.

Mr J.R. Hamilton submitted an Italianate design which was accepted on 19 July 1848. But before the building of the asylum was far advanced he left for New York and Daukes, his partner, took over. In November 1849, Mr M.P. Moore, Clerk to the Committee of Visitors, inserted advertisements in the County and London newspapers and in *The Builder* requesting tenders from contractors desirous of erecting the asylum. Moore had been busy. He had prepared 'voluminous conditions' for the terms on which tenders would be accepted. He had lengthy discussions with the County Surveyor, Mr Thomas Parry, he had corrected the printer's proofs for thirty-four folios, he had spent a whole morning discussing the water supply and he had drawn up the tender form. In December he wrote to fifty-four persons who had asked for particulars of the contract and he had enquired into the respectability of the applicants. Of these thirteen were allowed to tender, their qualifications having been examined by the Committee of Visitors. They were as follows: Mr Costar who, in partnership with Peto, had built the Great Northern Railway stations from Doncaster to Peterborough; Mr Trego who was building the City of London Prison; Mr Ward and Mr Bennet who had both built prisons; Messrs T. & W. Piper who were London builders of eminence; Mr Sissons who had built the railway dock at Hull; Messrs Hutchinson and Sons who built the Midland Railway Hotel and station at Hull; Messrs Neale and Wilson who built something illegible; Messrs Lucas and Sons who built large works at Lowestoft and, in addition, Mr Lucas had been foreman during the construction of the Houses of Parliament. Messrs W. & T. Cooper were building the Derby Asylum; Mr Charles Lindley was employed by the Duke of Portland; Mr Charles Bennett had built Wisbech Gaol; Messrs Royston & Robinson were recommended by Mr Balam but further enquiries needed to be made, and finally there was Mr George Myers, Ordnance Wharf, Belvedere Road, London who was building the Middlesex County Lunatic Asylum. These contractors were all asked to be present at the Northern Hotel, Lincoln on 28 December 1849 to discuss the specifications.

David Myers, George Myers' eldest son, who worked in his father's office, forgot to stamp the letter accepting this invitation, a serious matter when a contract of this size was concerned. He realised what he had done and wrote hastily:

> I am very sorry from some mistake or other the letter sent you this morning was not paid. In case you have not taken the same in, the contents were to say that my father would be at the Northern Hotel, Lincoln at the time specified also would be

Lincolnshire County Lunatic Asylum.

LIST OF COMPETITORS FOR THE BUILDING CONTRACT.

£	
36,452	Mr. J. W. Costar, 15, Parliament Street, London.
32,870	Mr. George Myers, Ordnance Wharf, Belvidere Road, Lambeth.
35,978	Mr. W. Tregg, 5, Coleman Street, London.
37,749	Messrs. T. and W. Piper, 173, Bishopgate St. Without.
36,241	Mr. W. Sissons, 9, Brook Street, Hull.
40,992	Messrs. Hutchinson and Son, Hull.
36,000	Messrs. Neale and Wilson, Grantham.
38,352	Messrs. Lucas and Son, Lowestoft.
40,050	Mr. Charles Ward, Lincoln.
43,064	Messrs. W. and T. Cooper, Derby.
38,500	Mr. Charles Lindley, Mansfield.
39,700	Mr. Charles Bennett, London Road, Lynn.
	Messrs. Royston and Robinson, Hulme Works, Manchester.

Figure 51   List of Competitors for the contract to build the
Lincolnshire County Asylum, 1849.
*Lincolnshire Archives, County Asylum, KQS Bracebridge Asylum,
Box 3.*

happy to dine with the Gentlemen present. I beg
to enclose your postage stamp in case you have
received the letter.
I am Sir
Your very obedient servant
David Myers.

When the time came for the Northern Hotel meeting, Myers
found it 'utterly impossible to attend' and sent twenty year-old
David to represent him. Despite the youthfulness of his
substitute all went well, Myers' tender of £32,870 was accepted
and in February 1850 the contract was signed, the
Commissioners in Lunacy and the Secretary of State having
passed the plans.

The usual preliminaries were attended to, and Myers
provided testimonials but only four this time. Perhaps he felt
less need to impress the Lincoln Committee. The names he
gave were:

> Mr Rotch, Chairman of the Visiting Justices at
>   Colney Hatch
> A.W.N. Pugin
> Mr Daukes who was soon to be taken on as
>   Architect at Bracebridge, and ...
> Mr Allen, the solicitor to the Colney Hatch
>   Building Committee.

The contract was drawn up on 'the most expensive parchment'
and was ready for Myers' signature when he demanded the
inclusion of an arbitration clause. He had remembered that two
builders had refused to tender for the Colney Hatch contract
because this had been missing. Myers' refusal to sign displeased
the Committee but after deliberating for some time 'it was
deemed advisable to accede to his demands'. His tender had
been nearly 10 per cent below that of his nearest competitor.
Once the contract had been signed the building of the asylum
progressed in an uneventful manner and so when, at a meeting
of the Visitors on Friday, 9 May at the Great Northern Hotel in
Lincoln, it was decided that extra work was needed to complete

the building, the contract was offered to Myers. The work required was:

    1.   the enlargement of the airing courts,

    2.   an adapted form of Harwood's patent windows in the galleries and the 'Colney Hatch' casements (presumably those patented by George Myers), were to be used elsewhere. (The Great Exhibition, where this window was exhibited, had been declared open by the Queen a few days previously.)

    3.   lighting the Asylum by gas: Myers was instructed to build the gasworks and supply the fittings,

    4.   the construction of a cowhouse and sheds and a boundary wall.

Enquiries about the drains and the drainage were to be made by Mr Moore, and by Mr Parry the County Surveyor. (Once again the discussion of this vital system was left until the building was nearing completion.)

The work had started in the summer of 1850 and the final payment was made in July 1853, 'after taking into account the rebate of the brick duty ...'. George Myers was paid a total of £35,573. This was about a quarter of the basic cost of Colney Hatch but Bracebridge was only expected to accommodate 250 patients, whereas Colney Hatch housed over 1,000.

The Essex County Lunatic Asylum was also built by Myers. In August 1846 the Committee of Visitors advertised for a site. Twelve offers were received and the Brentford Hall Estate of eighty-six acres was purchased. The Estate was eighteen miles from London and close to the Eastern Counties Railway. A competition was arranged between ten selected architects to choose the best design for a hospital to house 450 patients. Mr H.E. Kendall was the winner with F.G. Francis second and Daukes, who had built the other two asylums, third. In July 1851 Myers' tender of £57,920 was accepted. On 11 July, the *Essex Standard* reported the formal commencement of the building.   C. G. Round Esq., chairman of the Committee, 'dug the first sod' and addressing Mr Myers said:

> I now on behalf of the Committee authorise you
> to commence this great work.   The Committee
> have as much pleasure in receiving you as the
> builder as, I have no doubt, you will feel in
> executing the work.   From all we have heard and
> seen of you, we are perfectly satisfied.   I trust
> your artisans will have skilful heads and steady
> hands; and may God prosper the undertaking.

But despite this trust, a Building Sub-Committee was appointed with instructions to inspect the work daily.

The style of the outside of the building was medieval but the interior was modern with hot and cold running water 24 hours a day, lavatories, bathrooms and gas supplied from the town gasometer.   Once again Myers' 'patent windows' were installed.   They were described in *The Builder* on the 16 May 1857 as being 'of cast iron fancy patterns, the casement opening outwards above the transoms; but the frames being double, when open, one of them remains in position unglazed so that ventilation is combined with perfect safety'.   The surrounding countryside was beautiful and the buildings and gardens were encircled by a ha-ha to prevent stray animals from eating the newly planted shrubs.

The work progressed satisfactorily and was finished just two years, two months and two weeks after the starting date. Kendall wrote a report which ended:

> ... from the turning of the first sod to the laying of
> the last brick everything has gone very smoothly,
> notwithstanding a quicksand on the site which
> occasioned much extra work.   Everything was
> completed singularly free of extras ... with
> punctuality and success ... nor should the
> contractor be forgotten who has acted throughout
> with great liberality and laboured in every way for
> the benefit of the work.

Myers had now built three asylums which had been universally acclaimed.

Towards the end of 1855 it was decided to enlarge Colney Hatch and Mr Henderson, the asylum steward, drew up a plan providing accommodation for an extra 593 patients at a cost of £39,604. The Committee agreed to this but curiously, considering the eulogies lavished on Daukes and Myers three years earlier, decided to employ Mr James Harris, the architect of Hanwell Asylum, and the Committee Meeting Minutes of 7 November 1855 give no clue to the reason for this change of architect. At the meeting of 13 February 1856, the Clerk of Works reported that he had discovered cracks in the plaster of some of the inner walls of the Asylum and that '26 Ward was in a very dangerous state'. Daukes was sent for and assured the Committee that there was no danger, that there was nothing wrong with the construction of the building and that if there were he would repair it at his own expense. He reminded them that a settlement of the foundations had been discovered under 26 Ward in November 1851 and referred them to his report of that time. Finally he confirmed in writing that there was absolutely no danger to the patients.

At a meeting on 7 May 1856 Mr Armstrong, a member of the Committee, reported that he had received a communication from Mr Andrew Trimen (an architect who had written a book called *Architecture from the Earliest Period to the Present Time* which included articles about the Tower of Babel and the Pyramids) stating that he considered the asylum to be in a condition of great danger. He said he would be willing to meet Mr Daukes and Mr Myers to suggest an 'inexpensive way of preventing further danger'. He had noticed the cracks when he found himself 'accidentally' walking through the building. His accusations were taken seriously and on 27 May 1856 a meeting was convened at which Mr Trimen explained to the astonished Daukes that the building was unsafe because:

> it was built on London clay
> the site was on an incline
> the drainage was unsatisfactory
> the foundations were not as wide as they should be

the vibration of shutting doors weakened the
whole structure.

Daukes asked to have Trimen's report in writing and this was
forwarded to him. By this time the Committee was seriously
worried and decided to consult Lewis Cubitt, the architect
brother of Thomas and William. He was the designer of the
much lauded King's Cross Railway Station and of the line
which passed close to Colney Hatch. He was asked to give his
opinion on 'the supposed insecure state of the asylum'.[6] On 24
September 1856 Lewis Cubitt presented his report which said
that:

> the foundations of the asylum needed
> underpinning, the arched ceilings should be
> removed, because they were too heavy, the 'bad'
> roof carpentry should be taken away and the roof
> redone, and that the fireproofing of the ceiling
> should be abandoned to save expense, as gas light
> and nightwatchmen made fire unlikely ...

Cubitt added that all these recommendations could be deferred
until the Spring i.e. for six or seven months, as long as the Clerk
of the Works kept an eye on things.

The Committee wrote to Daukes and explained that it
was 'with great reluctance and much regret that they had come
to the determination of reporting to the Court on the state of
the asylum as reported'. Letters passed between all the
interested parties and on 5 November 1856[7] Cubitt was asked if
he would meet Daukes in the presence of another architect.
Cubitt declined to meet Daukes either alone, in the presence of
the Committee or in the presence of any other professional
person. Despite this extraordinary behaviour on the part of
Cubitt, the Committee instructed their solicitor Mr John William
Allen, of J.C. Allen & Son, 17 Carlisle Street, Soho, London,
W.1, to prepare and submit a case for the opinion of counsel as
to the liability of Mr Daukes as architect 'for the damage
occasioned by such defects and to report thereon'. Allen

submitted a draft of the case against Daukes, but advised caution and suggested that any decision should be postponed until after the next meeting. In the meanwhile, a report was printed and circulated to the Justices and a copy was sent to Daukes. On 27 November 1856 Daukes wrote to the Committee refuting the criticisms.

The receipt of this letter is noted in the Minutes but there is no record of what it said. Fifteen days later, as there had been no response to his letter, Daukes sent a copy to the editor of *The Morning Advertiser* with a covering note which said:

> Sir,
> You give a notice, in your Impression of this morning, of a meeting of the Middlesex Magistrates, and of a report of their Visiting Committee, relative to Colney Hatch Lunatic Asylum. I well know the value of your space, but beg that you will in fairness, publish my letter to the Magistrates which has been passed over in their report, but which, I think, varies the aspect of the matter.
>> I am, Sir, Yours obediently,
>> S.W.Daukes
>
> 14 Whitehall Place
> Dec. 5, 1856.

Then followed Daukes' letter to the Magistrates of about 1,000 words. He acknowledged the receipt of Trimen's report of the 4 November and the Magistrates' letter of 7 November which referred to Cubitt's report as having been corroborated by Trimen, and Harris, a colleague of his who was the architect at the other Middlesex Asylum at Hanwell. In fact it was Trimen who had suggested that Colney Hatch was badly built and Cubitt who had confirmed this. He went on to point out that the 'faults' listed by these architects differed, as did the remedies and the cost of the repairs. Trimen suggested that all could be put right for £5,888 whereas Cubitt quoted a figure of between

£30,000 and £40,000. Daukes proceeded to answer the criticisms of both reports and showed that the three architects had referred to details of which they could have had no knowledge, such as the drainage arrangements under the building. Having refuted the criticisms, he remonstrated against:

> ... the acceptance, by the magistrates, of the expression of a mere volunteered verbal opinion unfavourable to the construction of an important public building, and reflecting upon the reputation of another professional man, when merely casually visiting the building, and without having ever seen more that one ward ... .

Daukes went on to refer to Cubitt's refusal to meet him in the presence of any architect of eminence or any other professional man and concluded that this was evidence of Cubitt not being able to support his statements if submitted to the scrutiny of a competent judge.

There are several notable omissions from the Minutes during the next few months and the omission of any record of the contents of this letter is one of them. The Justices referred their Report back to the Committee and 'trusted that they would do what was necessary to protect the interest of the County'.

There were times when the Committee seemed to hesitate. They were in a dilemma. They had spent a great sum of public money on this much publicised asylum and now they were told by an architect that it was badly designed, badly constructed and dangerous.

But while they were making up their minds how best 'to protect the interests of the County', Allen, their solicitor, pointed out that if they wished to issue a writ against Daukes, they had better do so at once or this course of action would be ruled out by the time limit. So without more ado they instructed Allen to take Counsel's opinion and to issue a writ.

It is only fair to point out that Cubitt had been asked for a report whereas Trimen's report had been volunteered, but now that Cubitt had the Committee's ear he continued to say how unsatisfactory the building was, while at the same time making suggestions about its proposed enlargement.

Counsel consulted by Allen was Mr William (later Sir William) Atherton Q.C., M.P., 1 Paper Buildings, Temple, London, E.C. He advised on 6 January 1857 that 'one or two or more architects should be called upon to examine the building and report thereon'.[8]

Expert evidence was sought from two independent architects, who were not partners, Thomas Bellamy of Charlotte Street London W 1, and George Pownall of Bloomsbury Square, London W C 1, not known to be related to Mr H.J. Pownall, the chairman of the Court of Quarter Sessions.

On 14 January 1857 Mr Lewis Cubitt was appointed architect in charge of the additions and alterations to be carried out at Colney Hatch. The estimated costs were £47,643 exclusive of fittings, water, coal stores and work to the farm buildings. The work eventually cost over £67,000. Cubitt's fee was 4 per cent of the amount expended. On the same day a letter was received by the Committee from the architects Bellamy and Pownall asking permission to communicate with Daukes to get his explanation of the criticisms. Permission was granted. Also on this day, 14 January, Daukes wrote a letter to H. J. Pownall, Chairman of the Court of Quarter Sessions, in which he was sarcastic about Cubitt's qualifications. But Lewis Cubitt had worked not only for his brothers, Thomas and William Cubitt, but also for several railway companies and he had been a pupil of the well-known architect H.E. Kendall. The letter went on to complain of the way he, Daukes, was being treated. Mr Lewis Cubitt had taken the 'unusual course' of reporting to the Committee before communicating with him. Cubitt then declined to meet Daukes or any other architect prepared to refute his criticisms. Once again Daukes' letter seems to have been unanswered.

It was resolved that the architects Bellamy and Pownall should report on the defective state of the asylum and the 'evils arising therefrom'. Cubitt was asked to provide a report while, at the same time, continuing with his preparations to add an extra storey to the building which, he insisted, was in danger of collapsing at any moment.

In March 1857 Daukes called on his solicitor, Travers
Smith of 25 Throgmorton Street, and Allen was instructed by
the Committee to consult with Counsel as to whether he
recommended an action for damages against Mr Daukes and
Mr Myers, and, if so, 'on what points?' It was also at about this
time that Andrew Trimen, the first architect to criticise Daukes'
work, realised that he had been ousted by Cubitt who had now
been engaged not only to repair the supposed faults estimated
by Cubitt to cost £70,000-£80,000, but also to build the
extensions. Trimen, distressed by this turn of events, sent in a
bill for 'consultation' amounting to £265. 4s. 0d. and asked that
it might be settled promptly. The clerk was told to inform Mr
Trimen that the Committee would think about it.

Travers Smith, Daukes' solicitor, wrote to Allen, the
Committee's solicitor, pointing out that his client had still not
been informed of the points against him. The Committee had
not yet made up their minds whether to sue only Daukes or
'whether any or what proceedings should be taken against
Myers the contractor'. In the background Trimen was still
appealing for his money. Confusion was great. On 2 May
1857, Travers Smith was still not clear what was alleged against
Daukes. On the same day Allen wrote to Myers to inform him
that legal proceedings would be taken against him to claim
damages for bad workmanship. Myers replied that he had
received this letter with 'the utmost surprise' and that it was
seven years since he had completed the building of the asylum
at Colney Hatch at which time the magistrates had expressed
their entire satisfaction. Myers added that he had been about to
ask to be allowed to tender for the additional work at the
asylum. He had probably been expecting to be invited to
tender. One wonders how many people were looking forward
to gaining this valuable contract for themselves, once the main
contenders had been driven from the field.

Bellamy and Pownall produced their report which was
read by the Committee, but Travers Smith's request for a copy
was refused in a letter which ended:

> I have no objection to informing you that the
> defects particularised in our letter of the second
> inst. have (amongst other things) been certified by

> them (Bellamy and Pownall) and that they do
> condemn the design not the workmanship only of
> the roof of the Asylum ... .

Both Daukes and Myers were now the objects of grave criticism. This statement was completely at variance with the substance of the report to be disclosed later. Meanwhile Daukes requested and was granted permission to visit the asylum with two or three other architects. The architects he chose were:

William Tite later Sir William Tite, President of the Royal Institute of British Architects, 1861—1863

J. Hewsby 30 Great George Street, London

Anthony Salvin 30 Argyle Street, London

T. H. Wyatt 77 Great Russell Street, London, another future President of the Royal Institute of British Architects, (1870).

These architects visited and inspected the asylum. They drew up and signed their report which, on 21 July 1857, was handed to the chairman by Allen. The report confirmed that the four architects had carefully examined the structure of the building and had arrived at the conclusion that the repairs now in progress were unnecessary; that the few settlements that existed were of a very unimportant, even insignificant, character; that the alleged defects in the roof were of no structural importance ... . There was no danger, still less cause for serious alarm. They expressed the opinion that the heavy expenditure now being incurred was wholly ... . The clerk, at this point, when copying this passage into the minute book, left out the next few words.

Daukes' four architect colleagues stated that they would be prepared to support their testimony at any time. On 12 August 1857 Travers Smith asked for six printed sets of the various reports and that the trial should be deferred till 'next term'. Both these requests were refused.

On 24 November 1857[9] the Clerk laid before the Committee of Visitors a letter from Bellamy and Pownall. They had been called upon by the Colney Hatch Visitors' Committee to report upon Cubitt's and Trimen's allegations. Bellamy and Pownall had been informed by Mr Allen that the case against Daukes was being proceeded with and that they would be expected to give evidence on behalf of the Visitors' Committee. Bellamy and Pownall felt it their duty however, 'to state in justice alike to the Committee, to Mr Daukes and to themselves ... (that) ... it was not a case which called for further proceedings against the architect'.

Bellamy and Pownall went on to say that it had been alleged that the foundations of the principal walls needed deepening and underpinning, arches and galleries needed to be taken down and rebuilding carried out - none of which was necessary. Some trifling repairs were needed but these could be executed without inconvenience to anyone. They continued by saying that the 'prosecution' of Mr Daukes was wholly uncalled for and they would have no part in it and ended by saying that there was not the slightest impeachment of Mr Daukes' skill and referred to the asylum as 'this great work'. This was the substance of the report drawn up by the two expert architects who had been called upon to substantiate Cubitt's contention that the asylum at Colney Hatch had been badly designed and constructed and was dangerous to live in. Mr Allen showed this letter to the Committee and to Mr Atherton, Counsel, who advised that the trial should be 'countermanded' at once - for: 'to precipitate a trial at present would go very far to ensure defeat'.[10] The Chairman asked Atherton if he really thought it necessary to cancel the trial. But the trial was not cancelled, and the Committee, determined to proceed, turned for advice to Professor Hoskins, architect and civil engineer of King's College, London, and to G. E. Street. They were asked to report on:

> The depth of the foundations
> The roofs of the buildings
> The arched ceilings of the galleries with particular reference to Mr Myers' contract and the specifications.

Hoskins commented that:

> upon perusal of particulars of agreement with Mr
> Myers for erecting the buildings and a collation of
> several documents which go with the agreement to
> form the contract to that effect and which
> documents purport to make the work to be done
> plain and certain, I can find neither plainness nor
> certainty.

Hoskins found the contract imprecise, so presumably the smaller
details of construction had been left to Myers' judgement and
skill and any alleged deviation from what had been expected
could not be held against him. Hoskins produced two reports
and Street one, which were not particularly critical but they
satisfied Atherton that he had grounds for proceeding with the
case.

During the summer of 1858 the Committee's lawyers
were collecting their evidence while its members concerned
themselves with the enlargement of the asylum with Cubitt as
architect and Mansfield as contractor. There are very few
references in the Minutes to the case of Skaife (the Clerk to the
Committee of Visitors, who was to represent them in the action)
versus Daukes.

The trial of the case of Skaife v. Daukes began in the
Court of Queen's Bench on 1 December 1858. The action
brought was to recover damages against Mr Daukes for breach
of duty in not constructing or not seeing Colney Hatch Asylum,
constructed in conformity with his plans and specifications for
the erection of the building. Myers was not to be sued but his
reputation was at stake. William Atherton, William Browne and
Henry Maude conducted the case for the Visiting Justices of
Middlesex; William Bovill and Charles Hawkins represented
Daukes. The Judge was Lord Campbell, a distinguished lawyer,
writer and politician who was to end his career as Lord
Chancellor.[11] The trial lasted for three days. Mr Atherton
opened the case and described the circumstances: how Daukes
had won the competition and Myers had gained the contract to
build the asylum. The witnesses called for the plaintiff were

Mr Allen, Mr Skaife, Mr Johns, Clerk of Works who had only recently taken up his post and who in evidence stated that 50,000 yards of concrete had been saved by an alteration made in the plans (the Editor of *The Builder* was completely mystified by this statement[12]). Also called as witnesses were Mr Harris, the Hanwell architect, Mr Trimen, who had started the whole process 'by amusing himself walking through the building observing what he considered defects in the construction and addressing a report to the Magistrates in consequence ...', Professor Hoskins, Mr Street, and Mr Thomas Bellamy and Mr George Pownall the two architects who had previously stated that the case against Daukes was wholly uncalled for. Daukes was examined and cross-examined, and much evidence was presented in support of his case which impressed the Court, particularly that given by Myers. Mr Atherton, after presenting the evidence for the plaintiff, but before the defence had had a chance to put its case to the Court, rose and said that he was authorised by the Justices to say that the case had been satisfactorily answered and that they agreed to a verdict being entered for the defendant.

Daukes had a formidable group of witnesses prepared to give evidence in his support. There were four County Magistrates who had been on the Committee when the asylum was being built, four architects including Salvin and Wyatt, and three builders. But the case was withdrawn before any of them reached the witness box. Lord Campbell made a concluding speech in which he said:

> The case has been most properly conducted from first to last by the learned Counsel for the Plaintiff, and I think no discredit ought to attach to the Magistrates for the County of Middlesex in instituting this enquiry, but I think it has resulted in the entire exculpation of Mr Daukes from all imputation. The Magistrates have been misled, not by any bad professional advice as far as the Law is concerned, but by the advice of rival architects. We have heard a great deal of *odium medicum* and *odium theologicum*. I think the

> making of drawings seems greater than either.
> There were a number of witnesses on the part of
> the Plaintiff who evidently were rivals of Mr
> Daukes. I think they made a very ungenerous
> and ingenious attempt to ruin his reputation. I
> am very glad that the matter has undergone a
> public enquiry and the result is most satisfactory.
> It is creditable to Mr Daukes and I think that the
> Magistrates are absolved from all blame in the
> course that they have adopted.

The term *odium theologicum* is defined in Brewer's *Dictionary* in
the following terms:-   'The bitter hatred of rival theologians.
No war so sanguinary as holy wars; no persecutions so relentless
as religious persecutions; no hatred so bitter as theological
hatred'.

    It would seem that in Lord Campbell's estimation, even
such damning words do not adequately describe the behaviour
of Cubitt and Trimen towards Daukes, and of course towards
Myers. A footnote in *The Builder*[13] at the end of the account of
the trial pointed out that by his 'condemnation' of Daukes,
Lewis Cubitt had procured for himself a large amount of work.
    On 30 December Travers Smith wrote to Allen
suggesting that the Committee should pay Daukes' expenses.
The Committee refused on the grounds that 'as trustees of
Public Funds, they did not feel themselves justified in acceding
to his proposition'. The Magistrates felt it necessary to explain
to the public the actions which they had taken by publishing a
book.[14] They considered that they could not have acted in any
other way and expected their readers to agree with them. The
extension at Colney Hatch was completed with Lewis Cubitt as
architect and Mansfield as contractor.
    Colney Hatch, known as Friern Barnet Hospital since
1959, is now a listed Grade II building, and still stands solidly
on its foundations in vindication of the work of a great architect
and a great builder: perhaps the Folly in the park, which is also
listed, can be looked upon by those who know this story, as a
memorial to the events of 1857-58.

IX

Building for Miss Nightingale's Army: 1854-66

The contracts which Myers carried out for the Army were some
of the most interesting and valuable which he undertook. They
included the original camp at Aldershot, as well as the barracks
and garrison church; two military hospitals, one at Netley on
Southampton Water, and the other at Woolwich; the Staff
College at Camberley, and the Royal Military Academy
(Woolwich), which he rebuilt.

The Duke of Wellington has been quoted as saying that
the British Army consisted of 'the scum of the earth enlisted for
drink'. Living conditions for the rank and file were so appalling
and the pay so meagre that no-one with the possibility of any
other means of support would enlist. It was not until the Duke
of Wellington died in 1852, (the same year as Pugin and the
Earl of Shrewsbury) and was succeeded as Commander in
Chief by Lord Hardinge, that conditions started to improve and
some attempt was made to train an efficient army.

Up to this time, manoeuvres had taken place on
privately owned land and because of the damage done by the
soldiers, large sums of money invariably had to be paid in
compensation when they departed. The establishment of a
permanent training camp was the idea of Prince Albert and it
was to Lord Hardinge that the Prince made his suggestion
which was received with enthusiasm.

In the summer of 1853 Lord Hardinge rode over all the common land around Aldershot prior to recommending the area as suitable for a training camp. The War Office had wanted to establish the camp in the Reigate area so that the troops would be positioned between London and the South coast where a danger of invasion was perceived. Suitable land near Reigate was not available so the heathlands round Aldershot were chosen. The water supply was of good quality and abundant and it was agreed to purchase 8,000 acres at a cost of £12 an acre.[1]   On 13 February 1854, the Treasury approved the inclusion of £100,000 in the Army Estimates for 1854-5 to purchase the land at Aldershot for a camp.[2]

A month later on 28 March, 1854, the Crimean War started; all available regular troops were dispatched to the war zone and 50,000 militiamen were called out, but there was nowhere to quarter them. The billeting of soldiers on the civilian population could only be enforced when the safety of the Realm was at stake.[3]   Hostilities undertaken for the protection of the Ottoman Empire did not come into this category. It was therefore decided to build wooden huts on Aldershot Heath for their accommodation. The militiamen's training was a matter of some urgency. William Howard Russell's dispatches from the Crimea alerted the public to the conditions on the battle front and to the unprepared state of the Army. Instead of a 'brilliant and rapid feat of arms' resulting in the capture of Sebastopol and the ending of the war, the expedition turned into a disaster, the horrors of which became general knowledge. In the autumn of 1854, Henry Clutton, the architect, under the direction of Lord Hardinge, surveyed and marked out the land for the proposed camp.[4]   Good transport facilities were available, with the Basingstoke canal crossing the heath, the railway only a few miles distant and the Winchester road skirting the land.

The Royal Engineers were responsible for the design, construction and maintenance of Army buildings, but when large-scale or specialised operations were to be carried out, it was usual to seek civilian help. The leading architects of the day were consulted (on this occasion it had been Clutton) and civilian contractors were invited to tender. On 23 January 1855,

Figure 52   The Building of Aldershot.

Figures 52 & 53 are two of a series of photographs taken by an unknown photographer
during the building of Aldershot.

Reproduced by courtesy of the late Brigadier W.J. Reed, Director of the Aldershot Military Museum.

Figure 53   The building of Aldershot.

tenders were invited for the building of huts to accommodate 20,000 men, completion date being 23 April, just three months later. George Myers gained the contract to build the huts in the north camp. It is possible that Lucas Bros. of Belvedere Road worked at the south camp but the evidence is not clear.[5] On Tuesday 30 October 1855, a dinner of the Builders' Benevolent Association took place at the London Tavern and Mr Charles Lucas presided. It was reported that when the various loyal toasts had been drunk 'Mr Myers jun. returned thanks for the Army and Navy because of the hutting which he was doing'.

The Militia camp consisted of 1,260 huts. Eight hundred of these were the men's living quarters where they slept and ate. Their iron bedsteads had a break in the middle so that during the day the foot could be pushed under the head end thus increasing the area free of furniture in the centre. There were twenty-five soldiers to each hut. Four hundred huts were allocated to the officers, each of whom had a room to himself. There were also hut kitchens, wash-houses and hospitals, all built of wood except for one constructed of corrugated iron which, an article in *The Times* suggested, was intended for the General in Command.[6]

Once again Prince Albert intervened to suggest that a residence should be provided at Aldershot for the Royal Family, so that he and the Queen and the Royal children would have somewhere to stay when they came to inspect the troops. This was agreed upon and a letter dated 'June 1855' from Sir Frederick Smith R.E., who was in charge of construction work at the camp, suggested that, as the building of the Royal Pavilion was a matter of some urgency, tenders should not be called for by public advertisement, but that application should be made to some of the principal builders usually employed by the government, inviting them to submit tenders for the performance of the work at a lump sum.[7] Myers headed the list followed by seven other names   including Cubitt, Lucas, and Fox & Henderson of Crystal Palace fame. Myers had men and equipment engaged in the construction of the camp so could afford to offer a lower price than the others and he won the contract. Prince Albert pegged out the site with George Myers in attendance. The Pavilion was built in record time and was designated a Royal Residence. The *Illustrated London News* described it as follows:

> The building forms three sides of a square, and its ground plan resembles Buckingham Palace as it used to be before the late improvements. It has another point of resemblance also to its London compeer, viz; it is bald, cold and ugly to an extreme. The whole is built entirely of wood. We believe that except for one or two cases for the foundations, not a single brick has been used for the whole structure. The entrance is from the south. On the ground floor is a breakfast-room, a sitting-room, good sized dining room and a saloon. The upper rooms are of course all used as bed-chambers and dressing rooms for the Royal Family. The two wings are for the different Noblemen and Ladies in attendance on Her Majesty. The walls and ceilings of the different apartments are all formed by canvas stretched on frames and papered over. On every side there is merely a waste of boggy moor, dreary and repellent in its aspect. In the distance are the black huts of the camp quite in keeping with the moor on which they stand; and in the foreground is a long narrow piece of muddy water called the Basingstoke Canal, into which occasionally the waters of the surrounding bogs drain.

But the Queen was delighted with her cosy little palace which had stables, coach houses and a kitchen with access to the Royal Apartments via an underground tunnel. It was fenced with oak paling and planted with conifers and rhododendrons provided by Messrs Waterer of Bagshot.

Finally Prince Albert urged that permanent barracks should be erected on the land, so that in time of peace there would be no temptation on the part of the Government to sell.

On 22 February 1855, Lord Hardinge, who had acted on the Prince's advice, forwarded to him plans showing the ground on which the barracks should be built. Again it was Messrs Myers who won the contract. The building of the permanent barracks overlapped with the contract for the building of the hutted camp and Myers on his own initiative and at his own expense built a light railway, branching off the London to Southampton line, to carry bricks and other materials to the building site. The London & South Western Railway agreed terms with him on 15 March 1855.[8] The track went from Tougham to the camp and is marked on the Ordnance Survey maps of the time. There is a description of it in Charles Dickens' magazine *All the Year Round* which says:

> Along the High Street of this military village runs a single line railway devoted to the carriage of coal and building material, for the large barrack streets are still being erected for the accommodation of future Cavalry Regiments. Every hour of the day a train of luggage trucks is panting along this tramway, and the only wonder of it is that the driver who conducts the engine is not attired in some variety of Military undress costume.

The building of the railway was a necessity. *The Times* reported that the contract for making the camp roads had been forgotten until Myers moved in and his carts became stuck axle deep in the mud.[9] They went on to complain that the timber for the huts came from Riga, a Russian port; that the Board of Ordnance had insisted on the use of Greystoke bricks, hardly heard of outside London, for the construction of the barracks and finally that there was a clause binding Mr Myers, the contractor, to show a monthly expenditure of £15,000 in the summer months and £9,000 in the six winter months, 'either in labour executed or in materials placed upon the ground'. *The Times* was not impressed with the Board of Ordnance's arrangements for an undertaking which would cost the country more than half a million pounds and suggested that progress should be 'narrowly watched'.[10] There was confusion also over the signing of the contract. Colonel Bruce, a guards officer, signed on behalf of the Board although he had not yet taken out his patent and *The Times* raised serious doubts as to his authority to do so. The mud was appalling. The camp appeared to stand in 'the midst of an Irish bog' and anyone who wanted to see 'a miniature representation of what the mud was like in the camp before Sebastopol last winter, may have his curiosity gratified by going down to Aldershot after two or three wet days'.[11]

The construction of the barracks which had started in the spring of 1855 progressed rapidly. Col. Cole in his *History of Aldershot* gives a description of

> the red bearded, frockcoated contractor with his stove pipe hat, driving his high-wheeled gig, accompanied by an officer with mutton-chop whiskers in the dark blue undress uniform tunic, followed by a mounted orderly leading an officer's charger.[12]

On this occasion they were followed by 'a swirl of fine dust' so it must have been summer.

The north and south camp each had its own chapel and regimental schools. Quarters were provided for the General in Command, the Commander in Chief, the Minister for War and for the Queen, who had her little hut palace, the Royal Pavilion, situated on an eminence overlooking the camp.

These barracks introduced many improvements. The married men had separate quarters. Until this time soldiers' wives had been ignored: if they chose to share their husbands' beds in the dormitory, so be it. But in these barracks each married man was to have a separate cubicle and there were to be special washrooms for the women. Other 'luxuries' were day rooms and lavatories. These last were mentioned so frequently when eulogising Myers' buildings that one can only presume that when they were not mentioned, they did not exist. There were covered areas for drill in wet weather and a hospital. Mr Stapleton, 'the well known wine merchant' was allowed to establish a clubhouse for the officers, which was a great success.

Other tradesmen subsequently set up shops on the perimeter of the camp and many of the original businesses remain to this day. In fact, when news of the building of this great camp spread abroad, artisans from all over the country came to Aldershot. One Simes, a carpenter, walked from Torquay, a distance of nearly 150 miles, and opened a saddler's shop which was sold only a few years ago by his great grandson.[13]

As had happened at Colney Hatch, Myers' progress was so rapid that money to pay him ran out. At Aldershot this was a more serious matter than it had been at the asylum, as the Secretary of State for War had to obtain the sanction of the Lords Commissioners of Her Majesty's Treasury for the extra payment. It is odd that the money was not available because Myers' contract had stipulated exactly how much money he was to spend each month. But despite the fact that it was deemed of the utmost importance that the works should be pressed forward with all possible speed, it was decided, in consequence of the necessity that the army estimates for the current year should be kept as low as possible, that the amount proposed for the barracks should be considerably reduced.[14]

Myers pointed out that he would suffer a serious loss if his staff of clerks, foremen and first-class workmen were unemployed for four months till the next payment from the Treasury was due. The letter from the War Office to the Treasury confirmed that if it were not possible to proceed with the work, this would cause 'the greatest embarrassment, and possibly vitiation of the contract would result'. Their Lordships of the Treasury did sanction the payment of the extra money but

> could not refrain from suggesting to the Secretary of State for War whether when the vote was taken it might not have been known as well as it is now, that the sum proposed was inadequate for the service - that sum being £100,000 while the Department was under actual contract to spend £144,000.[15]

The infantry barracks were the first to be finished and occupied, but the cavalry barracks, 'certainly the handsomest, if not the most perfect in the world' with their stables, forges and riding schools, remained empty until the money materialised which the Secretary of State for War had failed to ask for in the first place.[16]   They were strikingly superior to the accommodation provided for the infantry. Each cavalry officer was allowed two rooms, one large sitting room and a bedroom. The mess rooms were as comfortable as any London club. The stables were finely built and admirably planned with the men's quarters above their horses, thus providing warmth in winter and unwanted heat in summer. Each Regiment had its own riding school. The largest of these, with its huge wooden roof beams, still stands and is used for the training of the Mounted Police.

The living conditions of the men serving in Her Majesty's Army were greatly improved for those stationed at Aldershot. But now the indefatigable Prince Albert was determined that the officers should have a library, and in 1857 he expressed a wish to build one for them at his own expense. It took him two years to persuade the War Office to allow him to buy a plot of land and commission plans for the erection of the building. Eventually Capt. Francis Fowke, (1823-65), a brilliant officer of the Royal Engineers who was highly regarded by Prince Albert and is renowned for his involvement in the development of South Kensington, was instructed to provide plans and specifications.[17]   But no drains of any kind were included in the plans even though a resident librarian, with a wife and family, was contemplated. A cess pit was eventually dug, being less expensive than 'modern' drains.

Tenders for building the library were invited from (Sir John) Kelk and George Myers. Myers' tender, of £1,484, was lower than that of Kelk, and was accepted. The work began in August 1859, but Myers was not asked to install the underfloor heating or the 'Italian tiling' for the roof. The heating was installed by a 'cowboy' engineer, who used the wrong-sized pipes, so that the system never worked and the roof tiles, put in place by a Mr Brown from Surbiton, proved too heavy for the walls which had to be held together with iron tie-beams. On 5 October 1860, the library was opened by the Prince accompanied by the Queen. The Royal couple also supplied the books (which were in three languages) on Military History and Army Law. The Prince Consort's Library has since been extended and is renowned worldwide.[18]

Once it had been established that Aldershot was to be a permanent camp, a site was chosen for the building of a church on rising ground adjacent to the Royal Pavilion. The architect was Philip Charles Hardwick of London who had recently built the Great Western Hotel at Paddington, and the contractor was Myers. The red brick Victorian Gothic church was consecrated by the Bishop of Winchester on 29 July 1863. There are many interesting memorials on the walls, one of the earliest being in memory of Sir James Scarlett who fought at Balaclava in 1854. It soon came to be known as the 'Cathedral of the Army'. It had seating for 1,250 men. In 1923, King George V gave permission for the prefix 'Royal' to be added to the name of the church to mark its diamond jubilee, so it is now the 'Royal Garrison Church of All Saints'.[19]

Little remains of George Myers' imposing buildings apart from a riding school, two or three lodges, the church and the Prince Consort's Library. The hutted camps were demolished in the 1890s and the 19th century barracks were replaced by blocks of flats in the 1960s. The Royal Pavilion remained in royal occupation until the second World War but has now been demolished.

Referring to Mrs Myers' scrapbook once again we discover that Myers was one of the ten firms who contracted to supply 1,000 huts for the troops in the Crimea, in the winter of 1855. The huts were designed by Brunel. Amongst the other contractors were W. Piper, Lucas Bros. and Messrs Cubitt & Co. There is no indication as to which newspaper the cutting was taken from.

The next contract Myers undertook for the Army was the hospital at Netley on Southampton Water. It was the first military hospital to be built in England and was intended to care for 1,000 soldiers. The laying of the foundation stone on 24 May 1856 was Queen Victoria's first public engagement since the conclusion of the Crimean War. She arrived for the ceremony from Osborne in the Royal yacht *Victoria and Albert* accompanied by the Royal barge *Fairy* and a flotilla of gun boats. Also in the Royal party were Prince Albert, the Prince of Wales and the Princess Royal. A temporary jetty was erected to make it possible for the Royal party to land. The Queen laid the foundation stone and Lord Panmure announced that the building would be called the Royal Victoria Hospital, the crowds cheered, the ships in the river fired a salute, bands played and speeches followed. The Queen, having walked through the tent where a substantial meal had been provided for the troops to celebrate the occasion, then boarded the Royal yacht once more and returned to her seaside home in the Isle of Wight. The *Illustrated London News* added a postscript to its account of the day's proceedings which said: 'We much regret to add that as the gun boats fired the royal salute a gun of the *Hardy* prematurely went off, two seamen were blown to pieces and several others were injured'.

The hospital was built on the water's edge close to the romantic ruins of Netley Abbey and was surrounded by trees. The site was chosen because this was the nearest point at which ships returning from foreign wars could land the wounded. Designed by Mennie, the War Department architect, estimated to cost £200,000 and to take three years to build, it was to be the first of its class in Europe. George Myers was the contractor for the main part of the building, E. Smith of Woolwich having built the foundations. The façade was to be a quarter of a mile long, built of red brick with Portland stone facings. The newspapers described the wards, offices and kitchens, apothecaries' and surveyors' stores, also the water closets and bathrooms, (which were not provided for the officers at the Staff College which Myers was to build a few years later) and the swimming pool. The descriptions were detailed. It was pointed out that a nurse's or orderly's room opened off each ward. Such rooms had no door, because 'if capable of being closed, irregularities were more likely to take place, and as there would be no fireplace, the orderly would be interested in looking to the fire and comfort of the ward for himself, as well as for the patients'.[20]

The construction of this building swallowed up 30,000,000 bricks made on site, as well as between 2,000,000 and 3,000,000 cubic feet of stone. It was not until the building

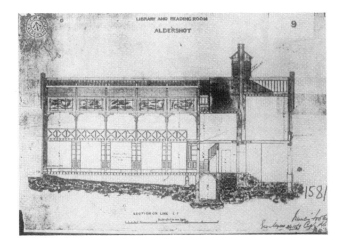

Figures 54a and b
Architectural drawings for the Prince Consort Library,
Aldershot, signed by Captain Francis Fowke
and George Myers.
Reproduced by permission of Paul H. Vickers, Librarian.

Figure 55 Netley Hospital, Southampton Water.

of the hospital was well advanced that Lord Panmure, later the Earl of Dalhousie, Secretary for War, as a matter of courtesy, showed the plans to Miss Nightingale, recently returned from the Crimea. Lord Panmure was not aware of Miss Nightingale's character or if he were, he seems to have forgotten that she had had fourteen years' experience of hospitals in London, France, Germany, Italy and Switzerland. She inspected the plans, consulted various authorities and then to Lord Panmure's amazement, condemned the hospital lock stock and barrel. He wrote her a soothing letter saying that her objections were no doubt sound, but that there were 'susceptibilities' to be considered. Florence Nightingale soon realised that she would get nowhere with the Secretary for War so she called on Lord Palmerston, the Prime Minister, whose house Broadlands was very close to that of her parents in Hampshire. Lord Palmerston, whose immediate concern this hospital was not, was quite easily persuaded that

> all consideration of what would best tend to the comfort and recovery of the patients had been sacrificed to the vanity of the architect, whose sole object had been to make a building which should cut a dash when looked at from Southampton River ... .[21]

Lord Palmerston told Lord Panmure to stop all work till the matter could be considered. A delegation of doctors from The Middlesex Hospital, London, was sent to inspect the building and they submitted an adverse report. But Lord Panmure was not prepared to face the questions in the House, or the bother and scandal that would ensue, so he pointed out that the contractor would have to be paid £70,000 to demolish the partly constructed building and start again. The building of Netley Hospital continued.[22]

It was only from the sea that this spectacular hospital could be admired. The effluent and drains of Southampton flowed into the estuary just upstream from Mr Mennie's masterpiece. Perhaps luckily the southwest facing windows with the wonderful view did not serve the wards but provided light for the corridors; the ward windows faced northeast. There was no through ventilation to provide fresh air for the patients as in the Herbert Hospital which was to be built later according to Miss Nightingale's 'Pavilion' plan. But there were enough bathrooms and lavatories on each floor to accommodate half the patients at any one time. There were dining-rooms where the patients who were well enough could eat, instead of having to sit on the edge of their beds. As far as the building itself went, only the best materials were used with windows of plate glass and frames of mahogany. The hospital stood in 193 acres of ground which was converted into terraced gardens and parkland. In spite of Florence Nightingale's objections the hospital was completed and occupied. It was a very spectacular building.

In the grounds, on 6 August 1864, the Prince of Wales laid the first stone of the Memorial to the Medical Officers who died in the Crimea, the death rate amongst whom had been higher than that of the officers who had led their troops in battle. The 56 ft Cross surmounting a series of arches supported by columns of marble and Portland stone was made by Myers' craftsmen.

The sick and wounded were cared for at Netley Hospital during both World Wars, but by 1958 it was realised that this vast Victorian edifice was not economic and it was no longer used. The empty building, seen from Southampton Water with the moonlight shining on the plate glass windows, appeared the habitation of ghosts. Then in June 1963 the building caught fire and was extensively damaged. Finally, in 1967 it was demolished except for the chapel which is now a small museum and a listed monument.

A military Academy to train young officers had been founded in 1802 at Great Marlow. It was moved to Sandhurst in 1812. But there was much opposition to the founding of a Staff College for Senior Officers. The conservative army officers of that time considered learning to be incompatible with a manly character. Even so, a senior College was set up, which, over the years moved from High Wycombe to Farnham and at last to Sandhurst where it was housed with the junior College in cramped quarters. The necessity for such a College does not seem to have been taken very seriously by the authorities. The lectures were given by a French emigré, General Francis Jarry. The General lectured in French, a language which none of his students understood, but there was no English officer capable of filling the post.

Eventually the Crimean War made those in authority realise that it was essential to have well-educated staff officers and the Duke of Cambridge, appointed Commander-in-Chief in 1856, took up the cause. In 1858, Sir James Pennethorne, one of the leading architects of the day, was asked to draw up plans for a College to be built in the spacious grounds of the cadet College. The contract was worth between £40,000 and £50,000 and was awarded to Mr George Myers who was described as the 'famous Master Builder'. In later years, the cynics were said to have pointed out that he had already built Netley Hospital, Colney Hatch Lunatic Asylum and Broadmoor Prison for the criminally insane. The Staff College designed by Pennethorne was 265ft long, 110ft broad and 55ft high. It was built of brick and stone. The heavy entrance doors have over them the Royal Arms and the Crest of the College whose main feature is an owl, the bird known for its sagacity and prudence which was the favourite companion of Minerva, Goddess not only of war but also wisdom. The principal apartments are the great hall, lecture rooms, study halls, libraries and mess room. A wide stone staircase leads up to the first floor and on the landing there is a balustrade surmounted by Ionic columns. Accommodation was provided for forty students, but despite the design of the entrance hall, which was that of a Roman bath, there were no up-to-date bathrooms in the College. Presumably the officers, if they wanted, had hip baths brought to their rooms by their soldier servants. The only hot tap was in the kitchen. The contract included the building of residences for the Commandant and Adjutant and stabling for forty horses.

The building materials were brought to Farnborough Station by rail or to Frimley by canal, whence huge horses hauled drays bearing enormous blocks of stone to the building site. Myers' masons were said to be the best in Europe, but they were not popular in the neighbourhood. They created a reign of terror and all public houses were closed to them except the Golden Farmer which was their special haunt.

One of the bricklayers working at the Staff College at this time was the brother of 'England's Champion', Tom Sayers, the last and most famous of the bare-fist fighters. Tom had been matched to take on the American John C. Heenan on 17 April, 1860, and 'The Great Contest' was to take place at Farnborough, a mere five miles from Camberley.[23] His brother with his mates, along with the College students and a large crowd from all walks of society, turned out to witness the contest. After a fight of thirty-seven rounds the referee declared a draw. The 5ft 8in. Tom Sayers had taken a tremendous battering from the 6ft 1in. American. He was given a grant of £3,000 by his admirers on condition that he never fought again. When Sayers died in 1865, at the age of thirty-nine, he was buried in Highgate Cemetery. At the base of his memorial reclines a stone effigy of his great dog, the chief mourner at the funeral. The procession from the East End of London to Highgate contained 10,000 people and took over three hours to pass. The horses were bedecked with black crepe and ostrich feathers, as at all important Victorian funerals.[24] In 1854 George Myers had built the wall round the new part of the Cemetery.

Four months before 'The Great Fight' took place, on 14 December 1859, His Royal Highness the Duke of Cambridge, Commander-in-Chief of the Army, arrived to lay the foundation stone of the College. In attendance were important members of the Military Establishment, the Chaplain of the Royal Military College, Colonel R.E.Chapman R.E. in charge of the work - and Mr Myers with his masons in spotless white coats and beaver hats, their craft clothing. With the scarlet coats of the soldiers, they created a dazzling effect. The chaplain said a prayer to bless the project and the Duke, under Myers' guidance, laid the first block of masonry in a truly professional manner. The band played the National Anthem and a salute of guns ended the ceremony.

The first students moved into the College in 1862. There were fifteen of them and during the next two years they were taught Mathematics, Military History, Art, Fortifications, Military Administration, French, German, Hindustani, Topography, Astronomy and Surveying.

Camberley, the home of the Staff College, was first named Cambridge Town in honour of the Duke of Cambridge but this caused confusion and the name 'Camberley' was adopted. The College still stands, a dignified memorial to the many great soldiers who come from all over the globe to study within its walls and also to the craftsmanship of George Myers and his masons.

In 1859 Myers not only commenced the building of the Staff College but also the enlargement of the Royal Military Academy at Woolwich. Work at Woolwich started at the end of that year on 13 December. *The Times* reported the removal of the Academy boundary wall and the demolition of the entire range of buildings comprising the cadets' workshops, the stables, sergeants' rooms, rackets courts and offices standing to the east and west of the Academy. These buildings were to be replaced by two wings affording additional sleeping accommodation thus allowing each student a room of his own, and there were to be extra class and lecture rooms worthy of the Institution. Mr Jones, Clerk of the Works from the Royal Engineers' Department, and Mr Pulley, representing Messrs Myers, were appointed to superintend the works.

The contract was worth £41,700. The completion date was May 1861 and there were severe penalties in case of failure to finish by the scheduled time. The demolished offices were to be replaced on a new site at a cost of £30,000 on completion of the first part of the contract.

The work was completed on time and Myers was allowed to continue in occupation of the stables, at the back of the Academy, as he had won the contract to build the new Military Hospital on Kidbrook Common, (the Herbert Hospital) about half a mile distant, where work was to start soon.

On the night of 14 October 1861, fire broke out in the stables which were built of wood and had recently been painted with coal tar, a wood preservative. The night sky was lit by the conflagration and the inhabitants of the neighbourhood were convinced that the Military Academy itself was ablaze. The Royal Artillery sentries sounded the alarm on their bugles; a detachment of the fire brigade commanded by Major Willard

R.A. and followed by a second body of men in command of Major Field, Deputy Assistant Quartermaster General, were quickly on the spot. But to no avail. The stables were reduced to ashes. Fourteen horses were burnt to death and two men in the building were saved with difficulty. Only one was expected to survive. It was presumed that the men had been smoking and this was the cause of the catastrophe. Once again a costly fire had taken place on a building site occupied by Messrs Myers. It was stated that one of the horses was burnt to a cinder.[25]

The hospital at Woolwich, which came to be known as 'The Herbert Hospital' was begun in 1861 and was to be 'the grand experimental test of Miss Nightingale's view ... as accepted by various Royal Commissions'. Miss Nightingale pointed out in her *Notes on Hospitals* that:

> It may seem a strange principle to enunciate as the first requirement in a Hospital that it do the sick no harm. It is quite necessary nevertheless to lay down such a principle, because the actual mortality in hospitals, especially those in large crowded cities, is very much higher than any calculation founded on the mortality of the same class of patients treated out of hospital would lead us to expect.

She considered that this situation was preventable if the hospital would observe the elementary principles of hygiene. The answer to hospital mortality was not prayer but better ventilation, cleanliness, good drainage and good food.

The architect of the Herbert Hospital was Captain Douglas Galton, R.E., the Army's expert on barrack construction, ventilation, heating, water supply and drainage. In 1851 he had married Florence Nightingale's niece, Marianne Nicholson. The hospital was to be constructed on the principles laid down both by the 1857 Royal Commission on the Sanitary State of the Army which had been set up on the insistence of Florence Nightingale, and by the Medical

Regulations of the Army of 1858.   The plans were examined by
Lord Herbert, then Under Secretary of State for War, submitted
by him to Miss Nightingale and finally presented to Queen
Victoria for her inspection.   Lord Herbert's letter to the Queen
said:

> The accompanying plans of the proposed Military
> Hospital on Kidbrook Common, Woolwich are
> most humbly submitted for Your Majesty's
> approval and signature
>
> > By Your Majesty's
> > Most Humble
> > and Devoted Servant
> > Herbert
>
> War Office
> April 1861

The Queen inspected the architect's drawings and signed her
name across the top of the letter.[26]
       At first all went well. Myers who had won the contract
to build the hospital, was to be paid monthly to the extent of
75% of the value of the work executed, until a certain reserve
sum was reached, by accumulation of the retained 25%, after
which payments were to be made in full, the reserve sum being
held over as a guarantee for the due performance of the work
until after its final completion.   But the work, as at Colney
Hatch and Aldershot, had progressed more rapidly than had
been expected.   Galton suggested that this was due to 'the
unusual warmth of the winter which had allowed the work to be
carried forward uninterruptedly'.   Consequently the Treasury
grant of £50,000 proved insufficient to meet the payments due
to the contractor, who once again pointed out that unless he was
paid, he would have to stop the work and in that event he
would claim compensation for his plant which would be idle.[27]
The argument was unassailable, and the Treasury sanctioned a
further payment of £10,000 to the contractor, to be deducted
from the next year's army grant, and the work proceeded.

148   *Pugin's Builder: The Life and Work of George Myers*

But, unfortunately, the site had been badly chosen and in the autumn of 1864, when the hospital was nearing completion, the ground showed alarming signs of subsidence. The work was halted and a committee of enquiry was set up which consisted of:

> Captain Douglas Galton, Assistant Permanent
>   Under Secretary of State for War,
> Colonel J.S.Hawkins, C.O., R.E., Woolwich,
> Captain W.Newsome R.E., Divisional C.O.,
> Mr Mennie, Surveyor to the War Department,
>   and architect Netley Hospital,
> Mr Ware and Mr Tait, Clerks of Works,
> George Myers, the Building Contractor.

Parts of the building were cracking and would need to be reconstructed. The committee decided that the cracking had been caused by the drainage pipes being laid below, instead of above, the concrete and rubble foundations.

It was said that the contractor was in no way to blame for this and *The Builder* pointed out rather smugly 'that the choice of site had always been wondered at by those acquainted with its boggy character'. Lord Panmure, now the Earl of Dalhousie and Secretary of State for War, had always disapproved of the whole project. He said that the hospital had been built 'on the glass and glare principle ... absolute cruelty to put an invalid in ... more suitable for a flower show or a museum ...'.[28] Once again the Treasury had to be asked for extra money as a sum of about £15,000 was needed due to the difficulties with the foundations, and alterations to the boundary wall. The day for completion of the contract had passed two months before, the building was nearly finished and the contractor would have to be paid very shortly.[29]

Myers was paid, the hospital was completed and *The Builder* reported, once again,

> as to the work generally in this building, it
> deserves the highest praise. Mr Myers who is the
> contractor, has had in his hands some

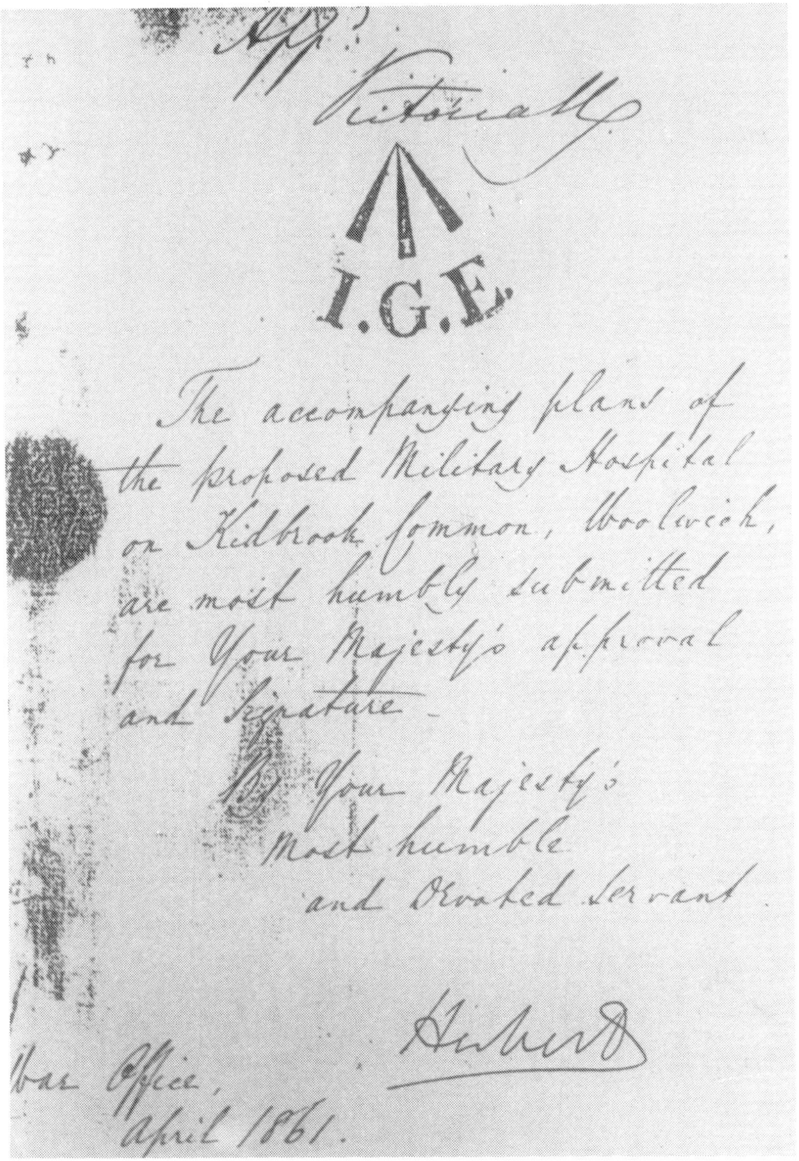

App?
Victoria R

I.G.E.

The accompanying plans of the proposed Military Hospital on Kidbrook Common, Woolwich, are most humbly submitted for Your Majesty's approval and Signature.

Your Majesty's
Most humble
and Devoted Servant

Herbert

War Office,
April 1861.

Figure 56 Sydney Herbert's letter to the Queen requesting her approval for the plans of the Woolwich Hospital, subsequently named the Herbert Hospital.
Courtesy of the Public Record Office WO 78/2893.

Figure 57   The Herbert Hospital, Woolwich.

undertakings of extraordinary magnitude, and he has never done better than the Herbert Hospital... The Government has provided a building in all respects worthy of the Nation, a disposition so seldom to be found as to occasion surprise when manifest.[30]

The Herbert Hospital was in use till 1975. The garden is overgrown but full of flowering trees and shrubs. There is a cemetery in the grounds and the whole site is surrounded by fine cast iron railings.

The Royal Victoria Patriotic Asylum for Girls was an orphanage for the daughters of the soldiers, sailors and marines who died in 'the Russian War', so a brief account of the building has been included in this chapter. News from the battle front shocked and horrified the British public. Accounts of the suffering and privation endured by their soldiers in the Crimea, where many more had died of disease and mismanagement than had been killed in battle, had turned the nation's thoughts to the widows and orphans of those brave men, many of whom were left destitute. A subscription fund, with Prince Albert as chairman of the commissioners, was set up in 1854, to help alleviate their suffering. Queen Victoria and Prince Albert headed the list of subscribers and money poured in from all parts of the British Isles and Colonies. Nearly £1,500,000 was collected and distributed to those in need. But the Executive and Finance Committee of the appeal, having acted with frugality, discovered that they had a surplus of £200,000 and so decided to build an orphanage for 300 girls under the age of fifteen.

Land was bought on the edge of Wandsworth Common, close to the Tooting Road. Mr Major (this was his 'Christian Name') Rhode Hawkins was chosen as architect and drew up a plan which resembled Heriot's Hospital in Edinburgh. George Myers' tender of £31,897 was the lowest to be submitted and was accepted. On 11 July 1857, Queen Victoria laid the foundation stone accompanied by the Prince Consort, various Royal Princesses and the Archbishop of Canterbury. The building of the orphanage was completed in two years. A clock had been planned for the central tower but it was replaced by St George killing the Dragon. The great hall where all 300 orphans dined together was decorated by Crace of Wigmore Street with the coats of arms of the cities, counties and towns which had contributed to the fund. There were schoolrooms, and dormitories with bathrooms and lavatories attached. The children were to be instructed in 'their moral and religious duties' and given an elementary education which would fit them for domestic service, and when they married, enable them to manage their households 'with economy, cleanliness and order'. Part of their education entailed doing the housework in the asylum, which doubtless effected a satisfying economy for the authorities.[31]

The central tower of the building is haunted by a child who was burnt to death while enduring the second of two days of solitary confinement in the superintendent's bathroom. The scandal caused by this tragedy resulted in a committee of thirteen ladies being formed to inspect the asylum regularly. They were horrified at what they found and were particularly shocked to discover that the superintendent of the orphanage was a man and that the chaplain inflicted corporal punishment on the girls.

During World War I the asylum was used as a hospital and the casualties were transported to the building, which overlooked the Southern Railway line, by train from the Channel ports. The orphans of those days were billeted out in nearby houses, but when the War was over they returned. In 1939 the building was evacuated once more. It is said that Rudolph Hess was imprisoned in the asylum during World War II. After the Second War, no use was found for the building and so in 1983, with various conditions laid down, the Greater London Council sold it for £1. It has now been converted into an art centre, a restaurant and flats.

George Myers' great buildings played a considerable part in the development of the modern army in the mid 19th century. But the imposing cavalry and infantry barracks at Aldershot, the two army hospitals, one which met with Florence Nightingale's approval and one which did not, have been demolished or are in danger of crumbling away. The Staff

Figure 58   The Royal Victoria Patriotic Asylum, Wandsworth, 1859.   The clock in the illustration was replaced by St George killing the Dragon.

College and Prince Consort's Library still stand, serving the purpose for which they were built, and the Royal Garrison Church of All Souls remains a peaceful memorial to 'The Fallen' of past wars and conflicts.

X

Changing Cities - Westminster and London: 1850-71

It was in Westminster and the City of London that the most varied and romantic contracts engaged Myers' attention. At Breadalbane House in 1854, he constructed a 'temporary Baronial Hall' for a dance at which Queen Victoria and the King of Portugal were present. This was one of several occasions on which Myers did the building and J.G. Crace the decorating. The Marquess of Breadalbane was so pleased with his temporary ballroom that it was not demolished until 1863, nearly ten years later.[1]

In 1858, Myers added an 82ft picture gallery and a ballroom to Dudley House, now 100 Park Lane, for Lord Ward and a conservatory overlooking Hyde Park. The architect was Daukes.[2] He also built the houses in Broad Sanctuary: G.G. Scott was the architect. These houses are beside Westminster Abbey and their designer could not resist producing a Gothic building. Today the much restored Abbey and the Victorian Broad Sanctuary Houses look to be the same age. Eighteen fifty eight was the year of the Colney Hatch Court Case against Daukes, when his competence and that of his builder had been questioned. It is interesting to note that they were still in demand: the building public had not lost confidence in either of them.

Just opposite the Abbey, Myers built the Westminster Palace Hotel. It was here, in 1859, that a very serious accident occurred.[3] In the 19th century accidents were commonplace on building sites and the average contractor showed little concern for his men's welfare. George Myers' safety record had been good, but on 14 May 1859 the *Illustrated London News* reported that a fatal accident had taken place at the Hotel site. It appears that soon after the men started work on the morning of Friday 13 May scaffolding broke and the unfortunate men who were standing on the platform, thirteen in number, were dashed to the ground. Four were killed instantly, one died on his way to hospital, the others were not expected to survive and the wife of one of the men who had been killed, died of fright on learning of the death of her husband. The final toll was seven dead and six seriously injured.

Myers arrived at the scene of the accident within half an hour and the police arrived soon after. Bricks and broken scaffolding had been removed from the site; but it was not clear whether this was to look for bodies or to hide the evidence. It was said that too great a quantity of bricks and mortar had been placed on the platform, and it was reported that the men were in the habit of jumping from one stage to another without using the ladders provided, that green wood had been used, etc., etc. There would of course be an inquest and Sir C. Russell, deputy chairman of the directors of the hotel, and his fellow directors 'were exceedingly distressed at this unfortunate occurrence and intended to contribute in a liberal manner to the wants and necessities of the wives and families of the deceased'.[4] There was no insurance for workmen in those days and little chance of suing the contractor in the unlikely event of his being found negligent. The inquest was adjourned until Monday 15 May 1859, and proved to be lengthy. The jury finally reported on 10 June that the catastrophe was: 'entirely owing to the accidental falling of an overloaded scaffold on which the unfortunate men were at work'. The report continued that there was not sufficient evidence to affix the blame of such overloading on any person or persons, but that blame attached to Mr Wm Coleman, the foreman, in not promptly carrying out the orders he had received from his employers to make a new scaffold. The jury expressed: 'an earnest and fervent hope that, where the lives of persons were to be jeopardised, more caution and circumspection should be exercised by the workmen in future'. They ended by commenting on 'the confused and unsatisfactory manner' in which the evidence had been collected and put before them.

The Westminster Palace Hotel where this dreadful accident occurred was situated at the east end of Victoria Street a few minutes' walk from the Houses of Parliament. It was the first of the very large 'modern' hotels and was erected by a company of 'noblemen and gentlemen' to provide accommodation for members of Parliament and those attending the Law Courts. Foreigners and the public at large were also catered for. The architects W. & A. Moseley had travelled abroad to inspect continental hotels and discover the most up-to-date furnishings and equipment. When finished the hotel had more than 400 rooms and the floors were reached by 'an ascending room' moved by hydraulic pressure. The building was fireproofed and the furnishing of all the principal rooms was on a scale of magnificence usually to be found in palaces.[5]

On 25 February 1860 the *Illustrated London News* published a picture of the new hotel which showed a chateau-like building with a shepherd peacefully shepherding four sheep past the main entrance and no sign of the dreadful tragedy which had occurred on the site such a short time before. In the early 20th century the building was taken over by the Conservative Central Office and renamed 'Abbey House'. The first Conservative Party Conference was held there in the 1870s when it was still a hotel. It has now been demolished. George Myers tendered for several other of these giant hotels but this was the only one for which he was the lowest bidder.

In 1851, Myers built Wyld's Great Globe. The preliminary skirmishes and legal arguments that took place before this was allowed were lengthy and acrimonious. James Wyld (1812-87) an M.P. and geographer, had wished to display a 'great model' of the earth's surface at the 1851 Exhibition, but he was not granted permission to do this and the Globe was eventually built in Leicester Square on derelict ground, the ownership of which was in dispute. On 11 February 1851,

Figure 59   Houses in Broad Sanctuary with Westminster Abbey and
Houses of Parliament in the background, 1858.

Figure 60   The Great Globe, Leicester Square, 1851.
Courtesy of the Guildhall Library, Corporation of London.

Wyld signed an agreement with the Tulks, part-owners of the land, which allowed him to erect his Globe and enjoy the use of it for ten years. At the end of that time, the building was due to be demolished and a garden laid out in the Square at Mr Wyld's expense.

The Great Exhibition was to open on 1 May, in less than three months' time. There was no time to be lost if Wyld was to benefit from the crowds expected to visit the Exhibition in Hyde Park. H.R. Abraham was chosen as architect. His design was accepted on 15 March and a week later George Myers, the contractor, had over a hundred men working day and night on the site. The Globe was opened on 2 June, just one month after the opening of the Great Exhibition.[6] Those who entered this extraordinary structure could study a large scale plaster model of the geographical features of the world.[7] An article in *The Art Journal* of 1851, pointed out that one of the advantages of this instructive and beautiful exhibition was that in great measure it avoided the laborious study of books. A model of the Great Globe can be seen in the Museum of the Moving Image on the South Bank, not far from the old site of Ordnance Wharf.

Myers' other contract in this area at that time was for the construction of a new roof for Exeter Hall. Until this Hall had been built in the 1830s, public meetings were held in taverns whose many disadvantages deterred the more particular members of society from attending. This Hall was unsectarian and a meeting place for both religious and scientific societies. It was there, on 1 June 1840, that Prince Albert made his first public appearance after his marriage when he presided at a meeting to promote the Abolition of the Slave Trade. He spoke there again at a meeting for the Promotion of Christian Unity. On that occasion the authorities sold twice as many tickets as they had seats, but though 3,000 people, most of whom had paid in advance, failed to gain admittance, there does not appear to have been a riot.[8]

In 1850 it was decided to improve the acoustics in Exeter Hall which were not satisfactory, and the architect S.W. Daukes was consulted. He designed a new higher roof which Myers executed. The result was a success and the Hall was used for concert recitals. It was demolished in 1907.

At the beginning of the 19th century the City of London had been a mixture of residential and business properties, but by the 1850s the bankers, merchants and other City dwellers had moved to live in the suburbs, returning only to work in the newly-built offices and banks, thus changing the whole atmosphere of the area. George Myers was one of the first of the big contractors to arrive on the scene. In 1852 he had erected offices for the Minerva Life Assurance Company in Cannon Street and a bank for Messrs Johnson & Co. in New Cannon Street. He was to be employed by other insurance companies and at least three other banks.

As well as erecting offices and banks, Myers, in 1858, was one of the six leading contractors invited to tender for the building of the Middle Temple Library and Chambers.[9] The other five were:

> William Cubitt,
> Lucas Bros,
> Piper & Son,
> Holland & Hannen,
> Jay.

Being lawyers, the Building Committee, wishing to guard against every eventuality, instructed Mr H.R. Abraham, the architect, to inform the contractors that they could not be held responsible for the quantity surveyor's inaccuracies. Myers wrote to say that he had complete confidence in Mr Crocker, the surveyor. He won the contract but construction did not run smoothly. Myers had worked for Mr Abraham when he built the Great Globe and that contract had been finished in record time, but on this occasion extra work was required which had not been included in the schedule. Mr Coles, of Essex Street, threatened proceedings against the Committee on account of expected obstruction of ancient lights and the orientation of the building had to be changed so that instead of lying east and west it came to lie north and south. But most disruptive of all was the fact that the contract was in progress at the time of the 'Great Lockout'. Myers, to show solidarity with his fellow Master Builders, and despite severe penalty clauses, dismissed his entire work-force. Building was at a complete standstill from 6 August to 26 September 1859. When work was resumed, Myers received a curt note from the architect requiring him to discharge the foreman, Mr Steel, whom he considered to be 'objectionable'.

Work proceeded. The interior of the library was decorated with the arms of the Chancellors and the Gothic roof was made of pitch-pine coated with boiled oil which created a splendid medieval effect and the hammer beams were carved with angels holding armorial shields. The outside walls were decorated with fantastic, grotesque animals which hid the ventilation inlets. The Bath stone came from Myers' quarries and his brother-in-law carried out the carving. The bookcases and other furniture were made in Myers' workshops.

Finally the work was finished, and, on 31 October 1861, the Prince of Wales, accompanied by the Duke of Cambridge, arrived to perform the opening ceremony. A long guest list was drawn up headed by Lord Palmerston. Both Gladstone and Disraeli accepted invitations. Myers was also invited and his son David was the last name on the list.

This beautiful building was bombed in World War II and all that remains are the steps that once led up to the main entrance and a Gothic desk which is in the librarian's office. Fortunately the books had been removed to a place of safety at the commencement of hostilities.

Myers built spectacular new premises for Messrs Sarl & Sons, Silversmiths, of Cornhill, the interior of which, with the glittering silver in the showcases, resembled a fairy-tale palace. Sarl had not wanted to close his premises while the old building was being demolished and the new was being built, presumably for fear of losing business. The scaffolding had been put up by Messrs Myers in conformity with the rules and regulations laid down by the Commissioners of City Sewers who licenced its erection, but despite the fact that it conformed in every way with the rules and had been erected at great expense, a stone weighing nearly two tons fell off the pier and landed on Samuel Wallace, aged 35, who was passing below. He died of his injuries a few days later. A verdict of accidental death was returned by the Coroner's jury, and Mr Sarl moved his shop to other premises for the duration of the building operations. Letters to the press offered much good advice.

Sarl was altogether an unsatisfactory employer. He refused to pay Myers on the dubious grounds that his weekly accounts had not been presented correctly. Myers sued. The editor of *The Builder* described it as 'a case of some mystery',[10] and as on the occasion of the Colney Hatch law suit, complained that if he said what he thought of the affair he might be liable to an action for libel. Myers won the case, but history does not relate whether or not he was paid.

In 1856, Myers undertook building work at the Tower of London. First built as a fort to guard the Thames by William the Conqueror in 1067, it has since been put to many uses: royal palace, mint, state prison, arsenal and menagerie. It had been renovated in 1660 on Charles II's return from exile and a permanent garrison quartered there. It remained a state prison and it was there that the crown jewels were kept and displayed to the public. When the Duke of Wellington was appointed Constable in 1826, the Monarchy was so unpopular and the situation in the country so unstable that he and many other members of the aristocracy feared that revolution was imminent. The Tower was seen as a centre of defence and during the next two decades the fortifications were strengthened and new barracks built. The Duke considered the sightseeing public a threat to security and wished to exclude them from the Tower, but in this he did not succeed. Gradually the fear of revolution receded and after his death, by which time the Tower was no longer needed for defence, it became the major tourist attraction it is today. But first, with the encouragement of Prince Albert, the authorities undertook a vast programme of restoration and rebuilding.

In 1856 the Office of Works and Buildings proposed to execute various works at the Tower of London 'in the repair and restoration of the Salt Tower'.[11] In its time the Salt Tower had housed many prisoners including John Baliol, King of Scotland, and in the reign of Elizabeth I many Catholic priests. The architect chosen to carry out the renovations was Anthony Salvin, the son of a General. He wrote to the Lieutenant

Figure 61 Middle Temple Library, 1860.
Courtesy of the Guildhall Library, Corporation of London.

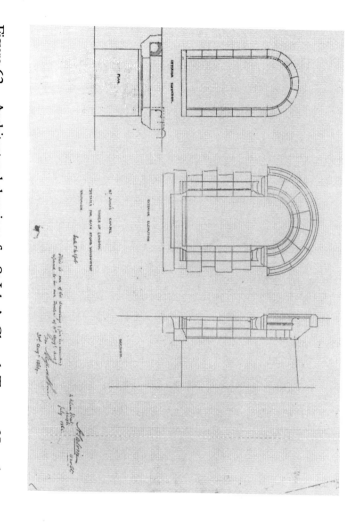

Figure 62   Architectural drawings for St John's Chapel, Tower of London,
signed by Anthony Salvin and George Myers.
Courtesy of the Public Record Office WORKS 31/527.

Governor of the Tower, Lord de Ros and suggested that the following three contractors should be asked to tender:

> Messrs Myers & Sons,
> George Smith Esq,
> J.Kelk Esq.

It is noteworthy that Myers' name was at the top of the list.

On 10 June 1856, the following letter was dispatched from the Office of Works and Buildings in Whitehall to the three contractors:

> Gentlemen,
> I am ordered by the P.C. (Privy Council) to inform you that it is proposed to execute various works at the Tower of London in the repair and restoration of the Salt Tower, and if you are willing to offer a tender for the same, that you can inspect the drawings and specifications at the office of the architect, Mr Salvin (no 30 Argyle Street) on or after the 12th inst. The tenders are to be delivered at this office on or before Tuesday 24th inst. at 12 o'clock endorsed: 'Tenders for Repair of the Salt Tower'.

On 24 June George Myers sent in his tender to the Commissioners of Her Majesty's Woods and Forests. It said:

> Gentlemen
> My estimate for the works proposed to be executed at the Salt Tower, Tower of London according to the drawings and Specifications, this will amount to £1,290. I am, Gentlemen
> Your obedient servant
> George Myers

His estimate was accepted.

Messrs Myers & Sons were to work at the Tower for the next twelve years. Their work there included the restoration of the Salt Tower and also the east and south walls of St Thomas' Tower. Some years before, the Board of Ordinance had installed a brick engine house which obscured the arch of the Traitor's Gate. The Constable ordered that the engine house should be removed and when this was done, it was discovered that St Thomas' Tower, which was over the Gate, had been damaged by the vibration of the engine. A very extensive repair was necessary including the restoring of the coping and the gargoyles on the exterior wall. As so much work was required, it was decided to convert this Tower into a residence for the jewel keeper and to clear the neighbouring Wakefield Tower of rubbish and to adapt it for the reception of the crown jewels. Myers carried out this conversion and the jewels were kept in the Wakefield Tower until the present Jewel House was opened in 1967.

Between 1864 and 1866 Messrs Myers worked on the restoration of St John's Chapel in the White Tower. This Norman Chapel had been built of Caen stone but Myers' masons replaced the jambs, head sills, caps, columns, bases, etc., with Bath stone, probably from his own quarries at Box. The sixteen windows were restored and the walling made good at a cost of £1,521. The chapel had once been richly decorated with painted walls, stained glass windows and a painted rood screen but all this was destroyed at the time of the Reformation. The austere beauty of the chapel is strangely moving even in the midst of a crowd of sightseers.

According to the official reports, all the work at the Tower was 'admirably' carried out under Mr Salvin's direction and the keys of the Jewel House and the Keeper's Residence were handed over to the Yeoman Porter by Mr McLeish, the foreman of Works, on 23 May 1869. But for Mary Anne Pope and Sir Spencer Ponsonby, who both lived within the precinct of the Tower, though in very different circumstances, the restoration work had not improved matters, as is shown by their letters still in existence 130 years after they were written.

Mary Anne Pope was the wife and then the widow of Warder Pope whose wash-house had been knocked down to make room for the new Jewel House. It was going to cost £30 to rebuild the wash-house on another site and it would take some time before this could be arranged, so in the meanwhile Warder Pope was to be granted an allowance of £2. 10s. 0d. a year. But Pope died before he got his allowance. His widow wrote to the authorities, apologised for bothering them and explained that she knew that in six weeks' time she would have to vacate the house she had occupied while her husband had been alive but - could she have that portion of the £2. 10s. 0d that was due to her late husband at the time of his death? She explained: 'my embarrassment would not I believe, be so painfully trying, were it not from my having a rather numerous family, consisting chiefly of helpless children'. She ended her letter:

> With the Utmost Respect
> I am Sir
> Your most humble and Obedient Servant
> Mary Anne Pope

She had written on Friday 20 July 1860 and a payment of £1. 13s. 0d. was authorised on Monday, 3 September, six weeks and three days later.

On 6 April 1864, Sir Spencer Ponsonby, Keeper of the Crown Jewels, wrote to Viscount Sydney (Governor of the Tower) and pointed out that it was eight years since he had first written to complain about 'this Matter'. Now that the restoration of the fortifications of the Tower had been undertaken, could not he, Ponsonby, have a comfortable house to live in? Ponsonby reminded Viscount Sydney that his house was adjacent to the soldiers' privies and urinals and so: ' the whole house is impregnated with the stench of these vicious places'. Viscount Sydney's reply is not extant.

While George Myers was still working at the Tower another very prestigious City contract came his way: the restoration of the Guildhall roof. In the Great Fire of 1666 the medieval roof of the Guildhall was completely destroyed. For some reason the architect, possibly Wren, replaced it with a flat one, totally out of keeping with the rest of the building. In 1862 the City Corporation decided to replace the 'miserable and unsuitable ceiling'[12] which had long disfigured their ancient hall.

Prominent architects were consulted and it was agreed that the roof should be restored in exact conformity with the original design. But it appeared that there was a lack of historical information as to what the original design had been. Despite this difficulty, the City Architect, Mr James Bunstone Bunning, drew up plans. Fifteen builders were invited to tender[13] amongst whom were Lucas Bros. of 6, 7 and 11 Belvedere Road, Holland & Hannen also of Belvedere Road, George Mansfield of 12 Henry Street, Greys Inn Lane, William Cubitt and Co. of Calthorpe Place, Greys Inn Road and George Myers & Sons of Ordnance Wharf, Belvedere Road, Lambeth. Twelve of these contractors submitted tenders. Edward Conder's of £24,150, for a roof of English oak and £23,210 for Quebec oak was the highest and George Myers' offer to build the roof of Quebec oak for £17,315 was the lowest and was accepted. His tender for a roof of English oak was £19,507. Other work at the Guildhall was included in the contract. This consisted of sixteen dormer windows in the roof, a centre lantern or louvre (whose cost was not to exceed £500), the roof and dormers to be covered with Westmoreland slating and to have cast iron cresting to the ridge, and the side walls and parapets were to be rebuilt from the tops of the capitals of the columns, using the old stone as backing and filling. There was to be a new plain Bath stone cornice between the trusses. On 15 March 1863, Messrs Myers & Sons signed a contract for the construction of the new roof and the execution of the other works.[14] Myers handed over £3,463 as surety. The work was to be finished by 'the first day of October next'. There was a penalty clause of £10 per diem for late completion, Sundays excluded and allowance was to be made for delays due to strikes. Messrs Myers were to work at the Guildhall from the spring of 1863 until the end of 1868, but there were to be interruptions.

The scaffolding was erected and the work had commenced when it was announced that a public meeting would take place in the Great Hall. Myers was instructed to remove the scaffolding and replace it after the meeting. He was to be paid £30 for this inconvenience and the completion date was postponed to 17 October. He rearranged his work schedule but was then told to halt all work until 18 November.

Figure 63 Chapel of St John the Evangelist,
Tower of London.
Courtesy of the Guildhall Library, Corporation of London.

Figure 64   Illustration of a civic reception in the Guildhall which shows the roof made by George Myers' craftsmen in 1864.
Courtesy of the Guildhall Library, Corporation of London.

Completion was once again postponed, this time until 31 July 1864. Myers was now to be paid £500 for removing the scaffolding and clearing up the builder's rubble and he was also to be paid a sum not exceeding £1,500 to be assessed by the architect, for wasted materials, labour, etc.

The reason for this disruption, as was eventually disclosed, was that the recently married Prince and Princess of Wales (the future King Edward VII and Queen Alexandra) had accepted an invitation from the Mayor and Commonalty and the Citizens of the City of London to attend a Ball at the Guildhall on 8 June, 1863. The building site had to be cleared and everything left in perfect order by 13 May so that Mr Crace would have time to decorate the rooms in a fitting manner.

The wedding of the Prince of Wales and Princess Alexandra of Denmark had taken place in St George's Chapel Windsor Castle in March. It had been necessary to build a temporary reception hall and retiring room at the West door of the church. An immense Gothic Hall was built under the direction of the Board of Works. Messrs Myers were the contractors, with Mr Turnbull, who was overseer of works at Windsor, as Clerk of Works. The hall was furnished and fitted by Mr Seebrook, Inspector of Windsor Castle. The walls of the hall were hung with chocolate, green and gold paper and the bride's retiring rooms had pink silk hangings trimmed with English lace. The Prince's apartment on the other side of the hall was simple and elegant, with blue wallpaper patterned with his crest in silver. Queen Victoria watched the wedding from the projecting wooden oriel window to the left of the altar. This had been added by Henry VIII and is decorated with the Arms of Queen Katherine of Aragon, who watched Garter services from a closet behind the window. Queen Victoria entered through the Deanery and a private covered way so that she could take her place unobserved.[15] She was still in mourning for Albert. The wedding, as was the custom in those days, was a family affair, cousins only were invited, that is to say most of the Royal families of Europe.

So when it was decided to hold a Ball at the Guildhall in honour of the Prince and Princess, George Myers was employed to erect the pavilion in the Guildhall courtyard for the reception of the Royal guests, as well as for dancing and supper. A commodious pavilion two stories high was required, but it was not until three weeks before the Ball was due to take place (on 8 June) that Myers was instructed to carry out the work. He wrote to the Chairman of the Entertainment Committee on 15 May 1863 agreeing to proceed, payment to be based on the London Printed Schedule of Her Majesty's Woods & Forests, (the predecessors of the Office of Works).

Mr Crace's tasteful decoration of the interior of the pavilion included cream and stone coloured walls relieved with gold, and ceilings of pale blue dotted with golden stars. The area reserved for the Royal Visitors was enclosed with ropes of purple silk. Gas lights illuminated the hall and on the night of the Ball the main rooms were hung with tapestries and decorated with massed flowers. The 'flat unsightly roof' could not be seen. It had been hidden by City shields and great baskets of ferns and flowers but, according to some, not as artistically as could have been desired.[16]

'Everyone' was invited. The Peers of the Realm, the Ambassadors, the Bankers and Merchants of the City and Mr George Myers and his lady. Some of those invited had dared to ask for extra tickets. One father wrote to ask for tickets for his 'three dancing daughters', and William Cubitt wanted six extra tickets. As he had been Lord Mayor of London in 1860 and 1861 he probably thought he was entitled to them.

Eventually the great day dawned and that evening at a quarter past nine a fanfare of trumpets announced the arrival of the Prince and Princess and the other Royal guests. They were received by the Lord Mayor and Lady Mayoress and then proceeded to the lavishly decorated hall where the formal business of the evening took place - the presentation of the Freedom of the City to the Prince and the documentary record of this event contained in a golden casket which opened by means of a secret spring.

The ceremony over, the Lord Mayor opened the Ball by dancing a quadrille with the Princess of Wales while the Prince led out the Lady Mayoress. The quadrille was followed by a valse, the lancers and a gallop and another quadrille in rotation until midnight when another flourish of trumpets announced that supper was served.

The Royal couple, the Lord Mayor, the Lady Mayoress and about forty of the most distinguished guests sat down to a lengthy and elaborate menu in the council chamber which had been decorated by Crace with large flower-filled gilt baskets. The end of the chamber was devoted to a display of the riches of the wealthiest corporation in the world. From floor to ceiling massive gold plate rose in glittering array, tier upon tier in a great pile over which the statue of King George III kept watch with outstretched hands. The other guests were divided into two groups and dined in separate rooms on menus adjusted to their station in the social order.

It must have been a memorable evening. Judith Myers kept her invitation for the rest of her life and today it is framed and hangs on the wall in the house of one of her descendants. George's got mislaid.

Seats had been erected along the processional route which was decorated with lights and flags. The Guildhall authorities set up a grandstand of 10,000 seats in St Paul's churchyard so that some of those people who could not be invited to the Ball would have a view of the brilliant spectacle. George Myers carried out this work too, at a cost of £6,905. 10s. 6d. The seats were covered with baize.[17] It was red baize not green.

The workmen who constructed the seating were filled with curiosity concerning the beautiful Danish princess who was about to marry the Prince of Wales and they longed to see her. So they wrote a letter to the chairman of the committee organising the reception saying:

> Lambeth
> Feb 28 1863
>
> To the Chairman & Committee of Reception
> Gentm,
> We have the honour as the Contractors for the seats in St Paul's Church Yard to ask you to be so kind as to favour us with 10 or 12 tickets for ourselves and families to view the procession. We have to devote very long hours to the undertaking which you entrusted to our hands, and we can

> only say if you will be pleased to let us have
> tickets we should be greatly obliged. We are,
> Chairman & Gentm.
> Yours very obediently
> Geo Myers & Sons

It is not known whether their request was granted.

When it was all over Messrs Myers had to return to the business of building the new roof, but the delays continued. Mr James Bunstone Bunning, the City architect who had drawn up the plans and was officially in charge of the preparations for the Ball, fell ill and, in March 1863, was granted six month's leave to travel to a warmer climate. But this did him no good and when he returned to London a few weeks later he collapsed on the Mansion House steps and died shortly afterwards. Horace Jones was appointed in his place. He altered the plans. When they were submitted to Myers he asked for a further £2,500 on top of the sum already agreed. He added that the four angle towers were not included in this estimate and that the taking down and removal of the cornices was to be charged as day work. The City Fathers had obviously hoped to get the new plan carried out for the same price as the old, but they called a meeting at which they decided 'to accede to Mr Myers' demands'. The new contract was signed and at last the work was able to proceed without further interruption. It was finished by November 1864 and all agreed that Messrs Myers & Sons had built a truly magnificent roof to replace 'the miserable and unsuitable ceiling'.

Two years later tenders were called for the restoration of the pillars and windows of the great hall. Once again Myers carried out the work, in Derbyshire alabaster at a cost of £808. Then in 1866, Myers was asked to provide a gallery to complete the medieval decoration of the newly restored hall. Designed by Horace Jones, it was considered of such importance that a deputation consisting of Mr W.J. Kelday, chairman of the Improvements Committee, accompanied by two other members, Mr Saunders and Mr Hewitt, proceeded to Belvedere Road to inspect the wood to be used. They must have had an interesting time because they paid at least three more visits to the workshops to inspect the progress of the work which they considered was proceeding rather slowly. They refrained from complaining to Myers as the craftsmanship was undoubtedly superb.[18]

On 3 November 1868, Myers was asked to present his account for work past and present.

There was another great Ball at the Guildhall for which Myers again built a temporary two storey pavilion filling the entire Guildhall Yard. With its staircases and fountains it cost £14,846. 6s. 10d. The occasion was the reception on Thursday 18 July 1867 of the great Ottoman potentate, His Imperial Majesty Abd-al-Aziz Khan. It was a glittering spectacle to which, as before, Mr Myers and his lady were invited. This time there were only two menus; the one for those entertained in the Council Chamber consisted of twenty-eight dishes, while the other bill of fare for the less important guests consisted of a mere twenty-one. The representative of the 'sick man of Europe', later to be deposed, was famous for his extravagance, and the City of London was no doubt anxious to impress him with the splendour of the occasion. All those present were magnificently attired but one cannot help wondering what the Sultan thought of the shapely English women with their bare arms and naked shoulders.

After the Ball in honour of the Prince and Princess of Wales, the pavilion had been demolished, and the 'timber, temporary fittings and decorations' sold for £3,794. 8s. 4d., but the sale, after the ball to entertain the Sultan only realised £1,144. 6s. 10d.[19]

This was not the only time in which Myers was involved with matters related to the Turkish Empire. Four years later, he constructed the London office of the Imperial Ottoman Bank in Throgmorton Street. This Bank had been set up in 1863, not, as its name suggests, by the Ottomans, but by French and English shareholders. The site chosen was next door to the office block which Myers was building in 1870 for Travers Smith, his own solicitors.

During the 1860s Myers built a series of bonded warehouses on or near Tower Hill. It was just over 80 years (1793) since Pitt's government had adopted the bonded warehouse system, a system of warehousing in bond which is governed by an intricate body of laws. The proprietor of the warehouse gives his bond to the government for the payment at the proper time of the prescribed duty, that is when the goods are to be released onto the market. In this way a large premature outlay is avoided. The doors of such warehouses are secured with crown locks and revenue officials are constantly present to check the movement of stock and to see that nothing is missing. Myers' warehouses were ideally situated on the edge of the new St Katherine's Dock and convenient for the Grand Union Canal when the time for the disposal of the goods arrived.

Myers owned the freehold of warehouses in Colchester Street, Savage Gardens and Coopers Row in the City of London. There must have been a considerable number of them as he had mortgaged them for a sum of £65,000 at an interest rate of 4.5 and 5 per cent. At the time of Myers' retirement in 1873, when a list of his assets was drawn up, there was no mention of a mortgage on his monster warehouse on Tower Hill or on his freehold property in Clapham (one of the rare occasions when he indulged in any speculative building). It is probable that his solicitors, Travers Smith, arranged the mortgages for him. In June 1873 the mortgagees were described as Henry Kebbel, Esquire and others, £35,000 and again Lewis Lloyd, Esquire and others £30,000.

It is not clear how many of these warehouses Myers used himself and how many he let. A newly erected warehouse consisting of seven floors, exclusive of the vaults and cellars, was situated on the west side of Tower Hill in the Parish of All Hallows, Barking. The ground on which it was built has a long history which can be traced in documents in the Guildhall Library to the 12th century,[20] to Matilda, Stephen's Queen, who in 1148 gave land near the Tower to the Master, Brothers and Sisters of St Katherine's Hospital for the care and protection of the poor of Poplar. This became a very wealthy foundation. It was exempt from the Secular Jurisdiction of the City which had grown greatly in power in the 12th century, and was under the Ecclesiastical Jurisdiction of the Bishop of London and through the centuries under the special protection of the Queen of England. Charlotte, George III's Queen, on her death in 1818,

Figure 65   Two floor pavilion constructed by George Myers for the reception at the Guildhall of the Sultan of Turkey, 1867.

Courtesy of the Guildhall Library, Corporation of London.

Figure 66   The Imperial Ottoman Bank, Throgmorton Street,
1871.

two years before that of the King, had appointed Sir Herbert Taylor as Guardian in her place as there was no queen to whom she could hand on her responsibility.

At the time of Queen Charlotte's death, St Katherine's Hospital and its buildings were in a very bad state of repair and the Community was in debt to the Master to the tune of £1,096. The Brothers had taken up more salubrious livings in the country and the Sisters had been left to fend for themselves. In 1819, only one year after Queen Charlotte's death it was decided to pull down the Bede Houses belonging to the Community. In 1823 when a scheme was launched to build a dock between Tower Hill and London Docks, Sir Herbert Taylor's only concern was to help the Master, who had not opposed the building of the new dock, to make as lucrative a bargain as possible. This he intended to do by selling the Hospital land to the Port Company instead of trying to save it for the charitable Community which had occupied it for 650 years. When the promoters of the new dock scheme presented their bill in Parliament, the only people to oppose it were the proprietors of the other docks in London who feared rivals. Unscrupulous means were used to obtain the passage of the Bill. The hospital and the church were demolished in 1826 and 2,624 inhabitants in the area were made homeless; all that remained of the Royal Hospital of St Katherine which had been established for the care and protection of the poor was the name which was transferred to the new dock. What remained of the Hospital Community was re-formed in Regent's Park, where it did not flourish.

To the west of Tower Hill stood the church of All Hallows by the Tower. There had been a place of worship on this site since the middle of the 17th century. In 1864 Messrs Myers & Sons leased the land just to the east of the church from the Crown and from the Master, Brothers and Sisters of St Katherine's Hospital and at a meeting of the Chapter on 30 June 1864, with the Master, the Honorable William Ashley in the chair, supported by the Revd George Hudson, John Glover, John C. H. Hill, Brother Wilson representing the Brothers and Miss Hilyard the Sisters, George Myers of Lambeth submitted drawings for a large double stack of warehouses, seven stories high, standing on top of two acres of underground vaults on three floors which he proposed to build on the ground belonging to the Master, Brothers and Sisters of St Katherine's Hospital on Tower Hill. Leases of varying length were held by tenants on the site. Myers wished to remove all the buildings on this property and take over the leases. The Hon. William Ashley said that he had no hesitation in advising the Chapter of St Katherine's Hospital to assent to the construction of Myers' buildings, as they would in every way be of much greater value than those which were now occupying the site. Without hesitation the Brothers, Sisters and the others present gave their consent to the erection of this vast building, which in later years was to be christened by the Revd P.B. Clayton, the founder of 'Toc H' and incumbent of All Hallows, 'The Nightmare of Tower Hill'.

The building was to be erected to the satisfaction of the Hon. William Ashley and that of the surveyor to the Chapter, Messrs Clutton of 8-9 Whitehall Place, Westminster, and was to be completed by 21 December 1865. The rest of the meeting was taken up with the financial side of the transaction, which was complicated. The land was divided into areas of unequal size, let for varying lengths of time at different rents.[21] Messrs Myers had acquired a parcel of freehold land amongst the maze of leases which they had taken on.

The warehouses were quickly constructed and the vaults beneath were cool and surprisingly dry. The building was supported internally by iron pillars each one with a collar of candle sticks, the drips of the candle grease still visible 125 years later. This edifice was bounded by Trinity Square to the north, Tower Hill to the east, Tower Street to the south and by Barking Alley with the Church Yard and All Hallows by the Tower, a short distance to the west. If objections were to be made to the close proximity of the warehouses to the church, they should have been made in 1864, to the Master the Hon. William Ashley, to the Brothers and to the Sisters of St Katherine's Hospital, but it is doubtful if any voices were raised at that time and in any case, would it have done any good? The Master and the Brothers and Sisters were only out to make money. There was no 'Ministry of the Environment', no

Figure 67   War-time destruction of All Hallows by the Tower and also of
George Myers' monster warehouse.
Reproduced from a drawing by Hanslip Fletcher, 1944.

'English Heritage' in the seventh decade of the nineteenth century.

The warehouses and vaults were built as an investment to be a source of income when Myers retired and, coincidentally, for his descendents for many years to come. Being well-positioned from a commercial point of view, they were soon let. Legal documents show that in 1873, on Myers' retirement:

> the Tower Hill vaults were leased to Messrs Robert Holdsworth Carew Hunt and others for £2,700 per annum.
> the warehouses above ground were leased to Messrs Waring and Wrightson and others at a rent of £2,255 per annum.

In 1890, fifteen years after George Myers' death, a warehouse and premises on Tower Hill were let to Messrs Densham and Sons, wholesale tea dealers of 11 Philpot Lane in the City of London for a yearly rent of £350, determinable by the lessees of first seven or fourteen years. But Messrs Densham retained the lease and with the brand name of their tea written in huge letters across the front of the building it became known as the 'Mazawattee Tea House'.

But in the 1860's no-one objected to this vast industrial building overshadowing one of the oldest of the City churches, except the Vicar who, it is said, called on Myers to lodge a protest. But it was too late, the warehouses were almost complete and it was not until 1922 when the Rev Tubby Clayton raised the question, that the siting of the warehouse was seriously considered. The great seven storey building was so close to the church that it blocked the light from the east window. Mr Clayton was determined that 'the nightmare of Tower Hill' should be removed and replaced by a peaceful garden. His plans depended on the fact that the lease of the 'nightmare' was due to terminate in 1948 which might make it possible to gain possession of the site. He interested public-minded men in his scheme: senior members of the Port of London Authority, his friends in the Tower, the Mint, the Trinity House, the Corn Exchange, the Customs House and the

Guildhall and even Sir G. H. Duckworth, a member of the Royal Commission on Historical Monuments. He wrote a book called *The Pageant of Tower Hill*, the purpose of which was to show that pageantry and warehouses did not blend with each other, or anyway not outside his church. Then, having done all these things, it is said that he knelt down and prayed that the 'nightmare' would go away. Eventually his prayers were answered but in a very unsatisfactory manner. At 1.20 a.m. on 17 September 1940 an air-raid set fire to the building which was totally gutted above ground. But Mr Clayton's satisfaction at this outcome cannot have been great because his own church was also destroyed.

But All Hallows has now been rebuilt and the site of the warehouse has been converted into a garden. The sun shines in through the east window at last, Mr Clayton lies at peace and Myers' underground vaults, which survived the bombing, have been converted[22] into an extension of the Museum of London recording the history of the City by means of a display called: 'A Pageant of Tower Hill, the City and its Port'. Here and there traces of George Myers' involvement in the site can be discerned - the bricks of his vaulted roofs, the ironwork and the cranes used for the movement of his merchandise. The Museum was opened to the public in 1991 by the Lord Mayor of London, Sir Alexander Graham.

XI

Building for the Rothschilds: 1851-73

In the autumn of 1851 George Myers tendered for the contract to build a mansion house at Mentmore for the Baron Mayer de Rothschild, the great City banker. Myers' tender of £15,427 to build 'the carcase of the said mansion' was the lowest of the three submitted and was accepted. The Mentmore contract was signed on 24 October 1851. The mansion was to be built according to the plans prepared by 'Sir Joseph Paxton of Chatsworth' who had just been knighted for his work at the Great Exhibition, and the contract shows that the designation 'Sir' was squeezed in by the clerk after the document had been drawn up. It contained all the usual clauses and the mansion was to be finished by 1 July 1853. There was a penalty clause of £20 per day for failure to finish on time. As we have seen, work started late and so was not completed by the designated date, but for some reason no penalty was invoked.

This was the beginning of Myers' long association with the Rothschild family which was to last until he retired in 1873. He worked for the three English Rothschild brothers, Lionel, Anthony and Mayer, for their nephew Ferdinand, who came from Vienna to settle in England, and for their uncle, James, who lived in Paris. During the twenty years, 1853-73, the Rothschild ledgers disclose that Myers was paid something in the region of £350,000 by the English members of the family.

Mentmore is situated forty miles north-west of London in the Vale of Aylesbury, in good hunting country. The London & North Western Railway provided transport to and from the Metropolis and the Grand Union Canal, passing west of the village, facilitated the carriage of building materials. Work on this Rothschild palace proceeded rapidly and, despite the late start, was finished in November 1855.[1] No expense had been spared. The huge plate glass windows in all the ground floor reception rooms, the result of the latest technology, can still be seen glittering in the sunlight from far away. The transportation of the glass must have caused Myers many an anxious moment as his packers were a rough lot,[2] but Mr Alfred Goslett of Soho Square, who supplied the glass, obviously had careful packers as the glass arrived safely.[3] The house had cold running water in all the bedrooms; to have running water at all in bedrooms was an innovation. The mansion was lit by gas. Gas lighting had been installed at Abbotsford by Sir Walter Scott as early as 1823 so this, though a 'modern' method of lighting, was not unusual.[4] It was of course necessary for the house to have its own gasworks. There was hot water central heating, though it is said that this did not prevent Mentmore from being one of the draughtiest houses in the county. Unlike many Victorian houses, Mentmore had no basement and the servants' rooms were comparatively light and spacious. The smoking room, for the sake of the ladies, was separated from the rest of the house by a large conservatory, and the Great Hall, decorated by Henry Brewer in 1863 is magnificent.[5]

Mayer continued adding to and improving Mentmore until his death in 1877 and, until Myers retired, Mayer continued to employ him. Over the years a dairy and a vinery were added, maid-servants' rooms were converted into guest rooms and new maids' rooms were built. Myers' craftsmen made built-in furniture and a pine wardrobe with a handsomely carved and moulded Elizabethan front and end pilasters for the Baroness de Rothschild's dressing room, as well as other furniture. Various adjustments were required in the house and the marble chimneypiece in the best bedroom was taken down and reduced in size and black marble slips and a polished grate supplied. Adjustments had to be made to the swing doors and a brass grating let into the billiard room door. At a cost of £26.

14*s*. 0*d*. Myers arranged for the carting of 14 tons of marble from the London docks to Mentmore in November 1866. Was this for fireplaces to convert maids' rooms into guests' rooms? Myers provided models of the proposed new lodges at a cost of £6. 10*s*. 0*d*.

In 1868 he sent in a bill for £4. 15*s*. 0*d*., the cost of two journeys to Newmarket and back 'taking dimensions for proposed alterations etc.'. Baron Mayer had bought Palace House, Newmarket, in 1857, and, in 1867, George Devey had provided designs for a new dining room, so it was presumably this house which Myers visited.[6]

In 1853 Anthony de Rothschild started planning the conversion of a farmhouse on land he owned at Aston Clinton. It was to be a residence fit for a gentleman and he too employed Myers. Mr James James, solicitor, of Aylesbury, the Rothschild's man of business in that area, was required to attend to the preliminary details. He met Myers on 3 September to consider the plans and specifications and the drainage. During the spring of 1854 Myers and James had several meetings to discuss the contract which was finally signed on 5 May.[7] James charged £2. 2*s*. 0*d*. for drawing up the contract, £1. 5*s*. 0*d*. for his rail fare and 3*s*. 0*d*. for cab hire. The work proceeded smoothly with Henry Stokes, Paxton's son-in-law, in charge. (Later George Devey was to take over as architect.) The basic alterations and improvements were soon complete including work to the roof, cellars, walls and of course the drains. A fanlight was required in the best W.C. on the first floor, slate shelves were needed in the beer cellar and the bell hanger (the bells were to summon the servants), had to be supervised. In October 1855, Myers signed a further contract to execute a conservatory, followed by stables and a billiard room.

There were bills for lesser items:-

	£	s.	d.
2 horses, van and driver, 10 hrs	1	0	10
Tolls and expenses for horses, van etc.	98	18	12 ½
Freight and canal dues on building materials	60	5	1 ½

In 1866 Myers laid out the gardens at Aston Clinton. Stone vases and figures were imported from France, Myers arranging transport from the docks. Marble bases and pedestals for the statues were made in the workshops at Ordnance Wharf and a fountain surrounded by groups of figures was arranged in the garden.

In 1873, His Royal Highness the Prince of Wales paid a visit to Aston Clinton. The fine specimens of camellias, lauristinus, bay trees, palms and a large variety of flowering plants in the conservatory as well as the orchids and other flowers which decorated the dinner table arrived the day before the great event, from the Royal Exotic Nursery in the King's Road, Chelsea.

Baron James de Rothschild, a member of the French branch of the family, heard of his nephews' grandiose building plans and, at the age of 61, was filled with an urge to build. In 1829 he had bought the property of Ferrières, located in the district of Seine et Marne about twenty miles east of Paris. The park and its small chateau had belonged to Fouché (1759-1820), Napoleon's minister of Police, who had also served Louis XVIII but fell from favour and died a naturalised Austrian. Baron James, who had seen Mayer's plans for Mentmore, decided that he too would employ Sir Joseph Paxton and George Myers. The agreement was signed on 20 March 1854.[8] Myers travelled to France with 140 English masons and engaged 200 local men on arrival. Work started and the foundation stone was laid on 7 July 1855, but there appear to have been problems. Paxton wrote to his wife from Paris on 19 March 1858 and complained:- 'We have had endless bother with the Baron and Ferrières. I am sick to death with it'.

There was serious trouble on 24 May 1859, when there was a fight between the English and French masons. One Frenchman and one Englishman were killed. Sir Joseph Paxton described the reason for the hostilities when he gave evidence before the Parliamentary Select Committee on Masters and Operatives in April 1860.[9] He explained that

the peculiar character of English masonry is much better than that of French masonry; and for the

Figure 68   Mentmore, 1857.

Figure 69   Ferrières, near Paris

highly ornamental work it was necessary to take a
very high proportion of masons from this country
(England) and they were paid very high wages.
The Frenchmen were given the same wages they
generally receive in France, for the best work in
France; but working with Englishmen they thought
they ought to be paid the same wages as the
Englishmen. Mr Myers found he could not afford
to give those wages; the men were not competent
to do the work that the Englishmen did, either in
respect of quality or quantity.

The French masons walked out and it was five or six weeks
before they could be enticed back by an offer of an increase in
pay.

Paxton wrote once again to his wife from Paris on 14
November 1859: 'We arrived here safe last night and have been
waiting about all day upon the Baron who will keep me as far as
ever from a settlement ... I write this in the chair in Rothschild's
office where I have been waiting for four hours'.[10] Baron James
was not as meticulous about settling his accounts as his English
nephews.

Despite everything, the chateau, which was expected to
take twenty years to build, was completed in five. It was
acclaimed on all sides. A modern French guide book describes
it as 'l'un des plus parfaits examples de l'architecture d'une
grande demeure de campagne anglaise en France ... ' and goes
on to say that it was decorated in 'le style Rothschild' and was
surrounded by a beautiful park. The inside of the chateau was
even more luxurious than Mentmore, the water in the bedrooms
ran hot as well as cold and, of course, there was central heating.
The kitchens were in a separate building linked to the pantry by
a small underground railway.[11]

On one of his last visits to Paris while building Ferrières,
George Myers took with him his wife and two young daughters,
Caroline and Ellie. They went shopping and to the Opera
where they saw the Emperor Napoleon III and his elegant wife
Eugenie drive to the door of the Royal Box in their carriage.
Many years later Ellie was to describe this dazzling occasion to

her grandchildren. Perhaps it was at this time that Mr and Mrs Myers visited the Sacré Coeur Convent in the Rue de Varenne (N77) and arranged to send their daughters there as boarders. Caroline and Ellie Myers spent several years at this fashionable Parisian school where they were very happy and learnt to speak fluent French. Much of the old school building still exists as a lycée. It is near the Invalides.[12]

In January 1863, Baron James de Rothschild invited Napoleon III to a 'family luncheon' to celebrate the completion of Ferrières. This repast cost one and a half million francs. Evidently it was necessary to spend this sum in 'preparations essential to the ceremonious display required by the dignity of the two great potentates'.[13] The Emperor was deposed seven years later and the Third Republic came into being. In 1982 the French branch of Rothschild's Bank was taken over by the State and Baron Guy de Rothschild gave Ferrières to the Chancellerie des Universités de Paris.

G. H. Stokes designed a chateau at Pregny on the shores of Lake Geneva for Baron Adolphe de Rothschild, but George Myers and his pugnacious masons were not engaged to carry out the building.

Between 1860 and 1870, Baron Lionel, the eldest of the three Rothschild brothers, paid Messrs Myers & Sons well over £170,000, which is what it would have cost to build ten Mentmores.[14] It is difficult to discover exactly what work Myers undertook for Baron Lionel, as the receipts, kept in the Rothschild archives, reveal the name of the Rothschild concerned and the amount paid and only rarely the work carried out.

Lionel had inherited Gunnersbury Park in Middlesex from his father Nathan, who had bought it just before he died in 1836. It is known that Myers worked here altering, improving and extending the house from the late 1850s until he retired.

In 1857 Baron Lionel's beautiful elder daughter, Leonora, married her French cousin, Alphonse de Rothschild. The wedding took place at Gunnersbury Park and a large extension was built onto the dining room for the occasion. Myers' masons were probably employed to do this work, but the only evidence that could possibly bear this out is the account of the wedding in Judith Myers' scrapbook. The happy couple spent the first days of their honeymoon at Mentmore.

The Rothschilds owned several houses in Piccadilly and its hinterland and once again Myers was employed to 'alter, improve and modernise'. Then, in the 1860s, Myers built a mansion at Hyde Park Corner for Lionel. It was next door to the Duke of Wellington's Apsley House. Nos 147 and 148 Piccadilly had been demolished to make room for one magnificent 'palace'. By this time Baron Lionel de Rothschild was an M.P. and needed somewhere impressive to entertain his parliamentary and banking friends. It was to be one of the most beautiful houses in London. The landings and stairs were of marble, one room overlooking Piccadilly was 62 ft long and the two principal drawing rooms opened onto a wide balcony over the garden and a view of Hyde Park beyond. There was a lift to the upper and bedroom floors, while the maids slept in the garret and the menservants in the basement. In the basement also were the servants' hall, pantries, still room, wine cellar and strongroom. Under the terrace in the garden were the kitchens and sculleries. On 15 March 1862 the 130 men working on the mansion sat down to a dinner to celebrate, as was customary, the completion of the first stack of chimneys. Mr Bawden, Clerk of Works, presided, and Mr Gardener, Clerk of Accounts, filled the chair. Toasts were drunk to Baron de Rothschild and family, Nelson and Innes, the Architects, and to Messrs Myers and Sons.[15]

Baron Lionel was impatient to have his house finished. He complained that Myers was 'so slow'. This was on 17 November 1863. Myers promised that the work would be finished by 23 February or he would hand over £3,000. The Baron, writing to his youngest son at Cambridge, commented: 'what do you think of that?'.[16] Presumably the mansion was finished by the required date - Myers did not make rash promises.

In the autumn of that year Lionel's wife, Charlotte, went to Paris to look for chimney pieces and furniture for the new house. This time it was Myers who was impatient, looking forward to Charlotte's return to London so that he could consult her about alterations in the kitchen.[17] One would like to be able to report that when Myers had completed the alterations in the kitchen and Charlotte had chosen the furniture, the Lionel de Rothschilds were able to live happily ever after in their beautiful house. But even Rothschilds have quite mundane problems which disturb their lives from time to time. In October 1869, Charlotte writing to Leopold, her youngest son, reported that something had gone wrong 'under the library floor'[18] - she feared a colony of mice had taken up residence there - or perhaps it was RATS. What should she do ? She sent for Mr Myers who had already done his best. As it was not until the turn of the century that grids were fitted to Sir Joseph Bazalgette's new drainage system, for fifty years the rodents of London had free passage into many of London's most fashionable kitchens. At 148 Piccadilly, Myers had spread $1\frac{1}{2}$ ft of concrete over the cellar floors to prevent this from happening.[19] This had also been done at Marlborough House which was being renovated at the same time. This fantastic mansion was demolished in the 1960s to make way for the Park Lane dual carriageway.

The third generation of the Rothschild family, for whom Myers worked, was Ferdinand, a member of the Austrian branch. He came to London as a young man, fell in love with the city and with his cousin Evelina, Lionel's second daughter, whom he married in 1865. They lived at 143 Piccadilly, but the next year Evelina died in childbirth and the child died too. The broken-hearted Ferdinand never married again. In 1874 he built Waddesdon. It was too late for him to employ Myers, who had had a stroke in the spring of that year and died the next. But Myers had been the contractor for the Evelina Children's Hospital, built in 1868, by Ferdinand, in memory of his wife. He had thought of building a maternity hospital but changed his mind and built a children's hospital in Southwark Bridge Road, at that time one of the worst of London's slums. Florence Nightingale did not approve: she considered that it was much better for children to be in adult wards, so that the women in the other beds could look after them, which would take the women's minds off their own diseases.

George Myers was also entrusted with the building of the mausoleum where Evelina, and eventually Ferdinand, were

Figure 70   Baron Lionel de Rothschild's Piccadilly Mansion next door to Apsley House.

buried. Designed by Sir Matthew Digby Wyatt, in 1866, it is a listed building and was described by Pevsner as 'a domed building on a circular plan with Baroquizing Renaissance details, (mixed style)'. It stands in the Jewish Cemetery in Forest Gate which was opened in 1858. Inscribed on the wall of the mausoleum in English and in Hebrew is:

> She opened her lips with wisdom
> And in her speech was the law of kindness
> My darling wife.

> If I ascend up into heaven
> Thou art there
> If I lie down in the grave
> Behold I find thee
> Even there thy hand leads me
> And thy right hand supports me.

From the building of Mentmore until the end of his working life, Myers undertook all the English Rothschilds' major construction work. He knew that when he worked for the Rothschilds he would be paid regularly and according to contract. This made their patronage particularly important.

XII

Death of the Great Builder

In 1871 George Myers made his Will. The money which he left to his sons was theirs absolutely, but the money which he left to his wife and daughters was in trust. This was the manner in which a responsible Victorian father drew up his will. But Myers went further and stipulated that if Judith married again, her income from the trust would cease. He gave £4,000 to each daughter and also to his brother, Mark Myers, whose address was not given and about whom nothing is known, and he bequeathed the lease of the River Lee Ironworks to his three younger sons, who already owned the under lease. He left his 'books of drawings, sketches, prints, correspondence, manuscripts and writings' to be equally divided between David and Joseph. He realised that his papers would be of interest to posterity but most of them have been destroyed. To his eldest son David, he left his dining room table, his portrait in oils, the drawing he made of 'the reredos as restored in Beverley Minster' and other pictures, and Owen Jones' *Grammar of Ornament*. To his second son Joseph he left his watch, his ebony and painted cabinet representing the life of St Joseph (David already possessed the cabinet ornamented with stonemasons' tools which had caused such a rumpus at the Great Exhibition), and L. Haghe's drawing of the Medieval Court.

At the age of seventy, in June 1873, George Myers retired. His solicitor, Mr J. Travers Smith of 25 Throgmorton

Street, London, drew up the document which dissolved the partnership between Myers and his sons David and Joseph.

Until 1872 no written partnership had existed between Myers and his two sons. The document of dissolution refers to 'an agreement bearing date 6 April 1872', and then records the fact that George Myers, David Benson Myers and Joseph Patterson Myers had 'for some time' carried on business together. The document stipulated that the two sons were to pay their father the sum of £20,000 for his share of the business and guarantee him an annuity of £4,500 secured on the Trinity Bonded Warehouses on Tower Hill.

In 1873, David Benson Myers was forty-four and Joseph Patterson Myers forty-one. Both were married with numerous children and lived in large houses, one in fashionable Clapham and the other in Ealing. The three younger sons, George, John and Edward who ran the River Lee Ironworks and the two daughters, neither of whom was married, all lived with their parents.

A month before he retired, in May 1873, Myers applied to be admitted to the Freedom of the City of London, 'by redemption in the Company of Carpenters'. Redemption required the payment of a fee which at that date was 5s. 0d. The fee was required because Myers' father had not been a Freeman of the City, he himself had not been born in the City nor had he been apprenticed to a Freeman of the City. If he could have fulfilled any of these three conditions, Freedom would have been his of right.

But joinery and cabinet making are aspects of Myers' work which have not been discussed at any length. His pews, stalls, lecterns, pulpits and other furniture once adorned Pugin's churches, but much of it has now been replaced. An example of his early carving can be seen in the little church of St Lawrence at Tubney, near Oxford. Even here in this small country parish, the detail and painstaking skill of the craftsmen can be discerned. The lilies on the stall ends deserve a larger audience than this small church affords. Perhaps the most beautiful of all the Pugin/Myers church furniture is to be found in those which Pugin restored for his friends Dean Alford, Vicar of St Mary's, Wymeswold (1845) and for Mr Hornby, Rector of St Oswald's, Winwick (1847). It is interesting to visit these three churches and to study the progression in style.

Furniture made for the Sutton family church at West Tofts, in Norfolk has, as already stated, been moved for safe-keeping to the Garrison church in Colchester. The carving in this instance, though designed by Pugin, was carried out several years after his death. It is the most elaborate and skilfully executed of all Myers' surviving work, but it has been stripped and varnished and so looks new and rather brash.

Other churches where the carving, though not designed by Pugin, was executed in Myers' workshops and was much extolled in the press, were St Mary's, Beddington, architect Joseph Clarke, and St Paul's Langlebury, near St Alban's, where the architect, Henry Woodyer, was, like Pugin, known for designing furniture for his buildings in a 'package deal'.

A great quantity of secular furniture was manufactured in the Ordnance Wharf workshops, but this is far more difficult to locate. Myers is said to have made furniture for Colney Hatch which housed 1,250 patients and the staff to care for them. Furniture was provided for Sir Joseph Paxton's house at Sydenham and furniture was also required at Mentmore. There were bookcases for the Middle Temple Library and for Windsor Castle. Myers made the furniture for the Grange, Pugin's house in Ramsgate. This furniture is now in the Speaker's house in the House of Commons. At Horsted Place, he was not only the contractor for the house itself, but made the beautiful linen-fold panelling and doors, and also the oak staircase, a section of which was shown at the Great Exhibition. This is an elaborate piece of craftsmanship with heraldic birds sitting sentinel-like on the newels. The panels of the balustrade are carved with leaves encircling the crest and initials of the owner, Mr Barchard.

There is much discussion as to what part A.W.N. Pugin played in the design of this house and the decoration of its interior. The house is now a hotel and the pamphlet listing its attractions describes it as 'built in 1850 by George Myers' and, almost as an afterthought, the name of the architect, Samuel Daukes is mentioned. It appears that Myers had more to do with the form of this house than is usual with a contractor. It is tempting to think that as it was contemporaneous with the Great

Figure 71 Pugin drawing of the Madonna and Child with
instructions to Myers concerning the style
(note the ghostly angels).
Courtesy of the Royal Institute of British Architects.

Figure 72   The result photographed in the Petre Chantry, St George's Cathedral, Southwark, 1992.

Exhibition, Myers' thoughts were full of Pugin gothic, whence the Pugin influence. But at the same time he was also building, again with Daukes as architect, two very un-Pugin-like buildings, the asylums at Colney Hatch and Lincoln.

Pugin's great influence can be seen in the beautiful dining room table which Myers made for himself and which is now displayed in the Victoria and Albert museum. It has been suggested that this table was designed by Pugin, but in his Will, when he bequeathed it to his eldest son David, Myers stated firmly: 'My dining room table designed by me . . .'. In the centre, facing towards the head of the table are the initials 'G M' in gothic lettering nine inches high; circling round these initials is written, still in the most beautiful gothic:

> Waste ye not or spoil
> the products of the fruit of toil.

Under the table, where the stretchers meet, there is a small carving of St George killing the dragon, with a brass spear. This table was probably made in about 1852 when the family moved to a larger house in Clapham Road.

Perhaps now that he was about to retire, Myers planned to become an Alderman and take part in City affairs. He had led a full and busy life and from the early 1850s and probably before, had been deeply involved in the politics of the building industry.

Myers lived at a time of revolution in Europe and of riots, marches and strikes in Britain. The strikes were for higher wages and a shorter working day (the Nine Hour Movement). In the autumn of 1853 the workers had carried all before them due to the lack of a co-ordinated front on the part of the Master Builders. Myers, Jay and Cubitt capitulated and agreed to pay their masons an extra 6*d.* a day, that is 5*s.* 6*d.* for a ten hour day, and the labourers 3*s.* 4*d.* The men worked from 6.00 a.m. till 5.30 p.m. with $1^1/_2$ hrs off for meals. The other Master Builders had no option but to follow suit.[1]

Myers had put forward the arguments that the men would price themselves out of a job and that it would mean a substantial increase in building costs for the general public. The

Master Builders proceeded to hold frequent meetings and agreed amongst themselves that they must all pay the same wages.   At one of these meetings a Mr Turner said that he would not be willing to pay 5s. 6d. a day without reference to the ability of the man but added that whatever men like Mr Myers and Mr Lee did would 'rule the trade'.[2]   The next decade was dominated by recurring strikes for a nine hour working day.

The Revd. Mr Cadman of St George's in the east had been asked to advocate the cause of the 'nine hour movement' from the pulpit, but had declined to do so as he considered the workmen's claims unreasonable and impracticable.   Sporadic strikes had continued.   The men working for Messrs Trollope and Sons had struck in protest because a member of the deputation presenting a memorial about working hours had been discharged without notice.   The workmen employed by Messrs Grissell and Peto on the Houses of Parliament had also struck.

In August 1859 a deputation led by Mr Alderman Cubitt M.P.   and Mr Tite M.P., which included Myers and other well-known Master Builders, called on Sir G.C. Lewis, the Secretary of State for the Home Department.   Mr Tite introducing the deputation, explained that they considered it right that the Home Secretary should be informed of the circumstances of the dispute between the Builders and their operatives.   The deputation went on to say that they did not expect the Home Secretary or the Government to interfere or legislate, but that it must be obvious to everyone that the question of wages affected not only the Master Builders but also the public who employed them.   The Master Builders had requested some sign of support from the Government.   Sir G.C. Lewis had replied that it was the duty of Parliament to preserve order and see that all persons had the ability to make a free contract, but that the Government must be impartial and must not appear to favour any class of the community.[3]   The Chartists had not been forgotten.   Mr Ayrton M.P., who arrived late, suggested that more might be gained by conciliation and the exercise of moral influence than by closing the shops and locking out the men. At this point the delegation realised that there was nothing to be gained by talking to the Home Secretary, so they thanked him politely and withdrew.

It was in 1859 that the Central Association of Master Builders had been brought into existence, and, as might be expected, Myers was one of the leaders.[4] This new solidarity of the Master Builders resulted in the great lockout of 1859 referred to by Mr Ayrton, when 24,000 London building workers were on the streets for eight weeks and 'the nine hour movement' came to an end for the time being. The situation had become so serious that a Select Committee of the House of Commons was appointed to decide the best means of settling disputes between masters and operatives at which Sir Joseph Paxton, in giving evidence, quoted Myers' experience at Ferrières when the French masons suddenly went on strike without warning and without making their grievances known to their employer. Paxton was in favour of establishing some mechanism whereby grievances could be made known before a strike was resorted to. The Committee agreed with his advice and when their report was published on 15 May 1860 it concluded that the formation of Councils of Conciliation would promote a more friendly understanding between all parties, but added that the regulation of wages was a matter to be decided between masters and men.

Myers was involved in other strikes. There was a strike at Windsor Castle when he was putting up the temporary saloons at the West end of St George's Chapel in preparation for the marriage of the Prince of Wales and Princess Alexandra of Denmark in 1863. Myers had paid his joiners and carpenters 4s. 2d. a day, whereas the Windsor Castle carpenters were paid 4s. 6d., that is, 8% more. He had to increase the pay of his men. One would think that he would have learnt his lesson at Ferrières.[5] On that occasion also he was compelled to pay the men more before they would return.

At about this time, a letter to *The Builder*,[6] signed 'A Builder's Son', pointed out that Master Builders worked fifteen or sixteen hours a day and that he and his father rose at 4.45 a.m. and started work. They often did not finish their estimates, planning and writing till 10.00 or 10.30 in the evening. The builder's son went on to explain that the Master

Masons had the anxieties associated with large contracts and the thought of Saturday afternoon coming round when they might be short of cash to pay their men. Some of their employers were not particular about paying their debts. The letter ended with the query: 'what would the men think of the hours of a builder's clerk ?'.

Though Myers had no sympathy with the strikers, he had been a leading member of builders charities such as the Provident Institution of Builders' Foremen, established for the relief of 'decayed members, widows and orphans'; in 1853 he had been chairman of the Operative Masons' Benefit Society and always gave generously to their charities: he supported the Architectural Museum in Cannon Row, established in 1853. Its object was 'to enable the working man who cannot go in his working dress to museums contained in palaces and marble halls', to study architecture in an atmosphere where he could feel more at home. He urged upon his masons the importance of education so that they would be able to 'carry out the spirit of the drawing rather than be content with a mere mechanical execution'.[7] And every year there was the Annual Dinner of Messrs Myers' Work People. On one occasion a press report described how Myers and a numerous assemblage of his work people dined together in the Crown Hotel, Loughton in celebration of their annual holiday, and how Mr Watt, one of the stewards, announced that Mr Myers had contributed £30 towards the outing and then eulogised him as a generous employer. It was then the custom for Myers to make a speech in which he thanked the other speakers for their compliments. He went on to say how much satisfaction he gained from the fact that many of the men who had trained in his establishment were now doing well. Being a man of his time, he felt it his duty to do a little moralising and added that those who were not doing so well should, however, enjoy a large amount of happiness in the situation in which they found themselves. When the toasts and speeches were over, the rest of the day was spent in playing cricket, quoits, racing and other sports. The outing terminated when the bell announced the departure of the last train.

Myers travelled ceaselessly by coach, train, boat, gig and brougham. His brougham one day collided with a dray which was damaged beyond repair. The driver of the dray took him to court where Myers accused the other man of being 'drunkish'. But to no avail, as damages were awarded against him. At the time of the accident, Myers was probably hurrying to visit a building site.[8]   During the 1860s Messrs Myers sometimes had eleven or twelve contracts in hand at one time, many of the buildings built with stone from their own quarries in Wiltshire.   In 1864, perhaps planning for his retirement, Myers bought and developed the extensive estate in Clapham that had once belonged to Florence Nightingale's great-grandfather[9] and more recently to Mr Allnutt, the wine merchant and art collector, who had died in 1863.

When Myers retired in 1873, his sons inherited a thriving family business. But looking behind the scenes it would seem that towards the end of the sixties, the firm was running down. It is not clear whether this was policy or accident. In 1866 Myers had sold his quarries at Boxhill, Kingsdown and Pickwick, and the plant that went with them, to the Bath Stone Company.[10] During the year before Myers' retirement Messrs Myers & Sons tendered twenty times and gained only one contract, which was to build 'a Porter's Lodge etc. at Wandsworth Union' for £1,100, while their other (unsuccessful) tenders were amongst the most highly priced of those listed, as if Myers had no wish to carry out the work, at least not at a competitive price. This comment should be seen in the light of data going back over twenty-five years, concerning Myers' success in bidding by competitive tender. In October 1873, three months after Myers retired, for the first time in nearly thirty years, the name of Messrs Myers & Sons did not appear in *The Builder's* list of tenders. It was never to do so again.

Work in progress, when Myers died, included the Provident Institute Society Bank in St Martin's Lane, Hall Place in Kent, and work to the value of £8,000 for various members of the Rothschild family. Myers does not appear to have been driving his sons, or even encouraging them, to undertake more work. As far as is known his health was good until about a year before he died, and he was accustomed to getting his own way.

There are many instances of building committees deciding that: 'it would be as well to accede to Mr Myers' demands'. Could he have had enough of working round the clock and wished his sons to have a leisurely and more 'gentlemanly' existence?

This great Victorian contractor had been intimately involved in many of the historic events which took place during his lifetime and in the course of his work he came to know numerous figures mentioned in the history books.

The Religious Revival, with the clamour to restore the old medieval churches and Catholic Emancipation, provided major components of his livelihood. He built the monument to William Wilberforce in Hull in the year of the anti- slavetrader's death; he built three of the asylums which conformed with the new lunacy laws with which Lord Shaftesbury's name is always associated; he built several hospitals including the Herbert Hospital whose plans were approved by Florence Nightingale and Sidney Herbert; he sent prefabricated huts to the war zone in the Crimea and carried out vast contracts for the Army at home. He worked for the Royal Family on many occasions, building pavilions for their weddings and funerals, and he enlarged the King Henry VIIth Library at Windsor as well as the adjoining Queen Anne's Closet, installing bookcases to provide room for more than a thousand volumes. Both the Queen and Prince Consort spent much time laying foundation stones for his spectacular public buildings, and at Aldershot Myers had pegged out both the Royal Pavilion and the Prince Consort's Library under Prince Albert's personal direction.

In the City of London he built offices, banks and warehouses for the new breed of City merchants, and he built their country houses too. In his later years it would have been impossible for him to have driven through the streets of London without passing one of his own buildings and most of the counties of England could display at least one example of his work. His warehouses encircled Tower Hill overlooking the Tower itself and, standing beside Samuel Wyatt's Trinity House, they played their part in the expansion and increasing prosperity of the City of London. Many of these buildings, despite wars and vandalism, can still be seen today.[11] There was great variety in Myers' contracts, and those who think of

Figure 73　George Myers in the summer of 1874, after his stroke, in his Clapham garden, with his second wife, Judith, and their five surviving children.
Courtesy of Malcolm Lysaght of Kilmacoom, County Cork.

Figure 74   Norwood Cemetery, 1849.

him only as 'Pugin's Builder' fail to appreciate the versatility of all that he accomplished. It has been said that, without Myers, Pugin's buildings would not have stood up. Pugin's drawings of etherial churches enchant, but so often the reality fails to realize expectations. His polemical writings inspired religious zeal and often rage in his readers. He had time to write and travel because Myers was in charge of his building sites all over the country. In January 1852 Myers wrote to Mr Hobson, churchwarden of St Mary's Beverley,

> I beg to inform you, that I intend being at St Marie's Church, Beverley on Friday morning and intend remaining there on that day and on Saturday, so that I shall be prepared to meet the Revd. Mr Sands and the churchwardens any time they please to fix during the two days.

The same pattern of visits was followed all over the country with Myers inspecting the work and listening to complaints and, one hopes, expressions of praise and satisfaction from his employers and work force.

It is difficult to imagine Pugin's working life without George Myers. They were true friends, and the sense of affinity and understanding which existed between these two remarkable people was not to occur again in Myers' lifetime. He would still, without Pugin, have been one of the great builders of the Victorian age - in fact his most spectacular works were carried out for other architects, but without the epithet connecting him with Pugin, his name would probably have fallen into oblivion like those of so many of his fellow contractors.

Myers gained an artist's satisfaction from the fulfilment of his contracts. Monetary gain was never his prime objective. He was comfortably off, but his wealth did not compare with the large sums accumulated by other Master Builders of the day. At Colney Hatch, he had fitted up the committee room 'very sumptuously' at his own expense,[12] and at Beverley he accepted a reduced offer in settlement of his account because the churchwardens had on all occasions treated him with great kindness and it is said that with his last breath he cancelled the large debt still owed to him by St George's Catholic Cathedral in Southwark . He died on 25 January 1875. He had had a severe stroke in March 1874 and the immediate cause of death, according to his death certificate was 'exhaustion'. He was buried in West Norwood Cemetery.

It is a strange coincidence that the lease of Ordnance Wharf also came to an end in 1875 and stranger still that there is no mention of Myers & Sons in the trade directories for 1876. The firm of Myers & Sons had ceased to exist.

Notes and References

Chapter I

1.   H.M. Sinclair Archive, Sutton Courtenay, Oxon.: Family Tree compiled by Rosalie Sinclair, née Jackson, granddaughter of George Myers.
2.   Mogg, Edward, *Patterson's Roads*, 18th edn (London, 1826) p. 465.
3.   Scott, Sir G.G., *Recollections Personal and Professional* (London, 1879) pp. 88-9.
4.   Comins, William, Day Book. Beverley Public Library: B/746R Y/726.5/BEV.
5.   Ibid.
6.   Brown, Philip, *Old Beverley* (East Yorkshire Local History Society, 1983) note 16.
7.   HCAO, PE1/773.

Note: The load of stone would probably have travelled in a flat bottomed boat known as a *Humber Keel* via the rivers Ouse, Humber and Hull to Beverley. The 'flush of water for one day' referred to by Archbell, was an expedient for improving the navigation of rivers by generating an artificial flood by opening sluice gates upstream.

8.   HCAO, PE 158, temporary no. 62.
9.   HCRO, ICS 167.
10.   Midland Bank Archives: Hull Banking Company Minute Book 48/2 etc., 16 December 1844.
11.   CERC, BC 59/131.
12.   HCAO, PE 158, temporary nos. 27, 28, etc.
13.   Powell, J.H., 'Pugin in his Home' (Westminster Diocesan Archives: Mss Sec. 21/491), pp. 37/67.
14.   HCAO, PE 158, temporary no. 62.
15.   *Hull Packet and East Riding Times* (10 December 1845).
16.   HCAO, Holy Trinity, Hull, Order Book no. 3, pp. 508-9.
17.   Note: The churchwardens did not mention in their letter that in 1846, their 500 year old cemetery, having risen several feet above ground level, had been condemned as a 'cholera manufactory', and that an epidemic had been predicted. In 1849 the prediction came about, and over 2,000 local people died of cholera. The churchwardens, with their pestilential graveyard were held to blame.

See *Hull Packet and East Riding Times*: 7 September 1849 and 9 September 1850, etc.
18.   Stephenson's *Directory of Hull* (1842) p. 302.   The Memorial has now been moved to Wilberforce Drive near the Guildhall and Law Courts.
19.   LRO, G/7/32/1; DE 418/33.
20.   Midland Bank Archives: Hull Banking Company Minute Book, 13 March 1843.
21.   Stanton, Phoebe,   *Pugin* (London: Thames and Hudson, 1971) p. 43.
22.   *Orthodox Journal* vol. 7 (21 July 1838) pp. 37-8.

Chapter II

1.   *The Builder* (1861) p. 567.
2.   Trappes-Lomax, M.,   *Pugin: A Medieval Victorian* (London: Sheed and Ward, 1932) p. 187.
3.   Crace Letters: RIBA, ref 1/6/17.
4.   Crace Letters: RIBA, ref 1/7/58.
5.   Pugin MS 528 (Magdalen College, Oxford).
6.   George Ruddock Myers was born at 9 Laurie Terrace, St George's Road, London on 1 January 1843.
7.   Baptismal Records at St George's Catholic Cathedral, Southwark, London.
8.   St George's Catholic Cathedral, Southwark was not built as a Cathedral: St Chad's, Birmingham was.   St Mary's, Newcastle, St Barnabas, Nottingham, St George's, Southwark and St Philip Howard's, Arundel, built as churches by Myers, are now cathedrals and are referred to as such in the text to simplify identification.
9.   Midland Bank Archives: Hull Banking Company Minute Book 48/2, 29 December 1843, 25 January 1845.
10.   Birmingham R.C. Archdiocesan Archives: B790.
11.   O'Brien, Terence,   *Education and Care of Workhouse Children in some Lancashire Poor Law Unions 1834-1930* (Manchester University M.Ed., 1975).
12.   HCAO,   PE 158, temporary no. 62.
13.   PRO, B6 118   County District General Docket Book: A-Z no. 1 (October 1849-December 1857).
14.   H.M. Sinclair Archive, Sutton Courtenay, Oxon.   Box 3: both letters.
15.   Midland Bank Archives: Hull Banking Company Minute Book J9, 1855.

16. Ibid.
17. HL, Box 1845.
18. Atterbury, Paul, *The Story of Minton* (In house publisher: 1978) explains that the word 'encaustic' comes from the Greek word meaning 'burnt in'. Minton's encaustic tiles were made in moulds at the bottom of which was a raised design. When the tiles were removed from the moulds, the design was indented in the clay. The tile maker then poured a thin liquid clay (slip) of a different colour into the depression. This was left to dry for twenty-four hours before scraping, tidying and further drying and processing.
19. HL, Box 1847.
20. Letters: Minet Library, Lambeth, London.
21. Ibid.
22. Legal document listing property of David and Joseph Myers at death of David in 1888 (held by Messrs Travers Smith, London, solicitors).
23. *Illustrated London News* (9 February 1850) p. 95.
24. U.K. Census returns, 1871.
25. HL, Box 1849.
26. Ibid.
27. AW, p. 75 note 39. R.W. Willson, brother of E.J. Willson of Lincoln, friend of the Pugin family and well-known to Myers.
28. AW, p. 108, letter 36; also MFT drawings.
29. This memorial to the two Connelly children, Marie Magdalene, who died as an infant and John Henry, who died aged $2^1/_2$ as a result of falling into a vat of boiling maple syrup, is believed to be the only occasion on which Pugin's work travelled to the USA.
The Connelly family's story is an extraordinary one. The Rev. Pierce and Cornelia Connelly, an Episcopalian couple living in Louisiana, converted to Catholicism. Quite soon he decided that he wished to become a priest and, despite the fact that they had several children, instructed his wife to become a nun. This she did. (It is indeed strange that this was allowed by the Catholic Church.) Cornelia became a devout nun and was invited by Cardinal Wiseman to travel to England to found an order of teaching nuns - the Society of the Holy Child Jesus, now a world-wide teaching order. Pierce Connelly before long decided that he no longer wished to be a Catholic and in 1851 sued his wife for restitution of conjugal rights. Civil law as well as canon law was on her side and he did not succeed.
See *Cornelia Connelly 1809-1879* by 'a Religious' (London: Longmans, Green and Co, date not known).
30. AW, p. 80, note 22.

31. MFT drawings.
32. Powell, J.H., 'Pugin in his Home' (Westminster Diocesan Archives: Mss Sec. 21/491).
33. A 'string course' is an architectural term for a continuous horizontal band set in the surface of an exterior wall or projecting from it and usually moulded.
34. Mould and Pattern Making information from Spretson, N.E., *A Practical Treatise on Casting and Founding* (London and New York: E. and F.N. Spon, 1878).
35. HL, Box 1847.
36. Ibid.
37. *Burke's Peerage and Baronetage*, 1848: p. 558.
38. RIBA, SC/NS1/84.
39. Girouard, M., 'Lismore Castle', *Country Life*, p. 391, (1964).
40. Letter from Kean, R.F., St Mary's Cathedral, Sydney, Australia.
41. Information about happenings at Ordnance Wharf from Myers' letters to Hardman.
42. *Illustrated London News* (9 February 1850) p. 95.
43. Crace letters: RIBA, ref 1/7/11.
44. *The Builder* (3 August 1867), pp. 561-2; 10 August 1867, pp. 587-8.

Chapter III

1. PRO, Work 11/6 174189.
2. HL, Box 1847.
3. H.M. Sinclair Archives, Sutton Courtenay, Oxon.: Box 3. This letter was copied into the Minutes of the Committee of Visitors, Colney Hatch Asylum: GLRO, vol. II, p. 77.
4. Midleton Papers: Guildford Muniment Room: 1248/33/9.
5. Ibid. 1248/33/43.
6. Ibid. 1248/33/19.
7. Ibid. 145 Box 67 bundle 1.
8. Ibid. 145/39c, 145/91/1d, etc.
9. General information about the Drummond family comes from: Walmesley, R. Charles, *Albury Park and the Old Parish Church of Albury* (London: Country Houses Association, 1986).
10. Drummond Papers: Alnwick Castle, Northumberland: C/17/3.
11. Ibid. C/17/6.
12. Ibid. C/17/42.

13. Ibid. C/17/88.

14. Ibid. C/17/131.

15. HL, Box 1848. P.J. Burton, Sacristan at St George's Catholic Cathedral, Southwark, writing to Hardman, 5 May 1848.

16. AW, p. 86, note 40.

17. Pugin MS 528, letters 147 and 153 (Magdalen College, Oxford).

18. Ibid. letter 57.

19. Powell, J.H., 'Pugin in his Home', (Westminster Diocesan Archives, Mss Sec. 21/491).

20. Pugin MS 528, letters 53 and 64 (Magdalen College, Oxford).

21. Hobhouse, Hermione, *Prince Albert - His Life and Works* (London: Hamish Hamilton, 1983) p. 97.

22. PRO, Works 6/126/1, PFF/9293.

23. There had been another 'row' at the Exhibition on 20 March, (see Pugin's diary for that day). Arthur Kinnard and Lord Ashley saw the Great Rood from Ware hung high above the Medieval Court and were alarmed that a 'Popish Chapel' was being erected. Ref. Alexandra Wedgwood, personal communication.

24. Crace letters: RIBA, ref 1/8/23.

25. HL, Box 1851, 25 May.

26. Lord Macaulay's *Life and Letters*:   quoted in Jennings, H., *Pandaemonium 1660-1886* (London: André Deutsch, 1985) p. 258.

27. Crace letters: RIBA ref 1/8/35 a. and b.

28. HL, Box 1851.

29. Sykes, Christopher,   *Two Studies in Virtue* (London: Collins, 1953) p. 67.

30. Jennings, p. 257. See note 26 above.

31. The entry in the Royal Academy Exhibition Catalogue 1769-1904, vol. V, Lawrence to Nye, compiled by Algernon Graves is as follows: 'Myers, G. Painter. Ordnance Wharf. 1853, 1188 Interior of the Medieval Court, great Exhibition 1851, etc.'

32. This cutting came from JMS. Judith Myers usually gave the name of the newspaper concerned, but on this occasion she did not.

Chapter IV

1   Gwynn, Denis, *Lord Shrewsbury and the Catholic Revival*, (London: Hollis and Carter, 1946) p. XII.

2.   Ibid. p. 73.

3.   Trappes-Lomax, M.,   *Pugin, a Medieval Victorian* (London: Sheed and Ward, 1932) pp. 103, 106.

4.   Champ, Judith: *The Turbulent Career of Thomas McDonnell* (Southamption: Recusant History, vol.18, 1987) p. 289.

5.   Archdiocese of Birmingham: letters.

6.   AW, p. 78, note 20.

7.   Newcastle RO, 30 letters: 2988/AWP 1-30.

8.   See note 3, pp. 207-8.

9.   St George's R.C. Cathedral, Southwark: all information concerning the building of the Cathedral comes from the Pugin MSS in Southwark Cathedral Archive Library, unless otherwise indicated.

10.   Brogan, Bernard,   *The Great Link* (London: Burns and Oates, 1948).

11.   HL, Box 1849.

12.   HL, Box 1846.

13   Clifton, Michael, *The Quiet Negotiator* (Liverpool: Print Origination, 1990). Fr Clifton puts the debt at: 'over £5,000'.

14.   Gifford, J., *The Buildings of Scotland - Edinburgh* (London: Penguin Books, 1984). See also the RIAS Collection, Edinburgh: doc. 747.

15.   HL, Box 1852.

16.   Ibid.

17.   HL, Boxes 1849, 1852.

18.   Pugin MS 528, letter 59 (Magdalen College, Oxford).

19.   St Oswald's Church, Winwick, Cheshire. Information about the building of this church comes from letters kept in the vestry, photocopies of which may be found in the Warrington Archive Library.

20.   *Wymeswold Church and Dean Alford* (church pamphlet, no author or publisher).

21.   HL, Box 1851.

22.   HL, Box 1852.

23.   HL, Box 1852.

24.   HL, Box 1847.

25.   HL, Box 1852.

26.   HL, Box 1852.

27.   Plans at Pantasaph Friary. Other information: *The History of Pantasaph* (Fr Paschal Burlinson, O.F.M. Cap.Min.Prov., 1975).

28.   JMS. There is a report of the Trial in 1854 of John James and Geo. Gawan indicted for stealing stone, etc. from St Mary's, Beverley. Mr P. Thompson, appearing for the prosecution, stated that the restoration work began in 1844, ceased in 1847 for want of funds, but

was resumed in 1849. The report probably appeared in the local press.

29. HCAO, Beverley: PE 1/836. St Mary's Church, Beverley: all information comes from the Pugin MS. in the Humberside County Archive Office unless otherwise indicated. Any church named 'St Mary's' was invariably referred to by Pugin as 'St Marie's'. Presumably he thought it sounded Medieval. Myers sometimes imitated him.

Chapter V

1. AW, letter 121, p. 102.
2. Drummond Papers (Northumberland, Alnwick Castle) C/17/42.
3. Pugin MS: letter 172 (Magdalen College, Oxford)
4. Powell, J.H., *loc. cit.*
5. Bethlem Archives, Beckenham, Kent: CB/56, Male, Morison (1852) p. 23.
6. Bethlem Archives:
    a) Myers' contract (28 March 1854).
    b) Alldridge Patricia, 'The Bethlem Historical Museum' (1976).
7. Wedgwood, Alexandra, RIBA Drawings Collection (Greg International, 1977) p. 117.
8. Watkin, D.J. (ed.), *Sales Catalogues of Libraries of Eminent Persons* (Mansell & Southeby, Parke-Bernet Publications, 1972) vol. 4, pp. 239-83.
9. Westminster City Libraries: Archive Dept. E 3360/4.
10. See note 6. above.
11. Rothschild Archive, London: Ledge 1/2/11 2-11, p. 92.
12. HL, Boxes 1855, 1856.

Chapter VI

1. HL, Box 1849.
2. Summerson, Sir John, *The London Building World of the Eighteen Sixties* (London: Thames and Hudson, 1973) p. 9.
3. Ibid p. 10.
4. Ibid p. 11.
5. CLRO, CL Deeds Box 119A no. 76.

6.   Hobhouse, H., *Thomas Cubitt, Master Builder* (London: Macmillan, 1971) p. 8. See also JMS.
7.   *Bath Herald* (23 October 1861).
8.   HL, different boxes.
9.   Hobhouse, H., p. 8.
10.   Chatsworth Archives: Paxton Group, no.1265.
11.   *The Builder* (23 July 1870) p. 585.
12.   County Record Office, Trowbridge, Box Rate Book, 1852.
13.   *The Bath and Cheltenham Gazette* (19 November 1851) p. 3.
14.   Pugin MS 528 (Magdalen College, Oxford).
15.   JMS.
16.   Pollard, David: Bath Stone Quarry Museum, Corsham, Wilts.
17.   *The Builder* (1858) p. 652.
18.   PRO, 113008 WORK 14/2/1.
19.   Pugin MS (unclassified): Shrewsbury Diocesan Archives.

Chapter VII

1.   CERC, file 17376, 65/129, etc.
2.   CERC, file 59/131.
3.   *The Times* (4 August 1990).
4.   Maunsel, Revd John and Peter Murray, *History and Description of St Joseph's Church, Avon Dassett* (Published by the parish, 1986).
5.   HRO, 37M 82W/33, etc.
6.   NRO, PD55/21 and Tricker, Roy, *History and Guide* (privately published 1987).
7.   Stanton, Phoebe, p.138. .
8.   Memorial Plaque on church wall, and Revd A.J. Rose, B.D., Senior Chaplain, HQ 19th Inf Brigade, Goojerat Barracks, Colchester: personal communication.
9.   Howell, Peter, *Eton Parish Church of St John the Evangelist* Publication 12 (London: The Victorian Society, 1987).
10.   CERC, file 17806.
11.   CERC, file 1 30862/2.
12.   HL, Box 1846.
13.   *The Builder* (1861) p. 560.
14.   Somerville, Peter, *A Guide to the Queen's Chapel of the Savoy* (Parish publication, 1977). See also *The Builder* (1866), pp. 117-19.
15.   Diamond, A.S., *The Building of a Synagogue* (West London Synagogue of British Jews, 1989) p. 7.
16.   CERC, file 15714.

17. GLRO, p. 93/CTC 1/104.
18. *Guide to the Cathedral of Our Lady and St Philip Howard* (Arundel, Parish publication, 1985).

Chapter VIII

1. Of the many contracts undertaken by George Myers, the Lunatic Asylums are the best documented. The minute books of the visiting Justices of the Peace (Magistrates) still exist and it is from these that most of the information in this chapter has been obtained.
The location of the minute books is as follows:-
   (a) Colney Hatch Asylum, (now 'Friern Barnet Hospital'): GLRO, MA/RS, 1/53-102.
   (b) Bracebridge Asylum: Lincolnshire RO, KQS Bracebridge Asylum.
   (c) Essex County Asylum: ERO, Q/ALC4.
2. PRO, MH 51/49.
3. *The Builder* (1847) p. 463.
4. The list of those who provided testimonials when George Myers won the contract to build the Colney Hatch Asylum in 1848 is given below. Only the letters of Lord Shrewsbury and Pugin, which are quoted were copied into the minute book, vol.2, p.77.
   (a) The Earl of Shrewsbury.
   (b) A.W.N. Pugin.
   (c) Revd Sir George Glyn, Bart., Rector of Ewell, Surrey. Myers built the new parish church of St Mary the Virgin, Ewell in 1847.
   (d) Ambrose Phillipps de Lisle Esq., Pugin's friend for whom Myers worked on many occasions.
   (e) Michael Forristall Esq., secretary to the building committee at St George's Catholic Cathedral, Southwark.
   (f) G.G. Scott Esq. (later Sir George Gilbert Scott), architect, of 20 Spring Gardens, London.
   (g) Revd George Proctor, D.D., Rector of St Mary the Virgin, Monken Hadley, Middlesex. Myers restored his church in 1848.
   (h) Revd John Bloxam of Magdalen College Oxford. Myers built the College Gateway in 1842.
   (i) Revd Richard Conway of St Nicholas Church, Rochester. No building work done for him by Myers has been discovered.
   (j) Revd James Hamilton of Beddington, Croydon. Myers restored his church, St Mary the Virgin in the 1840s.

(k)   Henry R. Bagshawe, Barrister of the Middle Temple of 2, New Square, Lincoln's Inn. Friend of Cardinal Wiseman and a member of the St Mary's, Derby, building committee. He came of a Derbyshire family.

(l)   Revd James Hornby. Myers restored his church, St Oswald's, Winwick in 1847-50.

(m)   Captain Washington Hibbert. Myers enlarged his house and built St Marie's, Rugby for him in the 1840s

(n)   Thomas Gabriel and Sons, of New Barge House, Commercial Road, Lambeth. A timber merchant who supplied Myers with wood.

(o)   John Locke and Co., St Peter's Chambers, Cornhill and Shad Thames, about whom nothing has been discovered.

The two testimonial letters referred to above were as follows:

a. Alton Towers: 11 November 1848

Sir,

I have great pleasure in complying with your request, for I can confidently affirm that all the works you have executed for me and all those I have known you to execute for others have been done with the utmost punctuality and in the most workmanlike style, and whilst I speak from my own knowledge and observation I can give infinitely greater weight to my testimony by knowing it to be more than fully corroborated by Mr Pugin.

> I remain Sir
> Your well wisher
> Shrewsbury

Mr George Myers
Builder Etc.

b. London: Nov 8th, 1848

Gentlemen,
Mr Myers having informed me that you are desirous of knowing my opinion on his capabilities, I beg to

state that I have employed him in the erection of my churches and other buildings for upward of twelve years, during which time he has not only given me the greatest satisfaction as a skilful and practical builder but I entertain so high an opinion of his integrity that I would not undertake any great work without stipulating for his engagement to carry out the same, as a sure means of ensuring a satisfactory result.

I am Gentlemen
Your Obedient Servant
A.W.N. Pugin

5.   *The Times* (2 July, 1851).
6.   Minutes of meeting held on 13 August, 1856 at Colney Hatch.
7.   Minute book 12, p. 130, Colney Hatch.
8.   Minutes of meeting held on 6 January, 1857 at Colney Hatch.
9.   24 November, 1857: Minute book 14, p. 29, Colney Hatch.
10. Ibid.
11. DNB, vol. 8, p. 379.
12. *The Builder* (1858) p. 831-2.
13. *The Builder* (1858) p. 832.
14. Special Report of the Committee of Visitors entitled 'Action Brought against Mr S.W.Daukes, Architect' (1859). GLRO: MA/RS/1/65. This printed book of 148 pages and numerous diagrams, describes the action taken against Daukes, whose 'trial' was stopped after three days when the plaintiff withdrew without hearing the defence witnesses. This publication is a covering exercise by the Committee, excusing themselves from indulging in a costly exercise at public expense.

Chapter IX

1.   Cole, Col. Howard N.,   *The Story of Aldershot* (Aldershot: Southern Books, 1980), p. 29.
2.   Murray, Maj. Gen. T.A.L., *United Services Magazine*, no. 782, p. 324.
3.   Reed, Brig. W.J., Aldershot Military Museum, Director.
4.   PRO, WO 44 572.
5.   Ibid.

6.   Much of the information concerning the building of the camp and barracks at Aldershot comes from *The Times* and other newspaper cuttings in JMS. Dates are not always recorded.

7.   PRO, 162 498 WO 44/611.

8.   Jenkinson, Sally, *The Ash Railway*, Ash Library ref 942. 21 Ash (p).

9.   JMS.

10.   *The Times* (14 April, 1855).

11.   *The Times* (9 May, 1855).

12.   Cole, Col. Howard N. Ibid., p. 38.

13.   Reed, Brig. W.J.: see note 3.

14.   PRO, T1/6105 B, 162498: letter from the War Office to the Treasury.

15.   Ibid. Letter from the Treasury to the War Office.

16.   JMS.

17.   SL, vol 38 (1975) pp. 86-9.

18.   Royal Archives, Windsor Castle: E38. Also P. Vickers, Librarian at Prince Consort's Library, Aldershot.

19.   Adams, T, Lt. Col., *The Royal Garrison Church, Aldershot* (Aldershot Military Historical Trust, 1979).

20.   *The Builder* (1856) p. 457.

21.   Woodham-Smith, C., *Florence Nightingale* (London: Reprint Society, 1952) p. 226.

22.   Ibid.

23.   Godwin-Austin, Brevet-Major A.R., *The Staff and the Staff College* (London: Constable, 1927) p. 120.

24.   *The Dictionary of National Biography*, vol. XVII (Oxford University Press, 1963-4), p. 881.

25.   RMAS Collection, Sandhurst, Camberley: letter book 46, letter 55. See also *The Times*, 16 October 1861.

26.   PRO, WO 78/2893. Brigadier Reed points out that this letter has been 'doctored' some time in the last 130 years. Under the broad arrow the initials are really 'I.G.F.' meaning 'Inspector General of Fabrications'.

27.   PRO, T1/6410 B 151406.

28.   *The Builder.* 1865, p. 184.

29.   PRO, T1/6513B 151406.

30.   *The Builder* (1865) p. 184.

31.   *London Journal* (1857) p. 392.

Chapter X

1   SL, vol 40 p. 270.
2.   Pearce, David, *London Mansions* (London: B.T.Batsford Ltd, London, 1986) p. 134.
3.   *The Builder* (1959) p. 348 et seq.
4.   Ibid.
5.   Charges at the Westminster Palace Hotel:

Single Room:	3*s*.0*d*
Dressing room en suite:	42*s*.0*d*
Hip bath in bedroom:	6*d*
Bath in bathroom:	1*s*.6*d*

Source: Souvenir Pamphlet, 1897. Westminster Library: 647, 94421.
6.   SL, vol 34 (1966) p. 435.
7.   *The Art Journal* (1851), p. 138.
8.   Holmes, F.M., *Exeter Hall and its Associations* (London: Hodder and Stoughton, 1881).
9.   *Building News* (1861) p. 138.
10.   *The Builder* (1859) p. 600 and many newspaper cuttings in JMS.
11.   PRO, 113008 WORK 14/2/3, etc.
12.   *The Builder* (1864) p. 281.
13.   CLRO, Comt CL Deeds box 119A, no. 67; Arch. Plans, G/MH/4-9 and 16, G/MH/44 and 45.
14.   Ibid.
15.   *The Builder* (1863) pp. 124, 181.
16.   *Illustrated London News* (1863) p. 678.
17.   CLRO, Printed Reports, A/103L and A/112D
18.   CLRO, Guildhall Improvements Committee Minutes 7 May 1867 *et seq.*
19.   See note 17
20.   GL manuscript 21,051 and Jamison, Catherine, *The History of the Royal Hospital of St Katherine by the Tower of London* (Oxford University Press, 1952).
21.   See note 20.
22.   The Contractors were 'Culverin Consortium Ltd' of London.

Chapter XI

1.   HL, Box 1855.
2.   HL, Box 1847.

3.   *The Builder* (1857) p. 738-41.
4.   Wainwright, Clive, *The Romantic Interior* (New Haven and London: The Yale University Press, 1989) p. 182.
5.   Allibone, Dr Jill, 'Escaping the City. The Rothschilds in the Vale of Aylesbury', *Country Life*, 12 February 1989, p. 80.
6.   Allibone, Dr Jill, *George Devey* (Cambridge: Lutterworth Press, 1991) p. 158.
7.   Rothschild Archive, London: XII/41/1.
8.   Markham Papers, Chatsworth. Information concerning Paxton's letters to his wife during the 1850s, kindly provided by John Kenworthy-Browne.
9.   Parliamentary Select Committee on 'Masters and Operatives' p. 96 548, British Library (24 April, 1860).
10.   Markham Papers, Chatsworth.
11.   Ibid.
12.   H.M. Sinclair Archive: Sutton Courtenay, Oxon. Box 3; and Archives de la Province, 9 Rue des Feuillants, F-86000 Poitiers, (list of past pupils).
13.   *Illustrated London News* (3 January 1863) p. 11.
14.   Rothschild Archive, London: Rothschild ledgers.
15.   *The Builder* (22 March 1862) p. 213.
16.   Rothschild Archive, London: RFamC/4/243.
17.   Rothschild Archive, London: RFamC/4/73 and 76.
18.   Rothschild Archive, London: RFam C/21.
19.   *The Builder* (1862) p. 786.

Chapter XII

1.   *The Builder* (1853) p. 566.
2.   Ibid. (1859) p. 285.
3.   Ibid. (1859) p. 540.
4.   Summerson, Sir John, *The London Building World of the Eighteen-Sixties* (London: Thames and Hudson, 1873), p.11.
5.   Minutes of evidence taken before the Parliamentary Select Committee on 'Masters and Operatives', Sir Joseph Paxton's evidence: 24 April 1860, p. 96 548.
6.   *The Builder* (1859) p. 319.
7.   JMS.
8.   JMS.
9.   Smith, E.E., *Clapham* (Lambeth: London Borough of Lambeth, 1976) p. 71.

10. *The Builder* (1866) p. 767.
11. Almost every Victorian Society Annual during the last few years, under the heading 'Buildings in Peril', has listed at least one of George Myers' buildings under threat, for example: The Royal Herbert Hospital, Woolwich (1989) p. 50.
12. *The Times* (2 July, 1851).

Select Bibliography

There are very few published sources concerning George Myers, the Builder; the following are the most important and also give background information.
Other sources are indicated in the References and Notes.

Aldrich, Megan (ed.), *The Craces; Royal Decorators 1768-1899* (John Murray, The Royal Pavilion, Art Gallery and Museums, Brighton, 1990).

Allibone, Jill, *Anthony Salvin* (1987) and *George Devey* (1991) (Cambridge: Lutterworth Press).

Belcher, Margaret, *A.W.N. Pugin, An Annotated Critical Biography* (London & New York: Mansell Publishers Ltd, 1987).

Clifton-Taylor, Alec, *The Pattern of English Building* (London: Faber and Faber, 1987).

Ferrey, Benjamin, *Recollections of A.W.N. Pugin and his Father Augustus Pugin* reprint, introduced by Clive Wainwright. (London: Scholar Press, 1978).

Girouard, Mark, *The Victorian Country House* (New Haven and London: Yale University Press, 1985).

Gwyn, David, *Lord Shrewsbury, Pugin and the Catholic Revival* (London: Hollis & Carter, 1946).

Hardman Letters: Birmingham Central Library.

Hobhouse, Hermione, *Thomas Cubitt, Master Builder* (London: Macmillan, 1971) and *Prince Albert, His Life and Work* (London: Hamish Hamilton Ltd, 1983).

Hunting, Penelope, *Henry Clutton's Country Houses* (Ph.D. London: 1983).

Jennings, Humphrey, (compiler), *Pandaemonium 1660-1886* eds M.L. Jennings and C. Madge (London: André Deutch, 1985).

Spiers, Edward M, *The Army and Society, 1815-1914* (London: Longmans, 1980).

Stanton, Phoebe, *Pugin* (London: Thames & Hudson, 1971).

Summerson, John, *The London Building World of the Eighteen-Sixties* (London: Thames & Hudson, 1973).

Sykes, Christopher, *Two Studies in Virtue* (London: Collins, 1953).

Trappes-Lomax, Michael, *Pugin a Medieval Victorian* (London: Sheed & Ward, 1932).

Wedgwood, Alexandra, *Catalogue of the Drawings Collection of the Royal Institute of British Architects* (Farnborough, Hants: Gregg International, 1977) and *A.W.N. Pugin and the Pugin Family* Catalogue of the Architectural Drawings at the Victoria and Albert Museum (London: Victoria and Albert Museum, 1985).

Woodham-Smith, Cecil, *Florence Nightingale* (London: Reprint Society, 1952).

List of Abbreviations in Appendices I and II

AW	Alexandra Wedgwood, *A.W.N. Pugin and the Pugin Family* (London: Victoria and Albert Museum, 1985) contains Pugin's diaries, his letters to the Earl of Shrewsbury, etc., and catalogues those of his architectural drawings which are in the Victoria and Albert Museum.
B	*The Builder*
BCL	Birmingham City Library
Berks RO	Berkshire Record Office
BRO	Bedfordshire Record Office
CERC	Church of England Record Centre, Bermondsey
CLRO	Corporation of London Records Office
DNB	Dictionary of National Biography
ERO	Essex Record Office
ERRO	East Riding Record Office
GLRO	Greater London Record Office
GM	George Myers
HCAO	Humberside County Archive Office
HCRO	Hull City Record Office
HL	Hardman letters - Uncatalogued in Birmingham City Library. These letters written to John Hardman and later to Messrs Hardman, date from about 1842 to the middle of the present century.
HRO	Hampshire Record Office
Lincolnshire RO	Lincolnshire Record Office
LRO	Leicestershire Record Office
JMS	Judith Myers' Scrapbook
MFT	Myers Family Trust - Hugh Myers, Trustee (Private collection)
North CRO	Northumberland County Record Office
NRO	Norfolk Record Office
PH	Penelope Hunting ('Henry Clutton's Country Houses' Ph.D.) London, 1983.
PRO	Public Record Office
PS	Phoebe Stanton, *Pugin* (London: Thames & Hudson, 1971)
RIBA	Royal Institute of British Architects, London
RMAS	Royal Military Academy, Sandhurst
SL	Survey of London
TCRO	Trowbridge County Record Office
WAL	Westminster Archive Library, London

Appendix I: List of Contracts

NOTES:

1.   Contracts are listed by modern Local Authority boundaries. Local Authorities are in alphabetical order. Greater London contracts (no 1-111) come before Provincial County contracts (nos 112-232). Foreign contracts (nos 233-40) come last.

2.   Within individual Local Authority areas, contracts are listed in chronological order.

3.   This list is believed to contain the principal contracts undertaken by George Myers, but it is not claimed to be complete. There is a further list, not included here, containing over fifty projects, with a global value in excess of £450,000, in which his tender was the lowest but in which there is no confirmation that the tender was accepted.

BARNET

1   Church of St Mary the Virgin, Monken Hadley, High Barnet: restoration

Date: 1848-9
Architect: G.E. Street
References: George Myers gave the name of the Rector of Monken Hadley, the Revd G. Proctor, DD as a reference when he won the contract to build Colney Hatch in 1848.

2   Colney Hatch Lunatic Asylum, Friern Barnet Rd

Date: 1849-50
Architect: S.W. Daukes
Cost: £139,982
References: Visitors' Minute Books: GLRO MA/RS Acc 1038/1, etc.
Note: Foundation Stone laid 8 May 1849 and keys handed over on 1 November 1850. Now the Friern Barnet Hospital, but it is due to close in March 1993. Listed Grade II.

3   Child Hill Church of England School, Cricklewood Lane, Kilburn

Date: 1870
Architect: Talbot Bury
References: GLRO Acc 1341/39/1-9
Note: Still in use, as an infant school.

BRENT

St Andrew's Church - *see* Westminster

4   Sewers in Kensal New Town in the Parish of St Mary's, Paddington, and St Luke's, Chelsea

Date: 1855
Architect: Sir Joseph Baselgette
Cost: £2,428
References: Contract, GLRO, M-C-S 2/2 104-5
Note: Still in use.

BROMLEY

5   Church of St John and Parsonage at Penge

Date: August 1848 - October 1849
Architects: Edwin Nash and John Nash Round
Cost: £4,058 + £1,519
References: CERC: 64/375. *The Builder* (1848) p. 143
Note: Also two houses in Adelaide Road, now demolished.

6   Work at the Crystal Palace, Sydenham: masonry and roads

Date: 1855
Architect: Sir Joseph Paxton
References: JMS (18 July, 1855) probably *The Times*
Note: Destroyed by fire 1936.

7   Rockhill House, Crystal Palace, Sydenham: alterations etc. for Sir Joseph Paxton

Date: 1857
Architect: Sir Joseph Paxton

Cost: £1,218. 18s. 4¹/₂d.
References: Bill for work done: Chatsworth Archives, Paxton Group
            1265.
Note: Demolished in 1970s.

The Wood *see* Lewisham.

CAMDEN

8   New College, Finchley Road, St John's Wood

Date: 1850
Architect: J .T. Emmett
Cost: £10,676
References: HL (1850). *The Builder* (1851) pp. 786-7
Note: Demolished 1934.

9   Holy Catholic and Apostolic Church and flats, Gordon Square

Date: 1851
Architect: R. Brandon
Cost: £33,267 in Bath Stone.
References: *The Times* (28 June 1851) *The Builder* (1859) p. 408
Note: Now the Church of Christ the King, of the University of
            London Chaplaincy (C of E).

10   London and Westminster Bank, 212-214 High Holborn

Date: 1853
Architect: Henry Baker
Cost: c.£10,000
References: *The Builder* (1853) p. 392
Present use: National Westminster Bank.

11   Highgate Cemetery Wall and Piers, (new part), Highgate

Date: 1854
Architects: Wehnert and Ashdown
Cost: £2,990
References: *The Builder* (1854) p. 540

12   St Alban's Church, Baldwin Gardens

Date: 1862
Architect: William Butterfield
Cost: £35,000
References: *The Builder* (1862) p. 442
Note: Bombed and rebuilt.

CITY of LONDON

13   Minerva Life Assurance Office and Warehouses, 1 Cannon Street

Date: 1852
Architect: John Foulton
References: *The Builder* (1852) p. 722
Note: Demolished.

14   Bank for Messrs Johnson & Co, New Cannon Street

Date: 1852
Architect: George Legg
Cost: £2,888
References: *The Builder* (1852) p. 189.

15   Corn Exchange: additions. Mark Lane

Date: 1852
Architect: George Legg
Cost: £4,761
References: *The Builder* (1852) p. 286.

16   New Building on the corner of Chancery Lane

Date: 1855
Architect: James Knowles junr.
Cost: £15,000
References: *The Builder* (1855) p. 389
Note: Demolished.

17   Law Union Insurance Offices, 126 Chancery Lane

Date: 1857
Architect: J. Warnham Penfold

Cost: £2,800 without fixtures and fittings
References: *The Builder* (1857) p. 119. *Building News* (1859) p. 218
Note: The back of the building has been rebuilt; the shop fronts
                  have been restored.

18   No 16 Cornhill: Rebuilt for Messrs Sarle & Sons, Silversmiths

Date: 1857
Architect: J. Barnett
Cost: £5,948
References: *Building News* (1857) p. 172
                  Many references in JMS
Note: Court case.

19   National Discount Offices, 33 Cornhill

Date: 1858
Architects: F. & H. Francis
References: *The Builder* (1858) p. 10
Note: Present use: The Banca Nationale del Lavoro.

20   Mutual Life Assurance Society's Offices, 39 King Street,
Cheapside

Date: 1859
Architect: J.M.K. Hahn
Cost: £5,979
Carving: Samuel Ruddock
References: *The Builder* (1859) p. 393
Note: Demolished.

21   New Library, Middle Temple

Date: 1858-61
Architect: H.R. Abrahams
Cost: *c.* £13,000 including the bookcases
Carving: Samuel Ruddock
Stone   From George Myers' quarries: ref. *Building News* (1861)
                  p. 138
References: Middle Temple Library, Box C19, 1 & 2, Contract etc.
Note: Bombed WW II.

22   Work at the Tower of London, including St John's Chapel

Date: 1856-69
Architect: Anthony Salvin
References: PRO 113008 WORK 14/2/3 etc. WORK 31/527,
              St John's Chapel
Note: George Myers was one of three invited to tender.

23   London and County Bank, basement and strongroom,
21 Lombard Street

Date: 1862
Architect: C.O. Parnell
References: *The Builder* (1862) p. 604.

24   Warehouses in Cooper's Row: also vaults and offices for
Mr Duncan Ervine

Date: 1862
Architect: Norman Shaw
Cost: £6,298
References: *The Builder* (1862) p. 396: tender accepted
Note: Demolished.

25   National Provident Institution, 48 Gracechurch Street

Date: 1863
Architect: Professor Robert Kerr
Cost: £12,907
Carving: Samuel Ruddock
References: *The Builder* (1863) p. 13: (also in-house publication,
              1985)
Note: Demolished and rebuilt, 1959.

26   Bishopsgate Police Station & Infirmary

Date: 1864
Architect: Horace Jones
Cost: £13,750
References: CLRO, CL Deeds Box 120A No. 76, contract, plans
              Surveyor's Justice Plans 803-17
Note: Demolished and rebuilt twice.

27   Guildhall New Roof, Windows and other work; Pavilion etc. for Ball to entertain the Prince and Princess of Wales

Date: 1863-4
Architect: James Bunstone Bunning, then Sir Horace Jones
Cost: Guildhall work, £24,200
References: CLRO, Comt CL Deeds Box 119A No. 67, & Arch. Plans G/MH/4-9 & 16, G/MH/44-45
Note: Roof destroyed by incendiary bombs 29 December 1940.

28   Seats in St Paul's Churchyard to watch the Prince and Princess of Wales pass by

Date: 1863
Cost: £6,905. 10s. 6d.
References: Printed report CLRO A/103L.

29   New City Club, and additions, George Yard, Lombard St

Date: 1864
Architect: J.H. Rowley
Cost: £19,000 + £5,670
References: *The Builder* (1864) p. 650-1
Note: Demolished c. 1953.

30   Warehouses and Vaults on Tower Hill

Date: 1864
Architect: No architect discovered in any of the documents
References: Guildhall Ms 21 051 p. 97 and documents with Messrs Travers Smith & Braithwaite, solicitors
Note: The warehouses were bombed 17 September 1940. The vaults were converted in 1991 into 'The Pageant of Tower Hill', part of the 'Museum of London'.

31   City Offices, Lombard Street

Date: 1866
Architects: F. & H. Francis
References: *The Builder* (1866) p. 752
Note: Demolished.

32   Guildhall, work in connection with the reception for the Sultan of Turkey

Date: 1867
Architect: Horace Jones
References: CLRO, letter 16 July 1867 from Horace Jones to the Entertainment Committee
Note: Dismantled.

33   Offices in Throgmorton Street and Austin Friars: for Mr Travers Smith

Date: 1870
Architect: T. Chatfield Clarke
Cost: *c.* £10,000
References: *The Builder* (1870) p. 230
Note: Building being restored (1992).

34   Imperial Ottoman Bank, Throgmorton Street

Date: 1871
Architect: William Burnet
Cost: £8,000
References: *The Builder* (1871) pp. 646-7
Note: Present use: National Westminster Bank.

EALING

35   Christ Church, Ealing Broadway

Date: 1852
Architect: G.G. Scott
Cost: £7,000
References: *The Builder* (1852) p. 440
Note: In use.

GREENWICH

36   St Peter's Church and Presbytery, New Road, Woolwich

Date: 1843
Architect: Pugin

References: Pugin diaries; HL (1843)
Note: In use.

37   Our Lady Star of the Sea, 68 Crooms Hill: Chancel only

Date: 1851
Architects: William Wardell/Pugin
References: George Myers book of drawings, MFT
Note: In use.

38   Royal Military Academy, Woolwich, additions etc.

Date: 1859-62
Architect: R E Department, Clerk of Works, Mr Jones
Cost: £57,735: £30,000 for further work
References: RMAS Collection, Sandhurst, Camberley, Letter
Book, Letter 55. *The Times* (16 October 1861)
Note: In use.

39   Royal Herbert Hospital, Shooters Hill Road, Woolwich

Date: 1865
Architect: Douglas Galton
Cost: £205,486
References: PRO TI/6410B 151406; *The Builder* (1865) pp. 183-5 etc.
Note: Closed. Being converted into flats and offices. A Listed
building.

HACKNEY

40   Chapel and Schools, Upper Clapton

Date: 1850
Architect: J.T. Emmett
Cost: £7,316 (tender)
References: *The Builder* (1850) p. 586.

41   St Mary's Church, Stoke Newington

Date: 1858
Architect: G.G. Scott

Cost: c. £15,000
References: CERC, file 13970 etc.; *The Builder* (1858) p. 618
Note: In use.

42   Imperial Gas Station, furnace and chimney shaft, Shoreditch

Date: 1864
Cost: £7,635
References: GLRO, Metropolitan Bd of Works
Minutes of Proceedings: (1864) p. 988, para 44.

43   St Matthew's Church, Warwick Grove, Clapton

Date: 1867-9
Architect: Francis Dollman
Cost: £15,000
References: *The Builder* (1869) p. 267
Note: Demolished 1976.

HAMMERSMITH

44   Convent of the Good Shepherd, Fulham Palace Road

Date: 1848-50
Architect: Pugin
References: AW p. 68
Note: Sold to the Peabody Trust in 1914. Demolished in
             1921.

45   St Thomas of Canterbury, Fulham

Date: 1849
Architect: Pugin
References: AW p. 68 and HL (1849)
Note: In use.

HARINGEY

46   St Ann's Church, Parsonage, School and Model Cottages
Stamford Hill, N16

Date: 1861
Architect: Talbot Bury

Cost: £8,398
References: CERC file 22169: Illustrated London News (1861) p. 173
Note: Church in use; parsonage rebuilt, school vandalised, cottages derelict.

47 Royal Masonic Institute for Boys, Lordship Lane, Wood Green, Tottenham

Date: 1865
Architects: Edwin Pearce and B. Wilson & Sons
Cost: £21,894
References: *The Builder* (1865) pp. 816-17
Note: Demolished in 1973: a Court House has been built on the site.

HOUNDSLOW

48 Gunnersbury Park: alterations and improvements for Baron Lionel de Rothschild

Date: 1860-70
Cost: Very large sums of money were paid to George Myers by Lionel during these years which would have been due for work on the Piccadilly houses as well as for Gunnersbury
References: Rothschild Archive, Ledgers: London
Note: Now Museum and Community Centre.

ISLINGTON

49 St Luke's Church, Hillmarton Rd, Holloway

Date: 1859-60
Architect: Charles Lee
Cost: £6,970
References: *The Builder* (1859) p. 489.

KENSINGTON AND CHELSEA

50 Christchurch, Victoria Rd, Kensington

Date: 1851
Architect: Benjamin Ferrey

Cost: £3,540
References: SL, vol. XLII (1986) p. 368
Note: In use (May 1988).

51   St Margaret and St John's Workhouses, Kensington

Date: 1852
Architects: Hunt and Stevenson
Cost: £22,374
References: Westminster Archive Library: E 3360/4
Note: Part of St Mary Abbott's Hospital; partly demolished.

52   Sewers in Kensington, Chelsea and other parts of London

Date: 1853
Architect: Sir Joseph Bazelgette
References: GLRO MCS - 212
Note: Still extant.

53   All Saints' Church, Talbot Rd

Date: 1855
Architect: William White
References: SL, vol. XXXVI (1970) p. 318; *The Builder* (1855) pp.
              486-7
Note: The client went bankrupt with the church half built and
              George Myers took possession. Building stopped. It was
              known as 'All Sinners in the Mud'. After much delay
              and difficulty the church was completed by another
              builder. Still in use.

54   St Mary's Church, The Boltons, tower and steeple only

Date: 1857
Architects: G. & H. Godwin
Cost: £883
References: *The Builder* (1857) p. 218
Note: Carving by Samuel Ruddock.

55   Chelsea Congregational Church, Markham Square

Date: 1858
Architect: J. Tarring

Cost: £4,600
References: *The Builder* (1860) p. 236
Note: Carving by Samuel Ruddock. Demolished

56   St George's Church, Campden Hill

Date: 1864
Architect: E. Bassett Keeling
Cost: £7,000
References: Plaque on the building; *The Builder* (1864) p. 102
Note: In use.

57   St Matthias' Church, chancel only

Date: 1869-72
Architect: J. H. Hakewill
Cost: £1,988
References: SL, vol. .XLII (1986) p. 378
Note: Burnt down soon after it was finished.

58   St Jude's Church, Courtfield Gardens

Date: 1870
Architects: G. & H. Godwin
Cost: £11,300
References: *The Builder* (1870) p. 546-7
Note: Box stone used.

59   St Augustine's Church, Queen's Gate

Date: 1870
Architect: William Butterfield
References: SL, vol. XXXVIII (1975), p. 350.

LAMBETH

60   St Barnabas Church , Guildford Road, Stockwell

Date: 1849-50
Architects: Isaac Clarke and J. Humphrys
Cost: £5,360
References: CERC, file 17747; SL vol. XXVI (1956) p. 63.
Note: Converted to Council flats.

61   Clapham Congregational Church, Mostyn Road, Brixton

Date: 1852
Architect: J. Tarring
Cost: £8,000
References: *The Builder* (1852) p. 671
Note: Demolished.

62   Water Works: tower and chimney shaft, Waterworks Street

Date: 1853
References: GLRO
Note: Demolished.

63   Camden Church, chancel only, Camberwell

Date: 1854
Architect: G.G. Scott
Cost: £2,800
References: *The Builder* (1854) p. 362.

64   All Saints Church, New Park Road, Clapham

Date: 1858
Architect: Talbot Bury
References: *Building News* (1858) p. 416
Note: Demolished.

65   St Stephen's Church and Parsonage, Albert Square

Date: 1860
Architect: J. Barnett
Cost: £15,000
References: *The Builder* (1860) pp. 688-689; SL vol XXVI (1856)
               p. 63
Note: Destroyed by barrage balloon, 1940.

66   St Saviour's Church, Cedars Road

Date: 1862-64
Architect: James Knowles

Cost: £9,714
References: *James Knowles*: Priscilla Metcalf (Clarendon, 1980) pp. 184-5
Note: Bombed 1944.

67 Allnutt Estate, shops and houses, Clapham High Street, Clapham Cross, Clapham Common and Elms Road

Date: 1864
References: Deeds etc. in possession of Messrs Travers Smith and Braithwaite, solicitors.
Note: Some buildings bombed, others still standing.

68 Wesleyan Chapel, Mostyn Road, Brixton

Date: 1868
Architect: J. Tarring
Cost: £8,293
References: *The Builder* (1868) p. 364
Note: Demolished.

69 Our Lady of the Rosary, Brixton

Date: 1869
Architect: Arthur Phelps
Cost: £10,242
References: Plaque on building; SL vol. XXVI (1956) p. 130
Note: Built for the C of E but bought by RC Archdiocese of Southwark in 1905. In use.

LEWISHAM

70 The Wood, now 16 Sydenham Hill: improvements and modernisation for the Duke of Devonshire

Date: 1854-5
Architect: Sir Joseph Paxton
Cost: £3,730.2s.8d.
References: Bill: Chatsworth Archives, Paxton Group 1265.
Note: For 'two fat ladies' (Lady Hunloke and her daughter). Converted into flats (1973), by Borough of Lewisham. A grade II listed building.

NEWHAM

71   Rothschild's Mausoleum (Evelina and Ferdinand) West Ham
Jewish Cemetery, Forest Gate

Date:	1866
Architect:	Sir Matthew Digby-Wyatt
Cost:	£2,030
References:	Rothschild Archive, London, Receipt
Note:	A listed building.

72   Stratford: Congregational Church

Date:	1866
Architect:	Sir Rowland Plumbe
References:	Stratford Express (16 June 1866)
Note:	Bombed WW II; demolished.

SOUTHWARK

73   St George's Catholic Cathedral: also Priests' House, Convent and
School, St George's Road

Date:	1841-8
Architect:	Pugin
Cost:	£20,000 without decoration, tower or spire. £6,000 for priests' house, convent and school
References:	Southwark Diocesan Archives (RC)
Note:	Built as Parish church. Bombed WW II and rebuilt. Very little of the Pugin/Myers church remains.

74 Bethlem Hospital (Bedlam), St George's Fields, additions to

Date:	1852 then 1854
Architect:	Sydney Smirke
Cost:	£3,867
References:	Royal Bethlem Hospital Archive Library, the Contract 1854
Note:	Now the Imperial War Museum. The part built by GM has been demolished.

75 St Paul's Church, Lorrimore Square, Camberwell

Date: 1857
Architect: H. Jarvis
Cost: £6,000
References: *The Builder* (1857), p. 17
Note: Demolished.

76 St Paul's Church, Westminster Bridge Road

Date: 1857
Architect: W. Rogers
Cost: £7,683
References: *The Builder* (1857) p. 716
Note: Demolished. There is now a Catholic primary school on
             the site.

77 St Matthew's Church, New Kent Road

Date: 1867
Architect: Henry Jarvis
Cost: £6,605
References: *The Builder* (1867) p. 52
Note: Closed, and may be converted into flats.

78 Evelina Hospital for Sick Children: New Kent Road, for Baron Ferdinand de Rothschild

Date: Main Building 1868; Outpatients 1869; Fever Wards
             1870
Architects: March, Nelson and Harvey
Cost: £13,292
References: Rothschild Archive, London. GLRO H.9/EV/Lib/1
Note: Demolished.

TOWER HAMLETS

79 Railway from South of the River Lea Cut Canal to the West India Dock. For the 'East & West India Docks and Birmingham Junction Railway Co.', later the 'North London Railway Co.'

Date: 1849

Engineer: H.D. Martin. Robert Stevenson (son of George S.) was
              the consultant engineer .
Cost: £37,832
Tender: George Myers' bid was lowest of 47
References: PRO RAIL 529/9: the Minute Book of the Railway Co.

80   London Hospital Medical School, Whitechapel Road; also
extentions and alterations to the Hospital

Date: 1853
Architect: Alfred R. Mason, surveyor to the Hospital
Cost: £15,450
References: London Hospital Archives: House Management
              Committee Minutes, LH/A/5/27-28 24 May, 1853 *et seq.*
Note: About £6,900 spent on the Hospital. In use.

81   City of London Hospital for Diseases of the Chest, Bonner Road,
Victoria Park

Date: 1855
Architect: F.W. Ordish
Cost: £17,200
References: *The Builder* (1855) p. 187
Note: In use; now part of the London Chest Hospital; rather
              dilapidated (1988).

82   Jews Infant School, 43a Commercial Street, Whitechapel

Date: 1857
Architect: Tillot and Chamberlain
Cost: £5,000
References: SL, vol XXVII (1936) p. 262.

83   Christchurch, Spitalfields: restoration of Hawkesmore's church

Date: 1866
Architect: Ewan Christian
Cost: £4,500
References: GLRO P93/CTC 1/104
Note: Being restored once again (1991).

WANDSWORTH

84   Royal Victoria Patriotic Asylum for Girls, Trinity Road

Date: 1857
Architect: M.R. Hawkins
Cost: £31,337
References: *The Builder* (1857) p. 579
Note: Much information in the thesis of S. McRoberts, School
              of Architecture & Design, Kingston-upon-Thames
              Polytechnic, 1937. Sold by the GLC for £1 (one
              pound) in the 1980s. Being converted into studios,
              workshops, flats, etc.

85   Chapel for the above

Date: 1864
Architect: M.R. Hawkins
Cost: £5,135
References: *The Builder* (1864) p. 892
Note: Sold with RVPA: part of the same convertion scheme.

WESTMINSTER

86   St Andrew's Church, Wells Street, Marylebone

Date: Nov 1845 - Jan 1847
Architect: S.W. Daukes and Hamilton
References: CERC, file 17376; *The Builder* (1847) p. 4
Note: Taken down and re-erected in Kingsbury, Brent, 1933.

87   Church of The Immaculate Conception, Farm Street;   the High
Altar and Reredos

Date: 1848
Architect: Pugin (Church itself by Scoles)
References: HL (1848-1852).

88   St Matthew's Church, Great Peter Street

Date: 1849-51
Architect: G.G. Scott

Cost: £12,000-£13,000
References: Council for the Care of Churches: PM 865.

89   Exeter Hall, The Strand: New Roof

Date: 1850
Architect: S W Daukes
References: *The Builder* (1850) p. 582
Note: Demolished, 1907.

90   Exhibits at the Mediæval Court: the Great Exhibition Hyde Park

Date: 1851
Architect: Pugin
References: George Myers' Prize Medal; many references in letters
              and journals
Note: *see* chapter 3.

91   The Great Globe House, Leicester Square

Date: 1851
Architect: H.R. Abrahams
Cost: £5,000
References: SL vol XXXIV (1966) p. 435 ; many other references
Note: Demolished 1861. Model in the Museum of the Moving
              Image, London.

92   St George's Baths and Wash House, Hanover Square

Date: 1853-54
Engineer: P. Pritchard Baly
Cost: £12,000
References: SL, vol XL (1980) p. 62
Note: Demolished 1910.

93   Eight Houses in Broad Sanctuary and Gateway, Dean's Yard, for
Dean & Chapter of Westminster Abbey

Date: 1853
Architect: G.G. Scott
Cost: £24,916
References: *The Builder* (1854) p. 114
Note: Now offices. Bath stone from the Box quarries.

94   Breadalbane House, Park Lane: temporary Baronial Hall

Date: 1854
References: SL vol XL (1980) p. 270
Note: Erected in garden of 30 Upper Grosvenor Street for a
              ball. Decorated by Crace. Hall demolished in 1863:
              House in 1876.

95   St Luke's Church, Nutford Place, Edgeware Road

Date: June 1854 - July 1855
Architect: Ewan Christian
Cost: £8,650. 7s. 0d.
References: CERC file 71/419; *The Builder* (1856) p. 246
Note: Bombed WW II.

96   Christchurch, Craven Hill, Lancaster Gate

Date: 1855
Architects: F. & H. Francis
Cost: £14,500
References: *The Builder* (1855) p. 30; CERC file 17806
Note: Converted to flats by Iranian Co.

97   Dudley House, 100 Park Lane

Date: 1855
Architect: S.W. Daukes
References: SL, XL (1980) p. 277-8
Note: Spectacular improvements, ballroom and picture gallery
              for Lord Ward. Now offices.

98   Burlington House, Piccadilly: new meeting room and library for
the Society of Arts

Date: 1857
Architect: Office of Works
References: *The Builder* (1857) p. 153
Note: In use

99　St James Workhouse: rebuilt a wing

Date:　　　　1858-9
Architect:　　Charles Lee
Cost:　　　　£6,190
References:　SL vol. XXXI (1963) p. 435.

100　Westminster Palace Hotel, Victoria Street

Date:　　　　1859
Architects:　W. & A. Moseley
Cost:　　　　£68,966
References:　*The Builder* (1859) pp. 348,366,381, etc.
Note:　　　　Eventually became the Conservative Party Central Office
　　　　　　and was renamed 'Abbey House'; now demolished.

101　All Saints, Margaret Street: stone carving only

Date:　　　　1859
Architect:　　William Butterfield
References:　*The Builder* (1859) p. 376
Note:　　　　The contractor was J. Kelk.

102　Metropolitan Board of Works, new offices

Date:　　　　1860
Architect:　　Frederic Marable
Cost:　　　　£16,000
References:　*Illustrated London News* (1860) p. 568
Note:　　　　Demolished.

103　Church of St James the Less, Garden Street, Victoria

Date:　　　　1861
Architect:　　G.E. Street
Cost:　　　　£5,634
References:　*The Builder* (1861) p. 410
Note:　　　　Listed building; in process of restoration.

104　St Peter's Church, Windmill Street, Haymarket

Date:　　　　1861
Architect:　　R. Brandon

Cost: £5,500 with furniture
References: *B* 1861, p. 561
Note: Demolished.

105 Rothschild Mansion, 147-148 Piccadilly, and alterations and repairs to others in Piccadilly

Date: 1863
Architects: Nelson & Innes.
References: Rothschild Archive, RFamC/4/243 and others
Note: Mansion demolished to make way for the Park Lane dual carriageway in the 1960s.

106 New Westminster Chapel, Buckingham Gate

Date: 1864
Architect: W.F. Poulton
Cost: £12,758
References: *The Builder* (1864), pp. 722-3
Note: In use. Spire removed due to bomb damage.

107 The Queen's Chapel of the Savoy, The Strand; rebuilt after a fire

Date: 1866
Architect: Sidney Smirke
References: *The Builder* (1866) p. 117
Note: In use.

108 East India United Service Club, St James's Square

Date: 1866
Architect: Charles Lee
References: *The Builder* (1866) p. 153
Note: In use.

109 The West London Synagogue of British Jews, 34 Upper Berkeley Street

Date: 1870
Architects: Davis & Emanuel
Cost: £12,730
References: A.S. Diamond: *The Building of a Synagogue.* Published by above (1990).

110   The Provident Institute Savings Bank, St Martin's Place

Date: 1871-5
Architect: D. Brandon
References: *The Builder* (1875) pp. 463-5
Note: In use - branch of National Westminster Bank.   George
               Myers was dead when building finished.

111   National Provincial Bank of England, 212 Piccadilly

Date: 1873
Architect: J. Gibson
References: *The Builder* (1873) pp. 487-9
Note: Facade of upper four floors unchanged: ground floor
               now a shop window.

BEDFORDSHIRE

112   Woburn: St Mary's Parish Church, for the Duke of Bedford

Date: 1865-8
Architect: Henry Clutton
References: BRO R5/916-17
Note: In use.

113   Husborne Crawley: School for the Duke of Bedford

Date: 1866-67
Architect: Henry Clutton
References: BRO R5/916-17
Note: In use.

114   Bedford: St Paul's Church: enlarged and restored

Date: 1866-8
Architect: Robert Palgrave (G.E. Street consulted)
References: BRO P1/2/140 & P1/2/132
Note: In use.

BERKSHIRE

115 Eton: Church of St John the Evangelist

Date:	1852-4
Architect:	Benjamin Ferrey
Cost:	£8,000
References:	Council for the Care of Churches, PM 1097
Note:	Converted: chapel, sanatorium, etc.

116 Crowthorne: Broadmoor Hospital and Chapel

Date:	1858-64
Architect:	Major General Sir Joshua Jebb
References:	PRO MH 51/49; JMS
Note:	In use.

117 Crowthorne: Wellington College Chapel

Date:	1861
Architect:	G.G. Scott
References:	*The Builder* (1861) p. 772
Note:	In use.

118 Reading: Assize Court and Central Police Station

Date:	1860
Architect:	J.B. Clancy, County Surveyor
Cost:	£15,614.
References:	BerksRO - the Contract; *The Times* 5 December 1859
Note:	Asked £1,000 for extra work.

119 Windsor Castle: St George's Chapel, alterations and fittings for the funeral of the Prince Consort on 23 December 1861. The Prince had died on Friday, 13 December

References:	*The Times* 20 December 1861.
Note:	*The Times* recorded that the arrangements were almost identical to those made for the funeral of the Duchess of Kent. Possibly George Myers was employed on that occasion also.

120 Windsor Castle: Royal Wedding. Temporary saloons at the west end of St George's Chapel, for the reception and accommodation of the Prince of Wales and Princess Alexandra of Denmark and the wedding guests.

Date: 1863
References: *The Builder* (1863) pp. 124, 181.

121 Windsor Castle: King Henry VII Library: enlargement; also the adjoining Queen Anne's closet. He provided bookcases for more than 1000 books and enlarged and improved the windows in the Waterloo Gallery.

Date: 1864
Architect: Anthony Salvin
Cost: £2,857
References: *The Builder* (1864) p. 168; Dr Jill Allibone, *Anthony Salvin*, (Lutterworth Press, 1988) p. 187.

122 Windsor: St Stanislaus College, Beaumont. New Chapel, refectory and dormitory

Date: 1870
Architect: J.A. Hansom & Son
Cost: £6,904
References: *The Builder* (1870) p. 274
Note: School now closed.

123 Sunningdale: Sunningdale Park for Charles Crosley

Date: 1865
Architect: Henry Clutton
References: Penelope Hunting in 'Henry Clutton's Country Houses': Ph.D. thesis, (London 1983).
Note: Demolished.

BUCKINGHAMSHIRE

124 Great Marlow, St Peter's Church & School

Date: 1845-8
Architect: Pugin

References: HL (1847)
Note: In use; enlarged.

125 Mentmore: Mansion for Baron Mayer de Rothschild

Date: 1853 (contract signed 1851)
Architect: Sir Joseph Paxton
Cost: £15,472: shell only, not including the foundations
References: George Myers' own copy of the Contract, c/o the Myers Family Trust; Rothschild Archives, RAL XII/41/5, etc.

126 Aston Clinton: enlargement and alterations for Baron Anthony de Rothschild

Date: 1853-70
Architects: Paxton, Stokes, Devey
References: Rothschild Archives, RAL XII/41/2, etc.
Note: Demolished.

127 Great Brickhill: Brickhill Manor, alterations and improvements

Date: 1854
Architect: E.B. Lamb
References: HCAO PE1/836
Note: Demolished.

128 Hedsor: Cliveden, Clock Tower, Stables, Porte-cochère and Garden walls

Date: 1857, 1861, 1869
Architect: Henry Clutton
Cost: Clock tower £2-3,000
References: Penelope Hunting
Note: Cliveden now belongs to the National Trust. Part of it is a hotel. The clock tower is to be restored.

CAMBRIDGESHIRE

129 Ely: Ely Cathedral Font

Date: 1850
Architect: G.G. Scott

References: RIBA SC/NSJ/93

130 Wilburton: Manor House

Date: 1851
Architect: Pugin ?
References: George Myer's book of Pugin drawings, Myers
              Family Trust; *Victoria County History of
              Cambridgeshire* (The Institute of Historical Research
              for the OUP, 1953) p. 168.
Note: Special School.

131 Wilburton: St Peter's Church, restoration

Date: 1851
Architect: Pugin ?
References: George Myer's book of Pugin drawings, Myers Family
              Trust.

132 Cambridge: London and County Bank

Date: 1866
Architects: F. and H. Francis
Cost: £7,739
References: *The Builder* (1866) pp. 426-7
Note: Now the National Westminster Bank.

CHESHIRE

133 Cheadle: St Giles' Church, the intricate carving only

Date: 1846
Architect: Pugin
References: Alexandra Wedgwood p. 58
Note: In use.

134 Winwick: St Oswald's Church, chancel vestry and furniture

Date: 1847-9
Architect: Pugin
Cost: £3,633, excluding the furniture
References: Pugin and Myers mss. in vestry, with copies in the
              Record Office, Warrington.

135 Widnes: St Bede's Church, Appleton - Lady Chapel, altar and reredos

Date: 1851
Architect: Pugin
Cost: £64. 7s. 9d.
References: HL.

CUMBRIA

136 Warwick Bridge: Church of our Lady and St Wilfred and Presbytery

Date: 1841
Architect: Pugin
References: Alexandra Wedgwood p. 54; PS p. 101
Note: In use.

DERBYSHIRE

137 Derby: St Mary's Church, Presbytery and church furniture

Date: 1837-38
Architect: Pugin
Cost: £8,027
References: Many
Note: Presbytery: demolished. Church: major renovation, 1989.

138 Bakewell: Burton Closes, decorating

Date: 1847
Architect: Paxton
References: Alexandra Wedgwood p. 180
Note: Pugin, Myers and Crace were involved in the decoration of this mansion.

139 Bakewell: Beeley Parsonage, for the Duke of Devonshire, Chatsworth

Date: 1856
Architect: Stokes

Cost: £1,743. 11s. 6d.
References: Chatsworth accounts, 1857.

DEVONSHIRE

140 Sidmouth: Chapel at Bicton, Rolle Mortuary for Lord Rolle

Date: 1849-52
Architect: Pugin
References: HL (many letters) 1851-2

141 Seaton: North Lodge, for Lady Ashburton

Date: 1864-5
Architect: Clutton
References: Penelope Hunting: 'Henry Clutton's Country Houses'
              Ph.D. (London , 1983) p. 103.

DURHAM

142 Durham: Ushaw College, Chapel and other buildings

Date: 1841-52
Architect: Pugin
References: Ushaw College, President's Archives, T.21
Note: R.C. Seminary.

143 Stockton-on-Tees: St Mary's Church, Cleveland

Date: 1841
Architect: Pugin
References: Timothy McCann - personal communication.

144 Ryhope, Sunderland: Wesleyan Chapel

Date: 1865
Architect: J. Tillmamn
Cost   £340
References: *The Builder* (1865) p. 473

ESSEX

145 Brentwood: Essex County Lunatic Asylum

Date: 1857
Architect: H.E. Kendall
Cost: £55,666
References: Essex County Record Library, Q/ALC 4
Note: Still in use as mental hospital.

HAMPSHIRE

146 Winchester: St Thomas' and St Clement's Church, Southgate Street

Date: 1845-7
Architect: E.W. Emslie
Cost: £6,060 plus
References: HRO, Contract 37M82W, PW33
Note: Converted into the County Record Office.

147 Aldershot: Hutted Camp, Cavalry and Infantry Barracks, Royal Pavilion and the Ash Railway

Date: 1854-8
Architect: The Colonel Commandant, Royal Engineers, Colonel Sir Frederick Smith was in charge
Cost: £144,000, + another £250,000
References: PRO 162 498. WO 44/611, T1/6105 B, Judith Myers' scrapbook.
Note: Mostly demolished and rebuilt but Riding School, gateways, etc. remain.

148 Aldershot: Prince Consort's Library

Date: 1859-60
Architect: Captain Francis Fowke
Cost: £1,484
References: Royal Archives, Windsor Castle, E 38 and signed architectural drawings in the Prince Consort's Library
Note: In use.

149   Aldershot: All Saints' Church - for the Troops

Date: 1863
Architect: Hardwick
Cost: £16,000
References: *The Builder* (1863) p. 173; Lt Col T Adams MBE: *A Short History of the Royal Garrison Church of All Saints*, (Parish publication, 1979).
Notes: 'The Cathedral of the Army'. In use.

150   Romsey: Melchet Court, alterations and reconstruction for Lord and Lady Ashburton

Date: 1863-6
Architect: Henry Clutton
References: PH p. 103
Note: Now an approved school.

151   Southampton: St Joseph's Church, Bugle Street

Date: 1841-2
Architect: Pugin
References: PS p. 202
Note: Only the chancel of Pugin's church remains.

152   Southampton: Royal Victoria Hospital, Netley

Date: 1856-63
Architect: Mennie
Cost: £200,000
References: *The Builder* (1864), p. 585; *Daily Telegraph* (21 October 1861) JMS.
Note: Demolished except for the Chapel, now a museum and listed building.

153   Southampton: Crimean War Memorial to Medical Officers who died during the War

Date: 1864
Architect: T.H. Lewis
References: *The Builder* (1864) p. 585
Note: Still stands in the grounds of Netley Park

HEREFORD and WORCESTERSHIRE

154 Hereford: Monastery and Abbey of St Michael, Belmont

Date: 1857
Architect: Edward W. Pugin
References: Alexandra Wedgwood *Catalogue of the Drawings Collection of the RIBA* p. 113 *Building News* (1859) p. 1094
Note: Also a school.

155 Malvern: Blackmore Park

Date: 1863
Architect: D. Brandon
References: *The Builder* (1863) p. 446
Note: Burnt down.

HERTFORDSHIRE

156 Ware: St Edmond's College Chapel

Date: 1845-51
Architect: Pugin
References: AW p. 73
Note: George Myers' three younger sons attended this college. Now a prep. school.

157 Ware: House for Mr Ward

Date: *c.*1851
Architect: Pugin
References: Alexandra Wedgwood p. 73

158 Langleybury: St Paul's Church

Date: 1865
Architect: Henry Woodyer
References: *Illustrated London News* (1865) p. 105
Note: All carving carried out in George Myers' workshops.

159 Tring: Tring Park for Baron Lionel de Rothschild

Date: 1874
Architect: George Devey
References: Jill Allibone, *George Devey* p. 167
Note: Arts Education Trust, a Ballet School.

KENT

160 Ramsgate: St Augustine's Church and The Grange with furniture

Date: 1843-8
Architect: Pugin
Cost: £7,146. 6s. 0¹/₂d.
References: List of Costs for church and house supplied by Dom
               Bede Millard OSB of St Augustine's Monastery,
               Ramsgate. Many others.
Note: Furniture now in the Speaker's House in the Palace of
               Westminster.

161 Ramsgate: Effigy of Pugin in stone on his tomb at St Augustine's

Date: unknown
Architect: E.W. Pugin
References: Alexandra Wedgwood, *Catalogue of the Drawings
               Collection, RIBA* p. 113.

162 Kilndown: Tomb of Marshal and Lady Beresford

Date: 1862
Architect: R.C. Carpenter
References: *The Builder* (1862) p. 421
Note: A model was exhibited at the Mediæval Court of the
               1862 Exhibition.

163 Westerham: Dunsdale, additions to, for Mr Kitchen

Date: 1861
Architect: Professor Kerr
Cost: £5,300
References: *The Builder* (1863) pp. 442-3.

164 Chilham: Parish Church restored

Date: 1864
References: *The Builder* (1864) p. 549.

165 Leigh: Hall Place for Samuel Morley, MP

Date: 1871-74
Architect: George Devey
Cost: £70,913. 15s. 1d.
References   Jill Allibone, *George Devey* p. 163.

LANCASHIRE

166 Manchester: St Wilfred's Church, Birchvale Close, Hulme

Date: 1838-42
Architect: Pugin
References: AW p. 81, note 39, drawing MFT.

167 Southport: St Marie's Church, Seabank Road

Date: 1839
Architect: Pugin
References: Drawings in George Myers' book of drawings, MFT.

168 Liverpool: St Oswald's Church and Convent, Old Swan

Date: 1840
Architect: Pugin
References: 150th Anniversary Parish of Old Swan publication with
             foreword by Archbishop Derek Worlock p. 4, 1992.
Note: Demolished to make way for a bigger church but the
             tower remains.

169 Liverpool: Tomb for Mr Sharples

Date: 1842
Architect: Pugin
References: AW p. 54.

170 Liverpool: St Mary's Church, Edmond Street

Date: 1845
Architect Pugin
References *Liverpool Mercury* (1 August 1845)

171 Kirkdale: Parish Schools, near Bootle

Date: 1843
Architects: Lockwood & Allom
Cost: £19,778
References: *Liverpool Mercury* (21 April 1843)
Note: Probable cause of breakup of Myers/Wilson partnership.

172 Wavertree: Chapel of the Sisters of Nazareth

Date: 1843
Architect: Pugin
References: Diaries 1842 and *Liverpool Mail* (15 April 1843).

173 Kirkham: Church of St John the Evangelist, Ribby Road

Date: 1845
Architect: Pugin
References: Drawings in George Myers' notebook, MFT.

174 Oswaldcroft: furniture for Mr Sharples

Date: 1845-6
Architect: Pugin
References: PS p. 204; AW p. 58.

175 Thurnham Lancaster: Church of St Thomas and St Elizabeth

Date: 1847
Architect: Charles Hansom
References: *The Tablet* (9 September 1848) p. 579
Note: Altars and other carvings.

176 Wigan: Memorial Cross for the Warmesley family

Date: 1852
Architect: Pugin
References: *The Builder* (1852) p. 323.

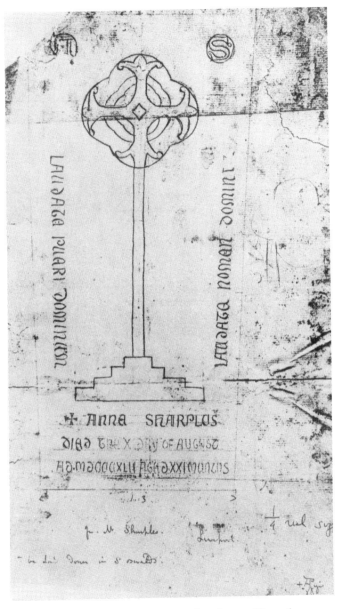

Figure 75   Tombstone for Anna Sharples.
Courtesy of the Myers Family Trust.

LEICESTERSHIRE

177 Loughborough: Workhouse

Date: 1838
Architect: G.G. Scott
Cost: £5,647
References   Contracts etc at Leicestershire Archive Library, G/7/32/1,
                 DE 418/33 Scott's *Recollections Personal and Professional*
                 (1879) pp. 88-9.
Note: Demolished.

178 Coalville: Mount St Bernard Abbey - the Chapel and Belfry

Date: *c.* 1840
Architect: Pugin
References: Laura Phillipps de Lisle's diary Minton MS 3058

179 Shepshed: St Winifred's Church and School

Date: 1842
Architect: Pugin
Cost: £500
References: AW p. 54
Note: Abandoned in 1928 (too small for parish), but purchased
                 and converted into a home and office in the 1980s.

180 Whitwick: School

Date: 1842
Architect: Pugin
Cost: ? £100
References: AW p. 54
Note: A small church was also built at Whitwick, ? by George
                 Myers.

181 Wymeswold: St Mary's Church, restoration

Date: 1845
Architect: Pugin
References: AW p. 61; *A History and Description of the Restored
                 Church of St Mary's, Wymeswold, Leicestershire* (Vizetelly
                 Bros, Fleet Street, 1846).

LINCOLNSHIRE

182 Lincoln: St Anne's Bede Houses

Date: 1847
Architect: Pugin
References: Pugin mss. Magdalen College, Oxford, letter 528 etc.
Note: Built without Pugin's supervision.

183 Bracebridge: Lincoln Pauper Lunatic Asylum

Date: 1850-2
Architect: S.W. Daukes (and Hamilton)
Cost: £32,870
References: Lincoln Archives, KQS Bracebridge Asylum Boxes 1-6
Note: Hamilton went to America soon after building started
             and Daukes took over. Now empty and up for sale

NORFOLK

184 Mundford: St Mary's Church, West Tofts, restoration and
furniture

Date: 1848-55
Architect: Pugin
References: NRO PD 55/21. Roy Tricher, *St Mary's, West Tofts - a
             Guide* (Private Publication, 1987)

NORTHUMBERLAND

185 Newcastle-upon-Tyne: St Mary's Catholic Cathedral

Date: 1842-4
Architect: Pugin
Cost: £7,918
References: North RO 2988/AWP1-30. Hexham and Newcastle
             Diocesan Archives, Album of miscellaneous mss 1790-
             1862. Letters in Archives of St George's Catholic
             Cathedral, Southwark.

NOTTINGHAMSHIRE

186 Nottingham: St Barnabas' Cathedral, Derby Road, also Presbytery, Convent and the furniture

Date: 1842
Architect: Pugin
References: Letters etc. Birmingham Diocesan Archives, References B.640, and B.913; AW p. 54.

OXFORDSHIRE

187 Oxford: Magdalen College Gateway

Date: 1843
Architect: Pugin
Cost: £679. 0s. 7d.
References: Pugin mss 528 Magdalen College, Oxford. Contract and letters
Note: Demolished in 1883 to make way for new building.

188 Oxford: St Aloysius' Church

Date: 1873
Architect: Joseph Hansom
References: The *Architect* (June 1873) p. 316
Note: Now the Newman Centre.

189 Tubney: St Lawrence' Church and pews etc.

Date: 1843
Architect: Pugin
References: Pugin mss 528, Magdalen College Oxford, letter 158 and others.

190 Culham: Oxford Diocesan Training School

Date: 1851
Architect: J. Clarke
Cost: £15,700
References: *The Builder* (1851) p. 754; Oxfordshire County Record Office, letter from John Gregson of Sutton Coutenay

Abbey to J M Davenport: 'Mr Myers' immediate demand is for £3,000 ... '. (Letter not indexed.)

Note: The building has been extended, but the original part is listed. It is now an International School for the children of parents who are working at the E.C. Atomic Research Centre at Harwell.

191 Cuddesdon: Rippon Theological College

Date: 1853
Architect: G.E. Street
References: *Illustrated London News* (1853) p. 308
Note: Additions have been made to the building.

SHROPSHIRE

192 Shrewsbury: The Cathedral Church of Our Lady. Help of Christians and St Peter of Alcantara. George Myers was consulted about the foundations.

Date: 1853
Architect: E.W. Pugin
References: Judith Hall: *Shrewsbury Cathedral, a Sacrament in Stone* (Cathedral publication, 1984) p. 22.

193 Shrewsbury: Ferney Hall, rebuilding for Willoughby H Sitwell

Date: 1855
Architect: Norton
Cost: £12,385
References: *The Builder* (1855) p. 560.

STAFFORDSHIRE

194 Alton Towers. GM paid frequent visits to Alton Towers and carried out various works for the Earl of Shrewsbury

Date: 1838-40s
Architect: Pugin
References: Colney Hatch letter, Minute book vol II, p. 77
Note: Now an Amusement Park and 'ruin'.

195 Lichfield: Church of the Holy Cross - screen only

Date: 1841
Architect: Pugin
References: AW p. 54.

196 Brewood: St Mary's Church, Presbytery and school

Date: 1843-4
Architect: Pugin
Cost: £2,010
References: Archdiocese of Birmingham Archives, letter B.470.

SURREY

197 Peper Harow: alterations and improvements to the House, Park
and Church of St Nicholas for Viscount Midleton

Date: 1841-8
Architect: Pugin
References: Guildford Muniment Room, 145, Box 39, bundle 6
             1248/33/51, etc.
Note: Now school for disturbed children.

198 Guildford (near): Albury House and Chapel, alterations and
other work for Henry Drummond Esq.

Date: 1846-56
Architects: Pugin 1846-52; E W Pugin 1852-57
References: Northumberland mss, Drummond Papers c/17/1-65 etc.
Note: Now the property of the Country Houses Association.

199 Ewell: Church of St Mary the Virgin

Date: 1847-48
Architect: Henry Clutton
Cost: £5,900
References: CERC 65/129; Colney Hatch testimonial; *The Builder*
             (1847) p. 533
Note: In use.

200 Beddington: St Mary the Virgin, restorations

Date: 1850
Architect: Joseph Clarke
Cost: £2,316. 19s. 7d.
References: Surrey Record Office, Kingston-upon-Thames, 2813/5/4
Note: In use.

201 Esher: Church

Date: 1853
Architect: Benjamin Ferrey
Cost: £5,000
References: *The Builder* (1853) p. 522.

202 Knap Hill (Nr Woking): Her Majesty's Male Convict Prison for invalid convicts (700) and Chapel

Date: 1858
Architect: Major General Sir Joshua Jebb, in charge of building operations
References: PRO MH 51/49 XC 194359, letter from Major General Sir J. Jebb
Note: This building replaced the last of the 'hulks'. In 1894-95 it was converted into a recreation centre for the Inkerman Barracks.

203 Camberley: The Staff College at Sandhurst, the Commandant's and adjutant's residences, and stabling for 40 horse

Date: 1859-62
Architect: James Pennethorne and Colonel Chapman, R.E.
Cost: £40,000 - £50,000
References: *The Times* (18 December 1859) p. 7; Major A.R. Godwin-Austen: 'The Staff and the Staff College'(Constable & Co., 1927) p. 119.
Note: The Staff College has been enlarged and modernised.

204 Croydon: St Saviour's Church

Date: 1867
Architect: Mullins, Lee and Mullins
References: *The Builder* (1867) p. 230.

SUSSEX

205 Little Horsted: Horsted Place, for Mr Barchard

Date:	1850-51
Architect:	S W Daukes
References:	Dr Mark Girouard, 'Horsted Place, Sussex, I and II', in *Country Life* (7 August 1958) p. 276 and (14 August 1958) p. 321
Note:	Now a hotel with a 'George Myers' suite.

206 West Tarring: Church restoration

Date:	1854
Architect:	Joseph Peacock
Cost:	£2,200
References:	*The Builder* (1854) p. 214.

207 Arundel: Cathedral of St Philip Neri for the Duke of Norfolk

Date:	1869-73
Architect:	J.A. Hansom
Cost:	£50,000 +
References:	Arundel Castle Archive Library, Architectural drawings signed by George Myers; *West Sussex Gazette*, 6 January 1870
Note:	St Philip Neri was built as a Church but is now the Cathedral of our Lady and St Philip Howard.

WARWICKSHIRE

208 Birmingham: St Chad's Cathedral and Bishop's House

Date:	1839-41
Architect:	Pugin
Cost:	c £20,000
References:	AW Note 9 p. 82; letters in Diocesan Archives, Southwark.
Note:	The Bishop's House has been demolished to make way for a ring road.

209 Birmingham: Springhill College, Moseley

Date:	1854-7
Architect:	Joseph James (of London)
Cost:	£12,985
References:	*The Builder* (1857) p. 166.

210 Kenilworth: St Augustine's Church and Presbytery

Date:	1842
Architect:	Pugin
References:	*Archdiocese of Birmingham Archives*, R 868; *The Church of St Augustine of England, Kenilworth*, by Elizabeth Meaton (Parish publication c. 1988) p. 44.
Note:	Paid for by Mrs Amherst.

211 Rugby: Bilton Grange, work carried out for Capt Hibbert

Date:	1841-51
Architect:	Pugin
References:	PS p. 176; AW Note 8 p. 98; HL (1847)
Note:	Now a private school.

212 Rugby: St Marie's Church, Convent and School

Date:	1844
Architect:	Pugin
References:	HL (1847) BCL
Note:	Has been enlarged.

WILTSHIRE

213 Box: the Railway Station

Date:	1849
References:	JMS letter to the *Bath Journal*.

214 Swindon: Christchurch

Date:	1851
Architect:	G.G. Scott
References:	*The Builder* (1851) p. 389

YORKSHIRE

215 Beverley: Beverley Minster, restoration work

Date: *c.* 1816-29
Architect: Fowlers of Winterton
References: William Comins' Day Book, Beverley Public Library, acc
               B/746R, class Y/726.5/Bev; G.G. Scott, *Recollections
               Personal and Professional*, (1879) pp. 88-9.

216 Beverley: St Mary's Church, restoration

Date: 1842-54
Architects: Pugin and E.W. Pugin
References: HCAO, PE1/744 etc.

217 Bishop's Burton: All Saints Church restoration

Date: 1853
References: HCAO: letter from George Myers to Mr Sands
               13 August 1853
Note: George Myers attended opening.

218 Cherry Burton: St Michael's Church, rebuilding

Date: 1852-3
Architects: Horace Jones and Charles Vickers
Cost: £1,700
References: Contract ERRO, DDCB 4/55.

219 Dalton Holme (South Dalton): St Mary's Church, built for Lord
Hotham

Date: 1858-61
Architect: J. Loughborough Pearson
Cost: £25,000
References: HCAO, PE54/11; Anthony Quiney, *John Loughborough
               Pearson*, (Yale University Press, 1979).

220   Hull: Between 1829 and 1842 George Myers and Wilson built many terrace houses and shops and paved new roads

References: Memoranda in HCRO, BE2, Book EP p. 295.

221   Hull: Holy Trinity Church, restoration, vaults and other work

Date: 1833-44
Architect: H.F. Lockwood from about 1842
References: HCAO, Holy Trinity Accounts, Book 5, temp no. PE
               158 27.

222   Hull: Wilberforce Memorial

Date: 1834
Architect: Clerk of Leeds
References: George Myers letter re foundations, CERC 59/131
Note: J.J. Sheahan *History of Hull*, 2nd edn (Beverley Green:
               1866) p. 674.

223   Hull: Public Baths

References: Midland Bank Archieves: Hull Banking Company Minute
               Book 48/12.

224   Hull: St Mark's Church in the Groves

Date: 1841-3
Architect: H.F. Lockwood
Cost: £5,086
References: CERC, 59/131
Note: Demolished 1958.

225   Hull: Great Thornton St Chapel

Date: 1842
Architect: H.F. Lockwood
References: Midland Bank Archives: Hull Banking Company
               Minutes, Book J, p. 146, London.
Note: Demolished.

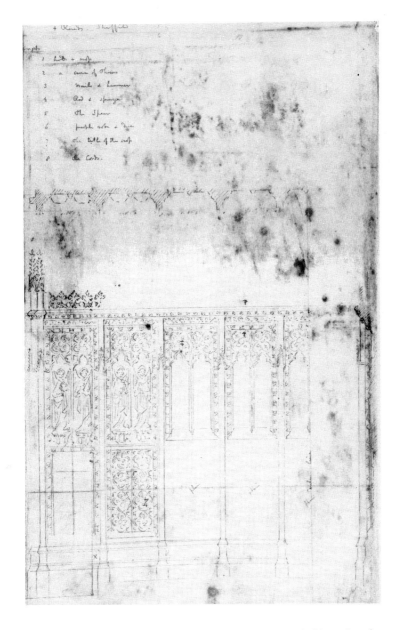

Figure 76   Reredos for Sheffield Cathedral Church of
St Marie.
Courtesy of the Myers Family Trust.

Figure 77   Tabernacle for Sheffield Cathedral Church of
St Marie.
Courtesy of the Myers Family Trust.

226 Hull: Flax and Cotton Mills

Date: 1843
References: Midland Bank Archives: Hull Banking Company
            Minutes, Book 48/2.

227 Leeds: Cathedral of St Anne, some carving only

Date: 1838
Architect: Pugin
References: AW pp. 54 and 88
Note: George Myers was not the contractor for the Cathedral
            but the altar, reredos and screen were made in his
            workshops.

228 Pontefract: Chapel at Ackworth Grange for the Tempest family

Date: 1842
Architect: Pugin
References: Pugin Diaries 1842; The *Tablet* (13 January 1844), p.6
Note: Demolished

229 Scorborough: St Leonard's Church, built for James Hall, MFH

Date: 1857-59
Architect: J. Loughborough Pearson
Cost: £5,000 +
References: Anthony Quiney (authority on JLP)
Note: In use.

230 Sheffield: Cathedral Church of St Marie, Norfolk Street

Date: 1850
Architects: Pugin; Weightman & Hadfield
References: *The Builder* (1850) pp. 448-9 and drawings MFT.
Note: The Cathedral was not built by George Myers but the
            High Altar, reredos, tabernacle, font, pulpit and founder's
            effigy were from his workshops.

WALES

231   Clwyd: Chirk Castle, restoration and decoration for Colonel Biddulph

Date: 1846-8; 1852
Architect: Pugin
References: HL 1852.

232 Pantasaph: St David's Church, work for Lord Feilding

Date: 1950
Architect: Pugin
References: HL 1851,1852
Note: Pugin and George Myers were called upon to convert this almost completed C of E church into a Catholic church.

AUSTRALIA

233   Church furniture designed by Pugin was sent to St Mary's Cathedral, Sydney and to other locations. It is possible that this furniture was made in George Myer's workshops.

234   Tasmania: Bishop Willson, in the 1840s, took with him to Hobart, a confessional made by George Myers, other furniture as well, and three model churches which could be taken to pieces.

CANADA

235 Newfoundland: for St John's Cathedral, oak lectern and marble altar table made in George Myer's workshops

Date: 1850
Architect: G.G. Scott
References: Scott's letters RIBA SC/NS1/93
Note: Burnt in the 'Great Fire' of 1892.

FRANCE

236 Ferrières (near Paris): Chateau for Baron James de Rothschild

Date: 1854-9
Architect: Sir Joseph Paxton
References: Markham Papers, Chatsworth; Paxton's evidence to Parliamentary Committee ... Paxton's obituary in *The Builder* (1865) p. 444; Mrs G. Cuffe, George Myer's granddaughter.

IRELAND

237 Lismore: Lismore Castle. George Myers made two fireplaces and perhaps other stone work and furniture

Date: 1851
Architect: Sir Joseph Paxton; Pugin designed the fireplace
References: Mark Girouard, *Country Life* vol. CXXXVI, (1964) pp. 336-40 and pp. 389-93.

238 Dublin: an altar and other carving for the Irish Exhibition of 1853

Designer: Pugin?
References: HL 1853.

RUSSIA

239 The Crimea: George Myers was one of ten contractors who sent huts to the Crimea for the Army in 1855. They were designed by Brunel, and a model was exhibited in the Great Western Railway station so the public could suggest improvements.

USA

240 New Orleans Tombstone for two babies, the children of Cornellia Connelly and her husband. She founded The Society of the Holy Child, Jesus - an order of teaching nuns.

Date: *c.* 1840?
Architect: Pugin
References: Drawing MFT.

Appendix II: List of Architects

NAME/ BUILDING	DATE	CROSS REFERENCE
1 ABRAHAM, H.R. The Great Globe House: Leicester Square	1851	Westminster
New Library: Middle Temple	1858-61	City of London
2 ALLOM, Thomas The Great Thornton Street Chapel: Hull.	1843	Yorks
Sub-workhouse and school: Kirkdale	1843	Lancs
3 BALY PRITCHARD, P. (Engineer) St George's Baths and Wash House.	1852	Westminster
4 BAKER, Henry London and Westminster Bank (Holborn Branch)	1853	Camden
5 BARNETT, John St Stephen's Church and parsonage: Albert Square.	1860	Lambeth
New building: for Messrs Sarl and Sons 16 Cornhill.	1857	City of London
6 BAZELGETTE, Sir Joseph William Sewers: in Kensal New Town, Paddington and Chelsea, Westminster. George Myers worked for the Metropolitan Commissioners of sewers; Sir Joseph Bazelgette was the engineer in charge.	1850s	Brent

7   BRANDON, David
Blackmoore Park: 1863   Hereford
Malvern.   and
                                                       Worcestershire

Provident Institution Savings Bank: 1871-5   Westminster
St Martin's Lane.

8   BRANDON, Raphael
Holy Catholic and Apostolic Church,   1851   Camden
and flats:
Gordon Square.

St Peter's Church: 1861   Westminster
Windmill St.

9   BUNNING, James Bunstone
Guildhall roof.   1863   City of London
James Bunning died before completion
and Sir Horace Jones (*q.v.*)
took over.

10 BURNET, William
The Imperial Ottoman Bank: 1871   City of London
Throgmorton Street.

11 BURY, Talbot
All Saints Church: 1858   Lambeth
New Park Road, Clapham.

St Ann's Church, Parsonage,
school, and model cottages: 1861   Haringey
Stamford Hill.

Child's Hill C of E school   1870   Barnet
(infants):
Cricklewood Lane.

12 BUTTERFIELD, William
Church of All Saints: 1859   Westminster
Margaret Street.
Carving only by George Myers
(contractor was Kelk)

St Alban's Church: Baldwin Gardens, Holborn.	1862	Camden
St Augustine's Church: Queen's Gate.	1870	Kensington and Chelsea
13 CARPENTER, R.C. Tomb at Kilndown. For Marshal and Lady Beresford.	1862	Kent
14 CHAPMAN, Colonel C.B., Royal Engineers, with Sir James Pennithorne Staff College, Camberley.	1859	Surrey
15 CHRISTIAN, Ewan St Luke's Church: Nutford Place, Edgeware Road.	1856	Westminster
Christchurch: Spitalfields. Restoration	1866	Tower Hamlets
16 CLANCY, J.B. Assize Courts, and Central Police Station, Reading.	1858, 1860	Berks
17 CLARK, John Wilberforce Memorial: Hull.	1834	Yorks
18 CLARKE, Isaac and James HUMPHRYS St Barnabas Church: Guildford Road.	1848-50	Lambeth
19 CLARKE, Joseph Oxford Diocesan Training College: Culham.	1851	Oxon
St Mary's Church Beddington. Restoration	*c.* 1850	Surrey

20 CLARKE, Thomas Chatfield Offices: Throgmonton Street and Austin Friars. For Mr Travers Smith.	1870	City of London
21 CLUTTON, Henry St Mary the Virgin: Ewell.	1847	Surrey
Cliveden, clock tower, etc.: Hedsor	1857, 1861, 1869	Bucks
Melchet Court: Romsey.	1863-6	Hants
North Lodge: Seaton. For Lady Ashburton.	1864-5	Devonshire
Sunningdale Park: Sunningdale.	1865	Berks
Woburn Parish Church: Bedford. For the Duke of Bedford	1865-8	Beds
School: Husborne Crawley. For the Duke of Bedford.	1866-7	Beds
22 DAUKES, Samuel Whitfield St Andrew's Church: Wells St, Marylebone.	1847	Westminster (re-erected in Brent)
Colney Hatch Lunatic Asylum: Friern Barnet Road.	1848-50	Barnet
Lincoln Pauper Lunatic Asylum: Bracebridge.	1849	Lincs

Exeter Hall, new roof: The Strand	1850	Westminster
Horsted Place: Little Horsted.	1850-1	Sussex
Dudley House Ball room and Picture Gallery. For Lord Ward.	1855	Westminster
23 DAVIS & EMANUEL West London Synagogue of British Jews: Upper Berkeley Street.	1870	Westminster
24 DEVEY,George Aston Clinton. Alterations and additions for Sir Anthony de Rothschild. (*See also* Stokes and Paxton.)	1870	Bucks
Hall Place: near Leigh.	1871-4	Kent
25 DOLLMAN, Francis St Matthew's Church: Warwick Grove, Clapton.	1869	Hackney
26 ELMSLIE, E.W. St Thomas and St Clement's Church: Winchester.	1845-7	Hants
27 EMMETT, J.T. Chapel and School: Upper Clapton.	1850	Hackney
New College: Finchley Rd, St John's Wood.	1851	Camden
28 FERREY, Benjamin Christchurch: Victoria Road.	1851	Kensington and Chelsea

St John the Evangelist: Eton.	1852-4	Berks
Church: Esher.	1853	Surrey
29 FOULTON, John Minerva Life Assurance Offices: 1 Cannon Street.	1852	City of London
30 FOWKE, Captain Francis The Prince Consort's Library: Aldershot.	1859-60	Hampshire
31 FOWLER, William and Joseph (of Winterton) Beverley Minster. Restoration.	*c.*1815-29	Yorkshire
32 FRANCIS, F. and H. Christchurch: Craven Hill, Lancaster Gate.	1855	Westminster
National Discount Offices: Cornhill.	1858	City of London
London and County Bank: Cambridge.	1866	Cambs
City Offices: Lombard Street.	1866	City of London
33 GALTON, Douglas Herbert Hospital: Woolwich.	1865	Greenwich
34 GIBSON, John National Provincial Bank of England: 212 Piccadilly.	1873	Westminster

35 GODWIN, George and H.

St Mary's Church:	1857	Kensington
The Boltons.		and Chelsea
Tower and steeple only.		

St Jude's Church:	1870	Kensington
Courtfield Gardens.		and Chelsea

George Godwin, FRS, Editor
of *The Builder* 1844-83.

36 HAHN, John M.K.

Mutual Life Assurance Soc. Offices:	1859	City of London
King Street, Cheapside.		

37 HAKEWILL, J.H.

St Matthias' Church, chancel only:	1868	Kensington
South Kensington.		and Chelsea

38 HANSOM, Charles

(brother of J.A. Hansom)	1847	Lancashire
St Thomas and St Elizabeth's Church:		
Thurnham.		

Altar and other carvings only by George Myers.

39 HANSOM, J A
(invented the 'Patent Safety Cab'. He also founded *The Builder* in 1842.)

St Philip's Cathedral:	1869-73	Sussex
Arundel.		

St Aloysius' Church:		
Oxford.	1873	Oxon

40 HARDWICK, P.C.

Church for the Troops:	1863	Hants
Aldershot.		

41 HAWKINS, M.R.

Royal Victorian Patriotic Asylum		
for Girls:	1857	Wandsworth
Wandsworth.		

Chapel for above:	1864	Wandsworth

42 HUNT and STEVENSON

St Margaret and St John's Workhouses:	1852	Kensington
Kensington		and Chelsea

43 JAMES, Joseph (of London)

Spring Hill College:	1857	Warks
Moseley, Birmingham.		

44 JARVIS, Henry

St Paul's Church:	1857	Southwark
Walworth, Camberwell.		
St Matthew's Church:	1867	Southwark
New Kent Road.		

45 JEBB, Major General Sir Joshua
(Senior Civil Servant in charge
of the Prison Service.)

Broadmoor Hospital and Chapel:	1858-64	Berkshire
Crowthorne.		
Her Majesty's Male Convict Prison		
(for invalid convicts):	1858	Surrey
Knaphill, near Woking.		

46 JONES, Sir Horace

St Michael's Church: rebuilt	1852	Yorkshire
Cherry Burton, near Beverley.		
Guildhall roof, windows etc.	1863-4	City of London
(*see* Bunning)		
Bishopsgate Police Station		
and Infirmary.	1863	City of London

47 KEELING, E. Bassett

St George's Church:	1864	Kensington
Campden Hill.		and Chelsea

48 KENDALL, H.E.

Essex County Lunatic Asylum: Brentwood.	1857	Essex

49 KERR, Professor Robert
(First President of the Architectural Association.)

Dunsdale: Westerham. Additions to, for Mr J. Kitchen	1863	Kent
National Provident Institute: Gracechurch Street.	1863	City of London

50 KNOWLES, James

New Building: Corner of Chancery Lane.	1855	City of London
St Saviour's Church: Cedars Road, Clapham.	1862-4	Lambeth

51 LAMB, E.B.

Brickhill Manor: Great Brickhill. Alterations and improvements.	1854	Bucks

52 LEE, Charles

St James Workhouse, (one wing only).	1858-9	Westminster
St Luke's Church.	1859	Islington
East India United Service Clubhouse: St James's Square.	1866	Westminster

53 LEGG, George

Corn Exchange. Additions to.	1852	City of London
Bank for Messrs Johnson and Co. New Cannon Street.	1852	City of London

54 LEWIS, T.H.
Crimean Memorial: to Medical   1864   Hants
Officers killed in the War.
Netley, Southampton Water.

55 LOCKWOOD, Henry Francis
Great Thornton Street Chapel: 1842   Yorks
Hull.

St Mark's Church in the Groves: 1843   Yorks
Hull.

Holy Trinity Church: 1833-44 Yorks
Hull. Restoration.

Kirkdale Parish Schools: 1843   Lancashire
Nr Bootle.

56 LOW, George
German Lutheran Church: 1856   Southwark
Champion Park, Denmark Hill.

57 MARRABLE, Frederick
New Offices Metropolitan Board   1860   Westminster
of Works:
Spring Gardens, St James' Park.

58 MARSH, NELSON and HARVEY
Evelina Hospital for
Sick Children: 1868-70 Southwark
Southwark Bridge Road.
For Baron Ferdinand de Rothschild.

59 MARTIN, H.D. (engineer)
Railway for North London   1849   Tower
Railway Company.   Hamlets

60 MASON, Alfred R.
Royal London Hospital   1853   Tower
Medical School and   Hamlets
additions to the Hospital in
Whitechapel Road.

61 MENNIE, Mr
Royal Victoria Hospital: 1856   Hants
Netley, Southampton Water.

62 MOSELEY, W. and A.
Westminster Palace Hotel: 1859   Westminster
Victoria Street.

63 MULLINS LEE and MULLINS
St Saviour's Church: 1867   Surrey
Croydon.

64 NASH, EDWIN
St John's Church and Parsonage: 1849   Sydenham
Penge.

65 NELSON and INNES
Mansion at Hyde Park Corner: 1863   Westminster
147-8 Piccadilly.
For Baron Lionel de Rothschild.

66 NORTON, Mr
Ferney Hall.   1855   Shropshire
For Mr Willoughby Hurt Sitwell.

67 OFFICE of WORKS
Burlington House extensions: 1857   Westminster
Piccadilly.

Windsor Castle.   1863   Berks
New rooms, repairs to private
rooms; furniture store.

St George's Chapel: Windsor Castle   1863   Berks
Saloons for wedding of Prince and
Princess of Wales.

Herbert Hospital: 1865   Greenwich
Woolwich (*see* Douglas Galton).

68 ORDISH, F.W.
City of London Hospital for Diseases
of the Chest: 1855   Hackney
Bonner's Fields, Victoria Park.

69 PALGRAVE, Robert
St Paul's Church: 1866-8   Beds
Bedford.
Restoration and enlargement.
In consultation with G.E. Street.

70 PARNELL, C.O.
London and Counties Bank: 1862   City of London
Lombard Street.

71 PAXTON, Sir Joseph
Burton Closes,   1847-8   Derbyshire
Bakewell. Carving only.

Mansion for Baron Mayer
de Rothschild.   1853   Bucks
Mentmore.

Ferrières. Mansion for
Baron James de Rothschild.   1854-9   France
nr Paris.

The Wood. Alterations and additions   1854-5   Sydenham
for the Duke of Devonshire.
Now 16 Sydenham Hill.
Listed grade II.

The Crystal Palace.   1855   Sydenham
George Myers was one of the contractors
when the building was moved to
Sydenham.

Rockhill House. Sir Joseph Paxton's   1857   Bromley
own house. Alterations etc.
Crystal Palace, Sydenham.

Aston Clinton.   1865   Bucks
Alterations, additions, etc.
for Sir Anthony de Rothschild
(*see also* Stokes and Devey).

72 PEACOCK, Joseph
Church: 1854   Sussex
West Tarring.

73 PEARCE, Edwin
(with Wilson and Son)   1865   Haringey
Royal Masonic Institute for Boys:
Wood Green, Tottenham.

74 PEARSON, John Loughborough
Scorborough Church.   1857-9   Yorkshire
For James Hall, MFH.

St Mary's Church: 1858-61   Yorkshire
Dalton Holme, (South Dalton).

75 PENFOLD, Warnham J,
Law Union Insurance Office: 1857   City of London
Chancery Lane.

76 PENNETHORNE, Sir James
Staff College: Camberley.   1859-62   Surrey

77 PHELPS, Arthur
Church of Our Lady of the Rosary: 1869   Lambeth
Brixton Road, Stockwell.

78 PLUMBE, Sir Rowland
Stratford Congregational Church: 1866   Newham
Stratford.

79 POULTON, W.F.
New Westminster Chapel: 1864   Westminster
Buckingham Gate.

80 PUGIN, A.W.N.
St Mary's Church and Presbytery: 1837   Derbyshire
Bridge Gate, Derby.

St Wilfred's Church: 1838   Lancashire
Hulme, Manchester.
George Myers helped with this church.

Alton Towers. Much work carried out for Lord Shrewsbury.	1838-50	Staffs
Metropolitan Church of St Chad and Bishop's House: Queen's Way, Birmingham.	1839-41	Warks
Mount St Bernard Abbey: Coalville.	*c.* 1840	Leics
St Oswald's Church and School: Old Swan, Liverpool.	1840	Lancs
Church of Our Lady & St Wilfred: Warwick Bridge.	1841	Cumbria
St Mary's Church: Stockton-on-Tees.	1841	County Durham
Church of the Holy Cross: Lichfield. The screen only.	1841	Staffs
Chapel of the Sisters of Nazareth: Wavetree.	1841-3	Lancashire
St George's Cathedral: St George's Road. Also church house, convent and schools.	1841-8	Southwark
Peper Harow near Guildford. Work for Viscount Midleton.	1841-8	Surrey
Bilton Grange: Rugby. Various works.	1841-51	Warks
Chapel at Ackworth Grange: Pontefract. For the Tempest family.	1842	Yorks

St Augustine's Church and Presbytery: Beehive Hill, Kenilworth.	1842	Warks
Cathedral of St Barnabas: Derby Road, Nottingham.	1842	Notts
Cathedral Church of St Anne: Leeds. Altar, screen and reredos made in George Myers' workshop. The building was finished in 1838.	1842	Yorks
School and probably small church: Whitworth.	1842	Leics
Tomb for Mr Sharples.	1842	Lancs
St Winifred's Church, Shepshed, Loughborough.	1842	Leics
St Mary's Church: Beverley. Restoration.	1842-54	Yorks
Cathedral Church of St Mary: Clayton St West, Newcastle.	1842-4	Northumberland
St Joseph's Church: Bugle St, Southampton.	1843	Hampshire
St Peter's Church: New Road, Woolwich.	1843	Woolwich
St Mary's Church, Presbytery, and School: Kiddemore Green Road, Brewood.	1843-4	Staffs
St Augustine's Church and the Grange: Ramsgate.	1843-8	Kent

Ushaw College: near Durham. Chapel, decorations, and additions to College.	1843-8	County Durham
St Lawrence's Church: Tubney.	1844	Oxfordshire
St John the Evangelist: Kirkham.	1845	Lancs
Magdalen College Gateway: Oxford.	1844-5	Oxfordshire
St Mary's Church: Wymeswold. Restoration.	1844-50	Leics
St Peter's Church and School: Great Marlow.	1845-8	Bucks
St Mary's Church: Edmond St, Liverpool.	1845	Lancashire
Oswaldcroft: Liverpool. Furniture for the house of Mr Sharples.	1845	Lancashire
St Edmond's College, Chapel, Ware.	1845-51	Herts
House for N.G. Ward: Ware.	1845-51	Herts
St Giles Church: Bank Street, Cheadle. Intricate carvings executed by George Myers.	1846	Staffs
Chirk Castle: Restoration and decoration.	1846-8	Clwyd
Albury House and Mortuary Chapel: near Guildford.	1846-52	Surrey

Alterations and other work
for Henry Drummond.

St Anne's Bede Houses: Lincoln. Built by George Myers from A.W.N. Pugin's designs without his supervision.	1847	Lincs
St Mary's Church, Convent and Schools and improvements to Bilton Grange. For Captain Hibbert.	1847	Warks
St Oswald's Church: Winwick. Rebuilding of chancel and vestry; also furniture.	1847-9	Cheshire
Convent of the Good Shepherd: Fulham Palace Road Hammersmith.	1848-50	Fulham
St Thomas of Canterbury: Rylston Road. Also the Gates.	1847-8	Fulham
St Mary's Chantry: West Tofts, near Brandon. Restoration of church and much furniture.	1849-54	Norfolk
The Rolle Chantry, Bicton Grange: Sidmouth.	1850-2	Devonshire
Cathedral of St Marie: Sheffield. Reredos, high altar, font, founder's effigy from George Myers' workshop.	1850	Yorks
St David's Church: Pantasaph. Decoration and furniture.	1850	Clywd

St Bede's Church: Appleton, Widnes. Altar and reredos.	1851	Cheshire
Lismore Castle. Fireplace and probably other stonework designed by Pugin for castle where Paxton was carrying out improvements.	1851	Ireland
The Great Exhibition. Many exhibits.	1851	Westminster
Wilburton Manor: near Ely.	1851	Cambs
St Peter's Church: Wilburton.	*c.* 1851	Cambs
Memorial Cross for the Walmesley family: St John's Chapel, Standish Gate, Wigan.	1852	Lancs

81 PUGIN, E.W.

St Mary's Church: Beverley. Restoration.	1852-4	Yorks
Albury House: near Guildford. Alterations and other work for Henry Drummond Esq.	1852-6	Surrey
Shrewsbury Cathedral: George Myers consulted when there were problems with the foundations.	1853	Shropshire
Monastery and Abbey of St Michael: Belmont	1857	Hereford and Worcestershire

Pugin's Effigy: *c.* 1854   Kent
St Augustine's Church in
Ramsgate.(In stone on his tomb.)

82 ROGERS, W.
St Paul's Church: 1857   Southwark
Westminster Road.

83 ROWLEY, J.H.
New City Club: 1864   City of London
Lombard Street.

84 SALVIN, Anthony
(Born in Co. Durham,
the son of an Army officer and
worked with Nash.)

Tower of London: 1859-69   City of London
Building works, restoration, etc.

Windsor Castle: 1863   Berks
New rooms and repairs to
private appartments.

85 SCOTT, Sir George Gilbert
Workhouse: 1838   Leics
Loughborough.

St Matthew's Church: 1849-51   Westminster
Great Peter Street.

Cathedral of St John the Baptist: 1850   Canada
St John's, Newfoundland.
Altar table and lectern.

Christchurch: 1850-1   Wiltshire
Swindon.

Christchurch: 1852   Ealing
Ealing Broadway.

Houses in Broad Sanctuary.   1853   Westminster

Camden Church: Camberwell. The Chancel.	1854	Lambeth
St Mary's Church: Stoke Newington.	1858	Hackney
Chapel at Wellington College.	1861	Berks
86 SHAW, Norman Warehouse: Cooper's Row.	1862	City
87 SMIRKE, Sidney Bethlem Hospital: Restoration and improvements.	1852, 1854	Southwark
Queen's Chapel of the Savoy: The Strand. Rebuilt after fire.	1866	Westminster
88 STOKES, G H Aston Clinton: Alterations and additions for Sir Anthony de Rothschild. *See also* Devey and Paxton.	1853	Bucks
Beeley Parsonage: Chatsworth. For the Duke of Devonshire.	1856	Derbyshire
89 STREET, G.E. Church at Monken Hadley High Barnet. Restoration.	1848-9	Barnet
Rippon Theological College: Cuddesdon.	1853	Oxfordshire
Church of St James the Less: Garden Street, Victoria.	1862	Westminster
90 TARRING, John Clapham Congregational Church: Mostyn Road, Brixton.	1852	Lambeth

Chelsea Congregational Church: Markham Square.	1860	Kensington and Chelsea
Weslyan Chapel: Mostyn Road, Brixton.	1870	Lambeth
91 TILLMAN, J. Weslyan Chapel: Ryhope, Sunderland.	1865	Durham
92 TILLOT and CHAMBERLAIN Jews Infant School.	1857	Tower Hamlets
93 WARDELL, William Our Lady, Star of the Sea: Crooms Hill. Chancel only.	1851	Greenwich
94 WEHNERT and ASHDOWN Highgate Cemetery. Boundary walls of new cemetery.	1854	Camden
95 WHITE, William Church of All Saints: Talbot Road, Kensington Park, Chelsea.	1855	Kensington and Chelsea
96 WILSON, B. and Son (with Edwin Pearce) Royal Masonic Institute for Boys: Wood Green, Tottenham.	1865	Haringey
97 WOODYER, Henry St Paul's Church: Langleybury, St Albans.	1865	Hertfordshire
98 WYATT, Sir Matthew Digby Evelina and Ferdinand de Rothschild Mausoleum: Westham, Forest Gate.	1866	Newham

Index

MP, 45
Sinclair, Archdeacon John, 47, 106-7
Smirke, Sydney, 81,105,279
Speaker's House, Palace of Westminster: furniture of, 38
Staff College: *see* Sandhurst,
Staircase, Horsted Place, 45
Stanton, Phoebe, 10,100
Stokes, Henry (Aston Clinton, Pregny), 175,178,279
Street, G.E., 103, 127,279
Strikes, Bath stone quarrymen (1849 and 1861), 91-2; Councils of Conciliation, 187; Crystal Palace, 1851, 41; Great Lockout (1859), 94,110; Guildhall Roof, clause in contract concerning, 162; Master Builders' working hours, 187; Middle Temple Library, 156-7; Nine-hour movement, 185; Non-intervention policy of Government, 186; Trollope and Sons, 186; Windsor Castle, 187
Stonemasons, 3
String course, 196
Summerson, Sir John, 82
Sunningdale Park, Berks, 236
Supper - roofing over, 55
Synagogue (West London, of British Jews), Westminster, 105,233

Tadcaster quarries,Yorks, 3
Tarring, John, 279-80
Tenders and tendering, 83-6; Aldershot Camp, 133,138; Guildhall roof etc., 162,166; last years - Myers less successful, 189; Mentmore, 173; Tower of London, 159
Tiles, encaustic, 195
Tillman, J., 280
Tillot and Chamberlain, 280
Timber supplies, 92, 135
Tite, Sir William, 126
Tomb of Marshal and Lady

Beresford, Kilndown, Kent, 244
Tomb for Mr Sharples, Liverpool, Lancs, 245
Tring Park, Tring, Herts, 244
Tower of London: tenders for, 86; Restoration of (1856), 158-61, 216
Trade Unions, 3
Trades, 87
Training under Myers, 188
Transport: *see also* canals; 88; Great Western Railway (1841) Bath stone by rail from Box, 90; Sandhurst Staff College, 143
Travers Smith (solicitors), 125,130,168
Trimen, Andrew, 120,123,125

Upset, Pugin by Captain Hibbert, 36; Crase by Myers, 42
USA: double tombstone to New Orleans, 24
Ushaw: *see* Schools

Verviers, Belgium, altar for, 27

Wages, 3
Wailes, William, (stained glass), 35,53,56,65
Walsh Dr., Bishop of Birmingham, 41,44,49,50
Wardell, William, 280
Warehouses, 168-72; Bonded, 183; Cooper's Row, City, 216; and Vaults, Tower Hill, City, 217
Waterworks, chimney, etc., Waterworks Street, Lambeth, 224
Watts, G.F., 103
Wehnert and Ashdown, 280
Westminster Palace Hotel, 153-4,205
West London Synagogue of British Jews, 105
West Tofts, Norfolk, 100
White, William, 280
Wilberforce, William, Memorial,

7,9,256; Memorial moved, 194

Wilberforce, Venr Archdeacon, 96

Wilberton Manor, Cambs, 238

Willson, E.J. of Lincoln:
antiquarian, architect, 4

Willson, Father Robert, Bishop of
Hobart (brother of E.J.W.),
23,50

Wilson, B. and Son, 280

Wilson, Richard, 5; Bankrupt
(1849), 16,112, *see* Myers and
Wilson

Windows for lunatic asylums,
45,119

Windsor Castle: Prince Albert's
funeral, 235; Henry VII Library,
Queen Anne's Closet, 190,236;
Temporary Hall etc., wedding of
Prince of Wales, 163,236

Wiseman, N., Cardinal
Archbishop of Westminster, 50

Women, exception taken to, 49

Wood, (The) Sydenham, for Duke
of Devonshire, 46,225

Woodyer, Henry, 184,280

Workforce at Ordnance Wharf,
and outside, 22,87; Recruitment
and lodging of operatives, 88

Workhouse: St James's,
Westminster, 232;
Loughborough, Leics, 247; St
Margaret's and St John's,
Kensington, 77

Workmen's Compensation (1862),
93

Wyatt, T.H., 126

Wyatt, Sir Matthew Digby (de R
mausoleum), 181,280